TRAVELLING HOPEFULLY

HELEN MURDOCH

Travelling Hopefully

THE STORY OF
MOLLY URQUHART

PAUL HARRIS PUBLISHING

EDINBURGH

© Helen Murdoch 1981

First published 1981 in Great Britain by

PAUL HARRIS PUBLISHING
40 York Place
Edinburgh

ISBN 0 86228 034 6

Printed by John G Eccles Printers Ltd, Inverness

CONTENTS

List of Illustrations

Foreword

When Helen Murdoch told me that she was writing a book on Molly Urquhart and wanted to have some of my memories of her, I was surprised to learn that Molly was having a whole book devoted to her. Much as we who had the pleasure of working with her loved her, an actor's life is as transient as a butterfly's, and a wide audience for books about even such luminaries as Alistair Sim and Duncan Macrae is in question.

As the book argues most persuasively, Molly's achievements were in many ways greater than the two men I've mentioned. She founded and ran her own theatre, and, as an actress, triumphed in fields as disparate as broad revue sketches and the fine playing called for if you play a nun in a film directed by Fred Zinnemann.

I took up Helen's manuscript with some misgivings — misgivings that were soon to give way to intense pleasure. Moreover, I realised that the book was telling a lot more than the story of one actor's life. It was, in fact, an account of the most exciting period in Scottish theatrical history, those thirty-odd years that saw the amateur movement give way to a full-time professional theatre company, housed originally in the Athenaeum, associated with amateur performances, before its transfer to the Royal Princess' Theatre, wholly professional in its background, which provided a stage for Macrae, Roddy Macmillan, Andrew Keir, Robert Urquhart, James Gibson, myself, John Fraser, Fulton MacKay, and, of course, our subject, Molly. The Glasgow Citizens' Theatre — all of us were there at the same time, and had strong reasons to feel that at long last the Knoxian ghost was being laid to rest, and we were in at the birth of a Scottish National Theatre. We spoke a lot of a Scottish playhouse that would fulfil the same needs as the Abbey Theatre in Dublin in the thirties.

Well, it didn't come to pass. The largely Scottish cast drifted south, as English directors with great skill and personal ambition but with little understanding of Bridie's dream, took charge. Or is that verdict unfair? When Micheal MacLiammoir once was asked what happened to the vanished magnificence of the Abbey and Gate's heyday, he said 'Oh, I tink all those happenings are like a little bird that lands on the shoulder and then flies away. Why it came in the first place is the mystery — and we should just be grateful for its brief sojourn with us.'

All of us who worked with her are grateful for our sojourn — however brief — with Molly Urquhart.

Stanley Baxter

Introduction

Molly Urquhart was in one of the first plays I ever saw, *The Pyrate's Den* by James Bridie at the Citizens' Theatre in 1945. Even as a child, I knew instinctively this was a great actress.

I first met her years later when I went backstage, a shy and gauche student, to show her my first attempts at dramatic writing. Although I recall one item was an incomplete drama about Catherine the Great, which contained the memorable line, "Why so pensive, Empress?", she looked over my scripts with a considerate, critical seriousness, that encouraged me to go on. From then on, we were friends.

She had always intended to write her autobiography, but she was too busy living her life. She did make some notes, which have been incorporated in these pages. The story of the MSU Theatre was what she was determined to record. The title she chose was 'Take a Pew', and during what were to be the last three years of her life, she talked to me a great deal about this proposed book, telling me story after story of her early life and her attempts to become established as an actress. Sometimes the talk would go on for hours, but when she laughingly said, "I'll never live to get all this down. You'll have to finish it!" I dismissed the idea.

She did not have time to write more than a few hundred words. Working from those, and using my clear recall of her own reminiscences, I began. Her son, Jim, and all the family gave me every possible help, and her friends and neighbours assisted me likewise in forming a picture of her early days.

My sincere thanks are due to: Kit and Len Cox; Lexy Rostek; Jim and Marion McIntosh; Jean McCallum†; Elizabeth Mallen; Lily and Dan Hepburn; Mairi Urquhart; Rev. David Stewart and Marie Dorman†. Also to: Miss Jessie Adamson; Miss Catherine Campbell; Miss Jessie Campbell; Mr and Mrs Edwards; Mr and Mrs King; Mrs

Hawthorn; Mrs Chrissie Inglis;† Mrs Anne McLeod; 'The Ladies in White' — Rosina McCulloch, Molly Blair, Barbara Blackwood, May Sinclair and Irene Thomson; Bruce and Nettie Whitelaw. When I contacted the many people she had worked with in the theatre and other media, I received the most tremendously helpful contributions, by letter, telephone and in several cases, tape recorded interviews. That they held her in high regard both as an actress and as a person is evident in the many letters and transcripts that have been invaluable in writing her story.

I wish to express particular gratitude to the following, who made invaluable and extensive contributions: Dame Peggy Ashcroft, Lea Ashton, Stanley Baxter, Joan Bridge, Andrew Crawford, Archie Duncan†, Joyce Edwards, James Gilbert, Begum Attia Hosain, Fulton MacKay, Elizabeth McKay, Roddy MacMillan†, Donald MacKenzie, James MacKenzie, Carmel McSharry, Ronald Mavor, Alan Melville, Nicholas Parsons, John Pollock†, Donald Ross†, Joan Scott, Ian Wallace, Fred and Renee Zinnemann.

My thanks also for the helpful contributions of: Professsor James Arnott, George Cole, Stewart Conn, Iain Crawford, Alan Dent†, Diana Dors, Jane Fonda, Giles Havergal, Laurence Hardy, Moira Heritage, Norman Holland, Waris Hosain, Dr Kenneth Ireland, Gordon Jackson, Phyllida Law, Moira Lister, Margaret Lockwood, Jimmy Logan, Peter MacDonnell, Nora McGowan, Mary McGuinness, Kay Macmillan, Ernest and Marguerite Mace, Amy Malcolm, Robert Morley, Helen Norman, Eileen O'Casey, Tony Paterson, Robert Pollock, Dr Gillian Rodger, Dorothy Roger, Elsie Russell, Jack Short, George Singleton, Anna Taylor, Richard Waring, Jim and Fiona Waters, Sheelah Willcocks, Marian Wiseman.

Thanks are also due to: The Librarians of — The Glasgow Room of the Mitchell Library, The National Library of Scotland, Baillie's Library, Glasgow University Drama Archive; *The Rutherglen Reformer*; The Scottish Arts Council for travel grant; the many subscribers who have supported this venture.

Grateful acknowledgements are due to the following copyright holders who allowed their work to appear in this volume: Ronald Mavor for the extracts from *Mr Gillie* and *The Forrigan Reel* by James Bridie; Stanley Baxter for 'Tatty Bacchante'; Winifred Bannister for the extracts from *James Bridie and His Theatre*; *The Glasgow Herald* for the photograph of Molly Urquhart and Duncan Macrae in *The*

INTRODUCTION

Tintock Cup; STV for the photograph of Molly Urquhart and Alec Heggie in *You're a good boy, son.*

To all these people, and to my own parents and friends, my sincere thanks. Their faith enabled me to go on 'travelling hopefully!'

This book, I hope, goes some way to recording the work of a lady who was a great Scottish actress, a pioneer in theatre, and yet was to all of us, Molly.

Helen Murdoch
September 1981

Chapter One

Prologue

The year was 1927. The scene was the Barrows, Glasgow's famous street market which sprawls between Gallowgate and the London Road. Every weekend to this day, the stalls spring up there, selling everything from old clothes to new carpets, bric-a-brac to light bulbs. It has always been known for its characters, and the sales-talk and repartée is as witty and original as any to be heard throughout the British Isles. The stall-holder with the potted plants was doing a splendid trade, calling her wares in a rich Glasgow accent, for no front parlour would then have been considered complete without its aspidistra, castor oil plant or scented geranium.

"There you go, china. A bargain at one and six. Give it a wee drink when you get home. It likes a gargle, same's yersell."

She turned to the next customer, a young woman with dark curly hair, who was waiting to purchase a small plant, popularly known as 'Mind-your-own-business'.

"That'll be ninepence, hen. Mind-your-own-business it is, but you'll no' mind me saying you've surely bought an awful lot of plants this while back?"

Blushing a little, the young customer agreed that she had. She thought of the red sandstone flat, two up, at 27 Caird Drive in the district of Partickhill in the west part of the city. Its front room was already bedecked with several such plants, standing on every available surface of the solid mahogany and moquette furnishings. "Not another plant, Mary!" her mother would almost certainly protest when she brought this one home.

The stall holder pursued the matter, "I mean, I want to sell ma plants, but your place must be like a hothouse!"

Rather hesitantly, in case she might give offence, the girl admitted her ulterior motive; speaking in the clear musical tones of the

1

Highlander, she explained that she was an amateur elocutionist, who gave readings and recitations, and was finding difficulty in capturing the true accent of Glasgow. "I would love to be able to speak like you."

"What an ambition! Just you come to see me any time, my dear. But you don't need to buy any more plants!"

So a friendship was formed, and with patience and observation, the young Molly Urquhart gradually mastered those resonant guttural tones with the elided consonants and broad tuneful vowels that somehow seem, in their plaintive quality, to belong in the minor key.

Then, as now, the originality of expression and the accent of Glasgow proved a superb vehicle for comedy. It is interesting to note that the lady who, despite the extensive vocal and dramatic range she could encompass, was seen very much as Glasgow's 'own' actress, was Glaswegian only by birth and had to make a conscious effort to master the accent which she loved so dearly and could employ so vividly.

Born in Glasgow on 21 January 1906, Mary Sinclair Urquhart was the eldest surviving child of Ann McCallum who came originally from the Isle of Tiree in the Inner Hebrides, but had lived most of her early years in Tarbet, Loch Lomond, before coming to Glasgow to work in the Post Office, and William Urquhart, a sea-going engineer who had been born and brought up in his parents' croft in the small community of Midtown, Inverasdale, on the shore of Loch Ewe in Wester Ross. After the couple married in 1902, Mrs Urquhart, as was frequently the custom in those days, sailed with her husband on board ship when it was engaged in coastal cruising so that they were sometimes living in rented accommodation in different ports where the shipping line traded.

Mary was the third child of the marriage and the third to be named after her maternal grandmother, Mary Sinclair. The first two children so named had died in infancy and had been buried in Cork where their parents had lived for some years. The merchant shipping company which then employed William docked its ships there.

A round-faced baby with dark hair, blue eyes and long slender limbs, she was not at first robust, but she responded to her anxious parents' care and she grew to be a sturdy child. Two other daughters were born at two year intervals; in 1909 Catherine, later called Kit, was also born in Cork where William had again taken his family, and Alexandrina, called Lexy for short, was born in 1911, in the Caird Drive flat which was to be the family home for many years.

Mary was a lively child who, from her earliest years, seemed to run towards life with open arms. She loved to hear her mother sing and say to her the old Scots nursery rhymes. Her father, a fine musician who played his bagpipes with the spirited verve of the Highlander, would play traditional airs on his chanter, so that she grew up well acquainted with her Scottish heritage.

Sometimes when accommodation on board ship proved suitable, the family would all sail together for a holiday. Such trips were often to European ports, and a memory which remained with Molly throughout her life was of one such occasion in her very young days when she wandered entranced, while shopping with her parents in an open market somewhere in Belgium. So intrigued was she with the different sights and sounds that she wandered off in the bustling crowd. Just before panic set in, her parents appeared to claim her, following the trail of broken eggs which had trickled from the basket that she had dragged heedlessly along the ground behind her.

She was always called "Mary" in those days and remained so to her family. "Molly" started as a nickname given to her by her mother's friends, the three Miss Watts of Dumbarton Road in Partick. They used to enjoy hearing her go through her repertoire of songs and poems, and were particularly amused by this four-year-old, rendering, with absolute seriousness, the old Irish ballad, 'Cockles and Mussels', especially the lines:

> "She died of a fever
> And no-one could save her,
> So that was the end of poor Molly Malone . . ."

So to Miss Jenny and her sisters, Nan and Nell, she became 'Molly Malone', and Molly was the name her friends always called her.

When Molly reached the age of five, the family rovings were curtailed. She was enrolled as pupil at Dowanhill Primary School only five minutes' walk away from Caird Drive.

William was at sea when, in 1913, just a fortnight before their next child was expected, Ann suffered a crippling stroke that paralysed her left side. A handsome woman with brown hair, blue eyes and a

3

fine complexion, she had been well and active during her pregnancy, and the doctor was taken aback by this sudden illness. Though secretly worried, he assured her that it was no doubt due to pressure on the nerves of the spine, because of the way the baby was lying, but in his heart he felt it unlikely that either mother or child would survive.

She did live, having given birth successfully to Alasdair, a healthy baby boy, but the condition of paralysis was unrelieved. Her strength was much diminished and the doctor prescribed complete rest, so the children had to be temporarily scattered. Kit went to elegant Great Aunt Sarah in Dennistoun, Lexy, not much more than a baby herself, was taken to her father's people in Inverasdale by Gairloch, while Aunt Effie, Ann's younger sister who had married Donald Stewart, a policeman, took Molly and the baby Alasdair to their home at Braeside, Arrochar.

Arrochar, a cluster of houses, cottages and a fine little church, stands at the head of the fiord-like stretch of water known as Loch Long. Across the loch there is a range of mountains, the highest named the Cobbler because the crags at its peak seem to resemble an old shoemaker hunching over his last. The two mile neck of land that separates it from Tarbet, Loch Lomond, is the corridor that the invading Vikings traversed in the thirteenth century, dragging with them their longboats, to scull along the inland waters of Scotland's largest fresh water loch, terrorising the people who lived on its banks and on the scatter of small islands along its twenty-three miles' length. And in Tarbet, at Shore Cottages, Molly had three cousins to play with, Mary, Jean and Duncan McCallum, the family of Aunt Mary and Uncle John, who was also a sea-faring man.

This first long visit to Aunt Effie's did not pass without incident. One evening her non-appearance home from the school at Tarbet caused a great hullabaloo. By six o'clock the whole village was out looking for the missing child who had been kept in school by a young teacher as a punishment. When she had gone to release her fifteen minutes later, she found a ram-shackle platform made of the teacher's high chair and a waste-paper box from which Molly had managed to reach the window. Two small boot prints in the soft ground underneath showed where she had landed before taking off into the countryside.

The furore arose when the new pupil was asked to read aloud.

PROLOGUE

Molly found that the reading book was the same one that she had used in Dowanhill School. Not so much because she had an exceptional proficiency in reading, but rather because she always had an exceedingly retentive memory, she acquitted herself well, her confident manner of speaking lending a convincing air to her 'reading' of the little story she knew by heart.

When confronted with arithmetic, it was a different story. She had as yet found sums fairly incomprehensible, and could not add up correctly, to the exasperation of the teacher who thought, with reason, that her attainment in reading implied she should have at least the beginnings of awareness in number. The teacher told her to sit down again at her desk, and to concentrate on the three simple sums on her slate, saying she would come back shortly to see how she was getting on.

Throughout her life, Molly had strong sense of justice and injustice. When she felt she was right, she would overcome opposition like a scythe cutting through cornstalks. Deciding even at this early age that this punishment was unfair, she resolved to escape.

As dusk gathered, the search party moved from the environs of the school to the lower slopes of the hills and the pebbled shores of the loch where the shallows at the edge soon gave way to dangerous depths and currents. The tramping feet of the men traversed the shore, backward and forward, but it was only young Duncan McCallum who heard the whisper, "I'm here. Ssh!" He lingered behind and saw under an upturned rowing boat the defiant face of the fugitive.

At supper that evening, his mother caught him slipping a scone into his pocket, and guessed the reason. The accomplice led Uncle Donald Stewart to the hiding place and Molly was carried back to Braeside. She was admonished of course, because one did not ever speak back to the teacher, but reassured, she was given her supper and put to bed, none the worse for her adventure. Then Donald Stewart went to see the anxious young teacher and peace was made.

The rest of the time spent at Arrochar was idyllic. A contemporary, Miss Jessie Campbell, remembers Molly as 'an awful bonnie wee girl, bonnie blue eyes, black curly hair in a kind of plait. She was a born leader. Things would be flat down at the shore and then someone would say, "Here's Mary coming. She'll stir things up." She was a wee bit bossy, and she would fight like the mischief. But

5

full of ideas. She always had to be organising us'.

The children used to sit on the jetty paddling their feet in the clear water, or making patterns with the round yellow pebbles that covered the shore. Molly was a born mimic. 'She could aye imitate onybody', recalled Danny Carmichael, a schoolfellow of those times. She was never short of things she wanted to do. Once she fired Jessie with her enthusiasm for doing good deeds, and the pair of them spring-cleaned a hen house on Stell Brae belonging to 'auld Jeannie' who was 'a wee bit wandered'. Not only did they put the hens off laying, but they threw out the old clothes and odds and ends that Jeannie treasured. For this they were severely chastised by Mr Grierson, the headmaster at the school.

Once young John McCallum got a rusty nail in his foot while they were playing near Coll McDermid's boats at the jetty. While they were waiting for Dr Imrie to come from Garelochead, the boy remarked, with commendable philosophy, "I'm awful glad that rusty nail's in my foot and not in my head."

"Aye. It would have been worse if it had been in your head. You'd've had to get the nail hammered in," said his cousin Molly, with dramatic relish.

Sometimes old Mrs Murray would take them out in one of her boats. Molly and the other children loved this hardy old lady who helped to row the boats that lay for hire at the jetty. Striking out from the shore along the renowned 'bonnie banks of Loch Lomond', she would entertain the children with one of her many stories. One of these concerned a young German tourist on holiday at Tarbet Hotel. He wanted to climb Ben Lomond, so Mrs Murray rowed him to the point nearest the approach to the mountain and went back for him later the same day. He was the son of Kaiser Wilhelm, and after 1914, when she was told that 'yon man you rowed across the loch started this great war', she said, with sincerity, "If I had kent that, I'd have droont the bugger half way ower!"

While her family were away, Ann, with the help of her husband who was at home for a spell, and her friends the Miss Watts, came to terms with her affliction. For the rest of her life, she held her left hand inert against her waist, and dragged her left leg. But she was able to walk and managed to cope with the cooking and some of the lighter household tasks, having a daily woman to help temporarily in the mornings.

PROLOGUE

At last the children came home again. They clustered around her, admiring baby Alasdair, with his fair curly hair and round beaming face. Aunt Sarah had dressed Kit like a little princess all in pink and white and she paraded before everyone with a frilly parasole, which was soon discarded. Little Lexy clung constantly to her mother in relief at being re-united with her. The Urquharts had lavished attention on her, but she was too little to comprehend the situation, and had missed her mother very much. Molly, then aged seven, saw with a shock of realisation, the great effort that it took for her mother, formerly so quick and spry, to heave herself to her feet and make her laboured way into the kitchen.

Ann knew that, as the wife of a sea-going engineer, her children's upbringing depended on her. She realised also that strict economy would have to be practised, because even in a nation that depended so much on trade, employment on merchant shipping was never easily obtained, even for a shrewd, highly skilled Clyde-trained engineer like William.

To compensate for Ann's impaired vigour, the household chores, which were, of course, at that time normally shared among members of any family in their social strata, fell on the shoulders of her children. The services of the daily help taxed the family income, so she had to go. It was Molly, the eldest, who became Ann's mainstay. She felt for her handsome mother, so cheerfully and determinedly coping with house and family, and was always there to help, holding her shoulder steady for her mother to lean on as they made their way downstairs to go shopping in Dumbarton Road.

Mrs Urquhart managed the preparation and cooking of the food, good plain Scots fare of home made soups with stock from a sheep's head, or hough, or ham bone with lentils added, and a main course of stewing steak, mince, or fish such as herring or haddock, with plenty of vegetables and potatoes. Puddings were often difficult for her to make, except for simple dishes like milk puddings or stewed fruit, but a great delicacy much enjoyed was a plateful of the shiny, round golden-brown 'plain cookies' bought at the local branch of the City Bakeries, two for a penny. Those split in half and spread thickly with home made strawberry jam and whipped cream delighted the children, who all had good appetites. A visit from Aunt Effie and Uncle Donald often meant a plump, boiling fowl for the soup pot, as well as some fresh country eggs with the creamy whites that only the free-range hens of bygone days could produce.

Formal family photographs show the children in the typical 'best dress' of the period, the girls in silk tussore dresses with sailor collars, with Panama hats and fine leather button boots. Winter week days saw them warmly clad in navy serge dresses and coats that would not soil easily, with white cotton pinafores to relieve the sombre colour. Black woollen stockings and boots completed the outfit.

Summer days meant washable cotton dresses in light colours and with, sometimes, canvas shoes to be kept white with Blanco, a solid chalk block which was moistened and a thin layer applied which hardened into a gleaming surface, which came off in little powdery clouds when the shoes were walked in. Mending was difficult for their mother, but their good friend Miss Jenny Watt on her weekly visit would come equipped with her needle, calling "Who's first?" as the children came home from school or play.

An atmosphere of friendship and hospitality always pervaded the household, and there were always visitors, neighbours' children and relatives. On Sundays, they went to the church in Gardner Street, a gathering place for exiled Highlanders, where an additional Gaelic service was held in the afternoon. William liked to hear the Bible read in his own tongue.

When father was at home, there would always be family gatherings. Loyal to his background, William always kept full Highland dress for 'best', and a magnificent set of bagpipes with silver decoration. His cousin, John Urquhart, who was president of the Highlanders' Association in Glasgow, would come over with his wife and three daughters, Jess, Lily and Anne, and there would be a musical evening, with songs at the piano, and the little girls dancing a vigorous Highland Fling to the skirl of the pipes. The neighbours had a great liking for the family, and never complained about the plaintive airs and joyful reels that, although the music making was kept to appropriate hours, would be more fitting among the mountains of Wester Ross than in a flat two up with five other families close by.

Once, when new neighbours had come to number 27, such a party had taken place on their first night. Mrs Urquhart realised this the next day, and sent Molly with a note welcoming them and expressing the hope that the pipe music had not disturbed them. Mr and Mrs Campbell had enjoyed it thoroughly, and it transpired Mr

PROLOGUE

Campbell's people had come from Tiree, from where Ann's forebears hailed. So another link was formed; their only daughter Cathie found herself with young friends to play with, and the parents were good friends from then on.

Kit and Lexy were the best dancers of the family and learned the intricate steps with ease, but Molly had an extraordinarily powerful voice and from the age of six or seven, sang the old Gaelic songs with an intensity of feeling almost unnatural in so young a child. Though she never had complete fluency in the language, the Highland airs seemed only right when the lyrics were sung in the original tongue, so her father taught them to her, and was so proud when she sang at the family gatherings. Realising that she had a special talent, her parents sent he to piano lessons, and Lexy, rather less enthusiastically, went to learn the violin. Kit and Alasdair were too lively a pair to concentrate on such activities when they could be out playing.

It was a very happy household, and other children always found an open door there and were drawn into the lively relaxed atmosphere. Although she had her household completely in control, Ann, as friends recall, seldom seemed to command or raise her voice; things flowed smoothly, and she was always at the helm, steering gently but firmly. She relied on Molly, but never let go of the reins, and she nurtured her daughter's growing love of poetry and music. She was also careful to send her for long holidays on her own to her sister at Arrochar and later at Bowling, where she could be spoiled.

Before the highway to Balloch had been built, Bowling was a quiet little village on the Clyde, situated just below a glen which was in a rugged, natural state, thick with wild flowers, buttercups, pink clover and harebells. The countryside was always dear to Molly's heart and she immersed herself in the sights, sounds and fragrances of a Scottish summer, which she herself recalled vividly over sixty years later:

> "Up the Glen" was Paradise. Still rugged and beautiful, wild flowers grew there in profusion, while in the marshy parts were great clumps of rushes which I loved to gather, to plait them and make a basket for flowers to present to my aunt.
>
> A burn came gurgling down from the hills and with bare feet, I'd wade in, shoes and stockings safely on the bank. There was a rock in the middle where, with great daring, I would sit and splash my feet, keeping time to the rhythm of the water.

9

Then there was the "Tarrie Boiler" where the men were busy all day boiling tar. I never discovered why, because the boiler was declared out of bounds since I seemed to manage to get tar on my clothes even if I only inhaled its pungent perfume, which, I argued, was supposed to be good for your lungs.

When the pangs of hunger assailed me, it was down the glen at the double, stopping at the little Toll House at the foot of the brae where old Mary lived. In her full serge skirt with its drugget apron and her little white cap perched on silver hair and tied under her chin, she seemed like the Old Woman who lived in a Shoe. With her rosy cheeks and her constant smiling, she was, in my eyes, eternally young. Her fund of stories was never ending, and I loved to hear her recite a poem called "The Boy who was half-past three", though it always made me sad. All the children loved her, because, although my aunt told me she worked very hard, she always had time to provide a freshly baked scone or pancake, spread thickly with butter by Mary's deft thumb — a knife would have taken too long!

Her one great treasure was her Cuckoo Clock. I would watch fascinated as she wound it by pulling down the weighted chain, then when the doors flew open, and the Cuckoo popped out to call five o' clock for tea time, Mary dismissed us with, "Awa hame wi' ye!"

By now she was back at school and an entry in the Dowanhill School Log Book for 1 September 1914 shortly after the outbreak of the First World War records:

All preliminary arrangements having been completed, the work of the school has now begun in earnest, though a good many pupils have not yet procured all the books required. In the case of over twenty families the father has gone on military service.

The war affected the lives of many households, whose fathers and sons of military age went to serve in the armed forces. Army pay was not princely. On average, the ranks received one shilling a day, with perhaps a slight extra for a special skill, for example, ability to handle a Lewis Gun, gave a man threepence a day extra.

The casualties in the War struck savagely and quickly and the war efforts of the families of this little district of Partick was indicated in the Log entry of 16 September 1914:

PROLOGUE

. . . This week all the pupils have contributed generously to provide for the needs of invalid soldiers in Stobhill Hospital and the Belgians who come to the city today. Three hundred pots of home-made jam, 4000 cigarettes, fruit, writing paper, chocolate, tobacco, pipes and several walking sticks have been collected.

In February, 1916, the Headmaster issued instructions to the staff to return to the more frequent use of slates in order to economise in paper. And in the same month twelve bewildered Belgian children were enrolled, their families being refugees from the German invasion of their own country. Mrs Urquhart was among the many who offered hospitality to these newcomers to the neighbourhood, and they joined in the spontaneous musical evenings and had suppers at her house. (This resulted in a strange coincidence when, many years later, sailing into Port Elizabeth with a film unit, Molly disembarked, to be greeted by a tall Roman Catholic missionary priest whom she could not recognise at all, till he said, 'Remember Mamma Urquhart's cream cookies!')

The war at first seemed only another adult preoccupation, for whispered items of news and family tragedies were kept from the children's ears as much as possible. Since they were used to their father being away on long voyages, his absence now with his ship, sailing with many others under convoy, carrying essential supplies, did not seem to be so very different to his young family.

The fact that the school's collection of £42 for the Lord Provost's Fund for Limbless Heroes was acknowledged by a letter of appreciation, read to the assembled classes, did not really register with the children as something that might relate to their own small world.

Yet in June 1916, the singular occurrence of being called to the headmaster's room in the middle of a school morning to find her mother there filled Molly with alarm even before she heard the fearful injunction "You must be a brave girl!" Her father's ship had struck a mine and all hands were reported lost. The little family sat together in their grief. Ann did not give way to tears when her children were there. She had great self-discipline, obtained from years of contending with her disability. Nor did she allow them to indulge in public sobbing. "Cry if you need to, but cry in your own room," she would say.

The news that arrived a few days later, that by some strange providence William had been transferred to another ship shortly before the ill-fated vessel sailed, came as a shock of joy. Yet in the midst of the relief and thanksgiving, Ann thought of all the other men lost and of their families, many of them their friends, suffering for ever the sorrow that had been miraculously taken from her door, and for once, she gave way to an ill-concealed depression. Thus Mary, always close to her mother, reflected this despair, so much so that, although it was only mid-June she was despatched to Bowling to Aunt Effie and Uncle Donald and the freedom of the countryside where her spirit gained strength again.

The long summer days were interrupted by an exciting intimation. Mr and Mrs Stewart had been invited to a grand wedding in Paisley Abbey. The bride was to be a Miss Flora MacDonald and a fleet of bridesmaids was to follow her down the aisle in full rig. To Molly's astonishment she was invited also; not only that, she was to be a 'stand-by train-bearer', since the little girl who was designated to carry the train was given to tantrums, and the bride's mother felt it necessary to have an older child standing by ready to step into the role at a moment's notice.

In preparation for that eventuality, Aunt Effie took her niece to call on Miss Selina Graham, a dressmaker who worked from her own little terrace house in Bowling. Molly recalled the visit vividly:

> We arrived at Miss Selina's on the stroke of three and were shown into her front parlour where, I noticed, a tea tray and cakes were set on a side table. Everything about her was flower-like. Small, slim, fragile as a piece of Dresden china, her age baffled me, but I don't think she was as old as I thought she was. Her hair was very fair, and looped over her ears, so that she looked exactly like one of the Victorian maidens in my scrapbook.
>
> A conscientious, painstaking seamstress, she was the acknowledged village dressmaker, and the thought of making a dress for even a stand-by trainbearer for a Paisley Abbey society wedding was a thrilling challenge.
>
> After we had tea, the cream shantung silk my aunt had bought was produced. This did not meet with Miss Selina's approval, nor with mine, since secretly I thought it had a funny smell. Her little white hands touched it with an air of rejection and she rustled with the whisper of taffeta underskirts, over to her cupboard, after winning my heart utterly by insisting I finish the last cake, my fourth, despite my aunt's silent disapproval of her greedy niece.

PROLOGUE

From one of a series of neatly docketed boxes, she produced a length of shimmering champagne silk, so beautiful that my sticky hands reached out to caress it. "No, no. Don't touch, dear!" cried Miss Selina.

I waited to hear the outcome. To my delight Miss Selina won, and instead of the smelly cream Shantung, my dress was to be of champagne silk!

My romping up the Glen was a bit curtailed, for I had to be clean and neat for fitting after fitting. Miss Selina worked with her mouth full of pins, which I was terrified she would swallow, and a whole armoury of equipment, a long inch tape round her neck, with little pouches fastened around her waist for thimble and scissors, and a small round red pincushion on her shoulder for storing even more of those jaggy pins.

Finally her creation was almost complete. I tried not to fidget as I stood in its glistening folds, Miss Selina darting here, there and everywhere viewing her work from every possible angle.

"You've caught the spirit, Miss Selina" said Aunt Effie in admiration.

Selina blushed, darted to her cupboard, and produced a delicate length of Valenciennes lace and a piece of Champagne satin. "This is for the sash, I think? And the lace will froth around the skirt like so . . ." and she attacked again with her pins.

Then came the final fitting. The completed dress, enveloped in tissue paper, was on the stand. As Miss Selina removed the tissue paper to reveal her work in all its glory, her canary, with a nice sense of occasion burst into song. I felt like joining him. Shimmering pale silk, scalloped hem with its froth of lace — it looked good enough to eat, a compliment sincere from a child so greedy as I was. Aunt Effie's words echoed my thoughts:

"Selina, it's not just a dress! It's a . . . a . . . a . . . *confection!*"

I felt suddenly shy. That dress and I did not belong together. But Miss Selina's fittings were expert, and as I looked in the mirror, I saw reflected a person who might well pass for a trainbearer at a grand wedding.

And marvellously, it came true. My aunt, in her best dress of lavender grey ("enlivened" by Miss Selina, with dusky pink trimmings) and in her old Leghorn straw hat, which she had scrubbed clean and left to dry in the sun, before covering the crown with a mass of artificial flowers, was a bright figure beside Uncle Donald in his bowler, and navy serge suit. I didn't, of course, travel in the dress but actually changed in an ante room of the Abbey, a building which to me was so magnificent that I felt it

13

must resemble Heaven itself. Miss Selina was there too, though not as a guest. She stayed with me while the others went into the church. The bridal car arrived. When I think of it, it seems a fearful situation to have had a ten year old waiting in the wings as an understudy for such an occasion. I smoothed down my flounces, looking with satisfaction at my satin shoes and white stockings dyed champagne colour with tea. When I looked at Miss Selina, she was standing with her eyes closed tight. A little alarmed, I was about to ask if she felt ill, when a gradual crescendo of crying began outside. Miss Selina's eyes opened; she beamed in thanksgiving and gave a last twitch to my sash. "Is that a tantrum?" I asked doubtfully. It was — and I was on.

Miss Selina vanished into the church, a lady rushed in and pinned a wreath of artificial buttercups on my head before ushering me into the foyer. "Hold the train loosely. Give it plenty of lee-way. And start off on your right foot!" I wasn't too sure what lee-way meant, but the bride appeared in a misty white radiance, like a princess from an ivory tower, I thought, beside her tall handsome father, who wore spectacles which were held together at the nose piece with a twist of black wool. I saw what were obviously his best ones in his breast pocket, but I only had time to suppress a giggle before the music started. The guests shuffled to their feet and the bride looked round, smiled at me through the delicate veil and said, "We'll count one — two — three — and away."

She seemed to glide forward and I straightened up and followed. The organ boomed, the congregation gave vent to oohs and ahs. I felt it was my moment, and carried the train with perfect 'lee-way' with the swish of the six adult bridesmaids' dresses coming behind like a gentle fragrant breeze.

I wished the aisle would stretch on forever but the bride was standing with her uniformed bridegroom. I carefully arranged the train before I was whipped aside while the adult bridesmaids moved in a V-shaped phalanx behind Miss MacDonald.

The service passed somehow. Then the longed-for 'Here Comes the Bride' called me back to my position and this time I caught sight of Aunt Effie and Miss Selina who had eyes for no-one but me as the wedding group passed their pew.

Chapter Two

School Days

'An average pupil.' That guarded assessment has been the label of innumerable small persons who have been difficult to categorise during their school days. Even nowadays, the school curriculum can highlight only the more obvious aptitudes and abilities shown by pupils. In the early part of this century Dowanhill Primary School was an educational establishment run by a series of forward-looking headmasters, and a glance at the School Log Books shows a concern to feature art, music, poetry and gymnastics as regularly in the curriculum as the basic 'Three R's'. It was a pleasant school to attend and, for its time, advanced in educational aims.

Molly was a dreamer, and often had to be chastised into giving her full attention to the everyday subjects. When it came to reciting poetry, she was alert and eager, and one teacher in despair over the disparity of effort shown by this pupil, uttered, with some accuracy, the prophetic remark, 'I don't know what on earth you'll be, but you'll be *something.*'

The idea of anyone from a good, solid Scottish, Presbyterian background becoming an actress was a possibility that neither family nor school would seriously consider. The stage was an exotic world and one still slightly suspect as being at least a sidepath on the road to perdition. Music was more respectable, but although piano and violin lessons were given high priority for the Urquhart children, a singing teacher who might suggest songs other than the traditional Scottish and Gaelic airs was not deemed necessary. Elocution lessons did not play a part in Molly's life until she was earning money herself, though she loved to learn poetry and found a ready-made audience when she called at the Miss Watts whom her mother visited weekly to play cards. They delighted in their 'Molly Malone's' ever-extending repertoire, and she gave harrowing renderings of the dramatic ballads of Longfellow and Thomas Campbell, particularly the latter's 'Lord Ullin's Daughter', with the tears shining in her grey-blue eyes as she told of the final tragedy of the lovers, who fleeing from the wrath of an angry father were drowned in the stormy waters of Loch Gyle:

> "Come back! come back!" he cried in grief,
> "Across this stormy water;
> And I'll forgive your Highland chief,
> My daughter — Oh my daughter!"

> 'Twas vain: — the loud waves lashed the shore,
> Return or aid preventing: —
> The waters wild went o'er his child,
> And he was left lamenting.

The two Miss MacFarlanes of Tarbet whom she visited during her holidays on Loch Lomondside likewise encouraged her to recite. They gave her a copy of Longfellow's 'Hiawatha' which she so loved to memorise that she could recite reams of it, throughout her life. They were very pretty, refined middle-aged ladies, quite beautiful in Molly's eyes, so much so, that one day she tentatively enquired of them why they had not married. "Well, Molly-Wolly-Doodle, the carriages passed us by, and we wouldn't go with the wheel barrows," was the reply, which mystified their young admirer for many years. They also told her stories about a famous actress called Mrs Pat Campbell who used to stay with friends at nearby Toberdarroch House. Moreover, the excellent Scottish fare of the Arrochar Hotel had always attracted the 'quality' and the elegance of Mrs Langtry who had appeared on the stage in London and in Edinburgh, and who had taken lunch there with the Prince of Wales, was still legend.

School did provide some outlets. One early effort at curricular integration began when the class had to learn Wordsworth's 'The Solitary Reaper' and her Highland accent sat well on the familiar lines:

> Behold her, single in the field,
> Yon solitary Highland Lass!
> Reaping and singing by herself,
> Stop here, or gently pass!

The next part was not so easy. The art lesson demanded that they should depict in water colour this same Highland Lass, a fairly daunting task for ten year old children: Molly's effort was woeful.

When a special allowance had been made to equip a primary school for an extra subject like art, a visit from the Inspectors of Schools came as a matter of course, to see if the materials supplied were being used to obtain worthwhile results. So it was that the visit of the Art Inspector coincided with the 'Solitary Reaper' venture. A selection of the paintings were set forth, and, as the best spokesman, one might say, Molly was called out to recite the poem.

Just before she began, the teacher handed her the relevant picture to hold while she recited. Beginning to blush at its remembered inadequacy she glanced down — to find, to her horror, that it was not her own smudged effort but the rather splendid work of a classmate who, it so happened, was not present at the school that day.

She looked at her teacher, who, apparently all unaware, said encouragingly, "Go ahead, Mary!" Somehow she got through the poem, with a heightened intensity but filled with a strange sense of guilt and a dread that she might be asked to demonstrate or comment on the artistic effort that she held. But in Yeats' phrase, 'the sixty-year-old smiling public man' simply said, "Well done", and moved on to the next classroom. The school's allowance for art was maintained, and only one small puzzled pupil rushed home to her mother to discuss tearfully the problematic exigencies of life.

During the next session, an enterprising young teacher let her class perform, at the end of term, a short play, that perennial favourite about boarding school girls by Violet M. Methley called 'Freckles'. Molly hoped she might be chosen to play the heroine, who tries unsuccessfully to eliminate her hated freckles with a dubious beauty preparation that stains her skin so brown that when the longed-for visit from her Godmother occurs, she has to pass herself off as 'Princess Salamanda Savanna' from Jamaica. Instead the budding actress had to content herself with the part of Joan, a 'best friend' of the 'Golly! I say!' variety, and never were such deathless lines as: "How I do hate getting up! I'm as sleepy as an owl!" uttered so fervently.

The First World War was drawing to a close in 1918; and the tension on the home front lessened. School charity drives to raise

17

money for Red Cross funds and other good causes were still being
organised, and to supplement the considerable sums already raised
by the children of Dowanhill School, Molly, aided and abetted by
her best-loved cousin, Lily Urquhart, put on a concert in the front
parlour for family and neighbours. Her rosy cheeks were powdered,
and a lace curtain framed an anxious face. As she pushed Lily on
ahead to play her accompaniment, she implored her in a whisper,
"You'll give me a clap, won't you — even if nobody else does!"

The night the war ended there were celebrations in the streets. The
great fleet of tram-cars, the mainstay of transport in the city, swung
through crowded streets, ablaze with triumphant light. The girls
from the munitions factories, still in their caps and overalls, were
singing on the open top decks, a ballad popular at the time, its theme
of parting lovers and hoped-for reunion set to the kind of yearning
melody so suited to the impassioned, intense nasal Glaswegian-style
rendition:

"We sailed away
To Suvila Bay . . ."

Molly standing beside her mother rejoiced in the sound. The
lassies gave it laldy, as they would have said themselves, and she
never forgot it. Indeed, nearly sixty years later, she set the B.B.C. in
Scotland scurrying to find a recording of it to play in an 'Autogram'
programme, where she was choosing melodies specially memorable to
her.

Her father came home safe and his future sailings were in peaceful
waters. Unfortunately the post-war depression soon began to take
effect, and he had to sail wherever he could get a berth, to Europe, to
Russia and for a period he sailed with a company in the Pacific plying
between Australia and New Zealand.

Times were hard and the family were growing up. Molly, on
reaching the age of twelve, went to Church Street School, which
offered a short course of higher education. There was no question of
her going to the fee-paying Hyndland School, which offered an
academic five-year course to take pupils to Higher Certificate
standard, nor, in fact, would she have wanted that, because already
she had formed her ambition.

"When I grow up," she confided to cousin Lily, "I'm going to be
an actress and my name will be Marie St Clair."

With an instinctive awareness of the kind of difficulties that would beset her path, she chose, even for her secret dreams, a more sophisticated version of her own Scottish forename, Mary Sinclair. The stage was a world of its own, of an elegance very remote from the front parlour concerts of her home. The touring companies which came to the King's Theatre and the Theatre Royal had glamorous leading ladies — Mrs Pat Campbell, Julia Neilson Terry, Marie Lohr, Marie Tempest, Gladys Cooper — all exquisitely rare creatures with the kind of prettiness often illustrated in the picture postcards that girls loved to collect. Their speech was silver-pure English, the celebrated forerunner of received pronunciation, that became a kind of Procrustean bed to which all voices had to conform, despite the best liberal intentions of speech specialists like Daniel Jones, who defined it as the form of English most easily understood. As Shaw had observed so shrewdly in *Pygmalion* a few years earlier, accent and social acceptability in Britain were inextricably bound together.

So Molly set her sights on a stage career. This she would have to achieve for herself since it was impossible for the family to contemplate any formal training for her, even if there had been a drama school in Scotland. There was anyway still a slight resistance towards the idea of 'actress', and so she concentrated gratefully on the music lessons which her parents always ensured were available.

She was still the mainstay at home and her younger sisters and their friend Cathie Campbell remember her chattering to them when they all got home from school, but dusting and polishing the while. Sometimes she was left in charge if her mother was out, and diverted them with a variety of activities, once making toffee which, since she read the wrong recipe half way through, turned out to be a syrupy pudding, which was happily eaten nevertheless. On other occasions, she sent them into paroxysms of enjoyable terror, by telling or rather enacting ghost stories and grisly legends. The neighbours would say, "I heard Mary keeping the wee ones quiet last night!"

She always supported them in any quarrels and for a young girl was strongly maternal and unselfish in the way she put them before herself if any treats or presents were offered. A quaint incident illustrating this occurred the Christmas after the war had ended. Her father was to have been at sea during the festive season, and it looked like being rather a bleak time, since her mother could only afford sensible presents, although in each small stocking there would be the traditional new penny, sugar mice and a tangerine. Then Uncle Sandy, a sea-going cousin of her mother's came to visit. 'Rich Uncle Sandy' the children secretly called this generous, jolly man, who never came without an armful of extras.

It being Christmas Eve, there was the usual sing-song round the piano, and he was so taken by his eldest niece singing 'Silent Night' with 'The Four Maries' as a moving but irrelevant encore that he presented her with a ten shilling note to "get some things for Christmas". This was an enormous sum, more, at that time, than many a working man's weekly wage. Molly was amazed at her good fortune, thanked him profusely, and got ready to go to the shops, which in those days stayed open late for the last minute Christmas purchasing. Ann got ready too, so mother and daughter made their way down Hyndland Street wrapped warmly in their blue serge coats, hats, and boots, for it was snowing lightly, and the pavements were covered with freezing slush.

Molly was intent on planning what presents she might buy. Her mother was strangely silent.

When they arrived at the shops, her mother stopped suddenly and pointed with her stick to a little group of three children, standing noses pressed against the window of the baker's shop, looking longingly at the various goodies displayed inside. They were quarrelling over which cakes they were going to have.

"Look, Mary." The stick pointed relentlessly. Bare feet! They were hopping from one foot to the other, holding each in turn against the warmth of the other calf, to try to dispel the chilling effect of the slush.

Mary's face fell. She knew what was coming.

"Wouldn't you like to make this a real Christmas for those children?"

Not at all sure that she would, she looked up at her mother with a petulant expression wondering if she could whisper aloud the refusal that was in her heart.

"I don't think we could enjoy our Christmas Day, remembering these little, cold, hungry children, could we?"

Molly's conscience was stirred, though she still longed to be the good fairy to her own family. But there was no refusing her mother. Silently, sullenly, she handed over Uncle Sandy's money.

Mrs Urquhart crossed to the little group who were stunned into silence when they were ushered into the shop and saw the Christmas cake they had fantasised over, being packed carefully into a cardboard carton for them. Then they all trooped over to the Outfitter's Department of the St George's Co-operative Store in Mansefield Street, where Mrs Urquhart was a regular customer. Such was the personal magnetism of Ann that when the manager became aware of her intent, he saw to it that the sum of money stretched quite amazingly so that the children went home warmly shod and with some toys, their faces full of glee as they marched along balancing their packages.

A thoughtful little girl climbed on Uncle Sandy's knee to explain the whole adventure. "So that's what we did," she concluded. With an unconscious exercising of that sense of timing that was later to prove so valuable in her chosen career, she paused and looked at him steadfastly for a moment. "Uncle Sandy, we learn texts at the Sunday School as well."

"Do you, my lass? What's the one you learned last Sunday?"

The blue eyes looked at him unwaveringly "Cast thy bread upon the waters; for thou shalt find it after many days."

Uncle Sandy guffawed loud and long — and gave her a pound note!

Chapter Three

Actresses happen . . .

'Actresses happen in the best regulated families.' Oliver Herford.

In 1920, at the age of fourteen Molly left school, without too much regret. She had by then gained a quick mind for figures, and with her pleasant out-going personality she obtained fairly easily a position in the cash desk of a local shop. It was while she was on holiday on the little island of Gigha off the coast of Argyll that she received the news that she had been successful in passing the entrance examination to get a job in the Post Office. This was quite an achievement, since there was not a wide variety of employment to be had for a young girl who had just left school. Young Kit and Alasdair, and their cousin David Stewart, also there on holiday with David's Aunt Elizabeth and Uncle Donald Duncan who lived in Newquay Cottage on the island, looked wide-eyed at Molly who, to them, seemed so unfortunate to be leaving early from a holiday in one of those one long hot summers that left a glow on memories of childhood. With every evidence of cheerfulness, off she went, waving to them from the little ferry-boat taking her to Tayvallich from where she would travel to Glasgow.

After a few months' basic training, her clear distinct voice made her a natural for the Telephone Exchange and that was the section in which she worked for many years. She tackled the job with enthusiasm and really enjoyed her work.

Social life was opening out. With her sisters, she joined the Girls Guildry in Church Street School which Lexy who was a fine runner much enjoyed, since it led to her friendship with Jessie Adamson, one of five sisters who lived in Hyndland. Together they joined netball and hockey teams and later the harriers, where Lexy, always rather shy, began to blossom and became a sprinter of real

22

distinction. Every Saturday afternoon, Molly with her cousin Lily Urquhart would be allowed to go into town to see a film at the matinee performance in the King's Cinema at Charing Cross where they watched everything from the high drama of *Lady Audley's Secret* to the cliff-hanging comedies of Harold Lloyd.

In summer they would play tennis in the public courts in Kelvingrove Park, first hiring, then later, proudly owning their 'bats' as tennis racquets were then called. This was one sport in which Molly excelled, later winning the Post Office Doubles Championship with a girl friend. She was a Sunday School teacher, at Partick Gardner Street Church, teaching the youngest class, members of which she would invite once or twice a year to her home for a party. She also delighted to teach any youngsters who were interested in poetry and rhymes, and looked on them proudly when they recited their party pieces, such as 'Time, You Old Gipsy Man' and 'Where are you going to, all you big steamers?'

Sometimes in the evenings, her sisters and friends practised dancing in the front room, not the Highland and country dances they had known for years, but the modern foxtrot and Charleston, which Kit, always so nimble, was first to master, and then teach to the others.

Lily's father was President of the Highlanders' Association in Glasgow, and one Christmas as a great concession, she and Molly, then fifteen years old, were allowed to go to the Highland ball. They were dressed in white, Molly with a peach satin sash and shoes, Lily with blue. Molly's father, resplendent in his full Highland dress, escorted both of them there; Lily's father was master of ceremonies and had to be early to welcome everyone. Thoughts of romatic meetings were soon squashed, when William, taking up Lily for the Gay Gordons, informed his daughter, "You will sit here till the dance is over, then I'll dance with you!" And so the whole evening went on, the girls, thus chaperoned, dancing in turn, only with him. Two young men did try to dance with the curly-headed vivacious Miss Urquhart, and although they were unsuccessful on this occasion their paths were to cross in different ways in future years. One tall dark-haired youth, just beginning his studies for an Engineering Degree at the University of Glasgow, was John Duncan Macrae, son of a Highland policeman. He was an enthusiast for the theatre and was already a keen amateur actor. The other, a handsome

23

boy, brown-haired with the misty blue remote eyes of the Highlander, was in Glasgow training to be an engineer. He was William McIntosh, one of a family of seven brothers and one sister, and his home was in Munlochy, Easter Ross. Older by six years than Molly, he was impressed by her glowing good looks. They were to meet again.

Now that she was earning a living, Molly was helping to pay for her own singing lessons. Her teacher was a Dr Seligmann who taught at the Athenaeum, the College of Music in Glasgow. Much impressed by her strong contralto voice, he thought she could make a career in light opera. She practised and practised, singing at churches and various burgh hall concerts. Never ungenerous with her talent, she did, however prefer the city hall concerts, since they usually paid their artistes a small sum (2/6d) as expenses, which went towards further lessons and music. A boy friend of hers had a job playing the piano as accompaniment to the silent films in a local cinema, the Rosevale on Dumbarton Road. The management suggested a musical interlude between the feature films, and he offered Molly a job as soloist. Absolutely delighted, she sang selections of old ballads, such as 'In a Monastery Garden' and 'Pale Hands I Love', for which she received the very welcome sum of five shillings for the evening. Alas, her mother, whom she had not informed of her exploit, heard from a neighbour of Mary's lovely singing 'at the pictures' — and that was the end of that! "No daughter of mine is going to sing in a cinema", pronounced Ann.

Some years later, Ann's strict views again came into conflict with her daughter's activities. A well-intentioned friend sent her a cutting from the *Kirkintilloch Herald*, of a review of a concert given in honour of Tom Johnstone, one of the finest Secretaries of State Scotland ever had. 'the *Internationale*' was given a beautiful and fervent rendering by Miss Mary S. Urquhart'. Mrs Urquhart was a Tory and she made her opinions felt quite forcibly when her teenage daughter came home from work!

To her great excitement Dr Seligmann got her a part in a good amateur production of *The Duchess of Danzig* which was to be presented for a week in a theatre in town. Watched from the gallery by all her friends and relatives, she sang her heart out and scored a small personal success. Unfortunately she had, with typical enthusiasm, over-practised; a few weeks later she was ill with a quinsy throat, an affliction that plagued her at intervals for many years. Her voice was over-strained, and she was told firmly she must not sing for at least twelve months.

That was a blow, but she could not rest without some outlet and so she began to take elocution lessons from a highly individual Glasgow teacher, Mr Percy Steeds. He schooled her in breathing and voice production techniques, and coached her in a series of diverse items, from Shakespeare to Burns, from the couthy comic verses of W.D. Cocker to dramatised readings from Dickens, of which her favourite was, with a fine disregard for physical appropriacy, Uriah Heep. That was not so strange, however, because she had one of the great actor's gifts, that of facial mimicry. In later years, she used little in the way of make-up aids to assume character on stage; "I do it from inside", she always claimed, and it certainly worked. That coupled with a strong, clear voice and a supreme instinct for timing made it evident to audiences that this was no ordinary elocutionist. Even allowing for the generosity of the local newspaper reporter, the reception her work received indicated its appeal.

The *Milngavie Herald* reviewing a concert at St Paul's Church in Milngavie, a little town just north of Glasgow, said:

> Miss Molly Urquhart, the elocutionist for the evening, deserves a paragraph all to herself. Her numbers were happily chosen, and she kept her listeners rocking with laughter throughout. Her first number, entitled "Gettin' Up," was a description of the morning experiences of Jimmy McFarlane of Brigton, culminating with the tragedy of "the cheenie dug". Needless to say she was peremptorily encored, and responded with "Two's Company" one of those mystifying readings that hold the audience in suspense until the very end, but the mystery was soon revealed in her finishing line, "You're the finest bottle of whisky I have had for a long time". Subsequently, she literally convulsed the audience when she narrated the adventures of "Wee Teeny" during a trip doon the "watter", and again being recalled, gave an amusing recital around the famous letters "R.S.V.P." Miss Urquhart undoubtedly proved her worth as an elocutionist, and is one of the most humorous we have heard in Milngavie for a long time.

Perhaps it is only fair to quote Two's Company here. It is a little curiosity of a piece of the type usually used as a brief encore:

TRAVELLING HOPEFULLY

We're sitting tonight by the fireglow
just you and I alone,
And the flickering light falls softly
on a beauty that's all your own,
It glows where the smooth round shoulders
from the graceful neck sweep down,
And I wouldn't exchange your beauty
for the best dressed girl in town.

I have drawn the curtain closer and from my arm-chair
I stretch my hand towards you, just to feel if you are there.
Your breath is laden with perfume and my thoughts
around you twine,
And I feel your pulses beating and your spirit
mingling with mine.

When the woes of the world have vanished and
I've pressed my lips to yours,
Just to feel your life-blood flowing to me is
the best of cures
Your purity of spirit inspires me thus
to rhyme —
You're the finest bottle of whisky I've had in
a long, long time!

In her late teens and early twenties she added to her repertoire constantly, printing each new item in her clear, neat script into hard-back exercise books. The aforesaid Dickens readings included, as well as Uriah Heep, Peggotty from *David Copperfield*, Fagin and 'The Death of Nancy' (from *Oliver Twist*); there were poems by Bret Harte, selections from *Songs of a Sourdough* by R.W. Service, Cockney monologues by A.P. Herbert, 'Highland' recitations by D.M. MacKenzie and others, as well as scenes drawn from that joyful saga of a Glasgow working-class family in Edwardian times, *Wee MacGreegor* by J.J. Bell. She had mastered the many varieties of the 'Glesca' accent; her meetings with the plant stall-holder at the Barrows marked the beginnings of a life-long habit of observing keenly and sympathetically every human voice that came within earshot. One of her favourite anecdotes in those books gave her the opportunity to reproduce, with deadly accuracy the ponderously sonorous tones of a certain kind of pulpit voice asking the hypothetical questions that, all too often, are scattered throughout a sermon. The reply in the tones and spirit of purest Glaswegian, convulsed innumerable audiences throughout her life:

A Perfect Being

At a Glasgow mission service, the minister addressing the congregation asked, "Is there anyone here tonight who considers him or her self perfect?" To this there came no answer.

He then asked, "Is there anyone here who considers anyone else here perfect?" To this query also there came no answer.

Then continued the minister, "Is there anyone here, who knows anyone who is perfect?"

There upon a woman's voice was heard from the back, saying, "Aye. Ma man's first wife was perfect!"'

The one accent that eluded her was that of upper class English. She could excel in the Irish, and could reproduce all the varieties of Highland, Lowland, urban and rural Scots, but the somewhat imperious detached tones of the English 'quality' sat uneasily on her, aand even in later years when a rôle demanded that she adopt such a voice, her performance lost something of the warmth, energy and veracity that so characterized her acting. Yet mastery of this variety of English was absolutely *de rigeur* for an actor who set his sights on leading parts, not only in sophisticated comedy set in Mayfair or drama with an English Country House background, but also for the classics. It was out of the question for a Hamlet, Prince of Denmark to speak his lines in an accent other than that of St James' Palace. Nor could Macbeth ever be permitted the intonations of his native Fife. So it was necessary, if one wanted to become established in the acting profession, to model one's speech on that of West End actors.

So, intent on the long term fulfilment of her secret ambition, she joined a local dramatic club and worked on with Percy Steeds, taking by now a few young pupils of her own on a Saturday morning. She was an operator on the Govan Telephone Exhange on the south side of the Clyde, and travelled across the city by the Glasgow Underground, that small but efficient system, linking various parts of the city by what is now nicknamed 'The Magic Roundabout'.

Her social life was bright enough. Tennis, walking with the Highlanders' Association Rambling Club in the summer, and parties, cinemas, theatres and dances in winter, rehearsals permitting.

One incident she often recounted was an occasion when she and cousin Lily had been invited to a dance with John Duncan Macrae and another student friend of his. The son of a Sutherland man who had come to Glasgow to join the police force, John Macrae met the Urquharts often at functions in the Highlanders' Institute, and he and Molly had become good friends. Although he grew to be an actor of spendid craggy appearance, he was not particularly dashing in his youth. Nor, at that time, was he much of a dancer, but he had taken pains to learn the foxtrot, then in vogue, so that he could keep up with his partner. Unfortunately he had learned the dance to one popular tune of the time, 'Happy Days and Lonely Nights' and found only that melody could keep him right. He knew someone in the band, and had persuaded him to have the number played as often as possible, but when, perforce, they moved on to another selection he was flummoxed, and the little group were forced to sit out.

Much to the girls' excitement, a very suave, good-looking fellow, impeccably dressed in full evening rig, with dark hair sleeked back, and narrow moustache in the mode of the current film stars, such as John Boles or Don Ameché, hovered near.

"He's looking at you!" whispered Molly to her cousin.

"No, he's going to ask you up." said Lily. "What a smasher!"

He glided over and with a questioning eyebrow raised to her partner, who nodded an unwilling acquiescence, he bowed deeply to Molly. With superb footwork, he swung her round the floor, gazing down into her eyes, looking almost continental with his dazzlingly perfect smile.

As the music finished, they were just beside the others. In the purest native wood-notes wild, he remarked, "S'awfy hoat in here, int'it? Thae windaes should've bin opened, sure they should."

With a scarce concealed shudder, his partner thanked him and returned, nose in the air, to the triumphant Macrae, who hooted with laughter over this incident many many times, even on the last occasion they were ever to chat together in 1967, shortly before his death.

Although they were both deeply enthusiastic about Scottish culture and tradition, they were also aware of the necessity of acquiring and sustaining an English accent. The reasons for this problem deserve further exploration: partly historical, partly cultural, partly social, they are connected with important issues of national identity. For the moment, let me simply observe that at that time, to paraphrase George Orwell 'some accents were more equal than others'. So Molly went to the theatre and revelled in performances by 'The Great English Tragic Actress Mrs Patrick Campbell and her London Company' at the King's Theatre in 1923, with Mrs Pat as Edith Cordelier in *Uplifted* by Henry Bernstein, in which she wore dresses specially made by Captain Molyneaux, 5 Rue Royal, Paris.

The same year she saw Marie Tempest in *The Marriage of Kitty*, Martin Harvey in *Via Crucis*, a hugely spectacular production adapted from *Everyman*, and in *The Only Way*, that most popular version of Dickens' *Tale of Two Cities* in which he played Sidney Carton. A Scottish Drama, *The Borderer* by Madge and Leslie Howard Gordon, brought to Glasgow those darlings of the London stage, Julia Neilson and Fred Terry as Mary Queen of Scots and the Earl of Bothwell.

As a present from her mother, Molly was given an expensive seat to go to hear Melba, the world famous soprano, sing in a celebrity recital (in a bill that also featured the superb pianist Wilhelm Backhaus.) As well as singing the expected arias as the 'Jewel Song' from *Faust*, *'Addio'* from *La Bohème*, and Rimsky-Korsakov's *Chanson Indoué* she gave, as an encore, 'Home, Sweet Home', sitting at the piano to play her own accompaniment. Though entranced by that silver-true voice singing, with ease and fluency, lieder and excerpts from grand opera, the aspiring young performer admired most of all the simplicity of the old favourite sung with a naturalness that seemed to reveal that all the pomp and circumstance that surrounded the prima donna was only part of an image assumed for show-business purposes. "She was beautiful, Mother. So simple!" was Molly's final judgement.

However, even after she had rested her voice, she gradually dropped the singing lessons in favour of the elocution training, because acting had become her passion. Not that she gave up her singing: indeed her voice, with the training it had received, was always a feature of her work, whether in musical plays or revues, and in the register at her London agent's office in later years, her 'strong, contralto voice' was a listed asset.

A strange little adventure occurred about that time. She decided to enter a verse-speaking competition to be held in the Synod Hall in

Edinburgh. This was an expensive venture, since it involved an entrance fee and the train fare to Edinburgh. Mrs Urquhart insisted she should take Lexy along for company.

There was in vogue in the the Edinburgh of the time a certain kind of vocal sound, very smooth, very melodious and controlled that characterised most of the competitors' work. Entrant after entrant came forward and enunciated the set piece, which was the opening lines of Burns' 'Tam o' Shanter.' Molly listened incredulously. This was in no way like her own planned presentation. It was the voice beautiful, certainly, but too refined for the poem, she felt. 'The Singing Sands', she mentally labelled the style.

Her turn came. She stuck to her guns and attacked the poem with all her considerable vigour, as she felt it should be said, in broad Ayrshire Scots:

> When chapman billies leave the street
> And drouthy neibors, neibors meet. . .'

At first, there were titters at this hearty vocalising coming from a young girl, but then the people began to laugh, really laugh at the humorous lines. She felt she was winning her audience, and finished in fine style.

The adjudication was perhaps predictable. Comment was made on the 'unusual approach' and 'vigour of delivery' but it was an impossible taks to assimilate this highly individual effort into the finer canvas of the other contributors. 'A very interesting rendering'. But she wasn't placed.

Molly always had a temper and she nursed her anger on the train home. But she learned something that day and greeted her family cheerfully enough when they rushed to hear how she had faired. Only Lexy, her loyal little sister, announced, in quivering tones of indignation, "M-m-molly's been rejected!"

Solo work was all very well and it did bring in a little money to pay for her lessons but the play was the thing. In Scotland, the Scottish Community Drama Association was founded in 1926 and was immediately popular as David Hutchison's most useful book, *The Modern Scottish Theatre* (Glasgow, 1977) makes clear:

> The sudden rise to popularity of the amateur theatre in Scotland
> can be seen by comparing the number of entries for the one-act

festival in 1926-27 (35), 1928-29 (88) and 1930-31 (243); by the 1932-33 season the entry had reached 307. By 1937 there were more than one thousand amateur clubs in Scotland.

Molly, therefore, found her way to the amateur clubs just at the beginning of this boom time. There was tremendous interest in the plays and the clubs had large, loyal followings, so that for the competitive Festivals held annually, tickets could often only be obtained by ballot.

Many actors who later became established, popular figures in the Scottish theatre also gained their first experience in the amateur clubs. Macrae was among them, his tall, thin rangy figure and saturine countenance was seen often in the more seriously ambitious productions. He was highly intellectual in his approach, and rather despised the light comedies some of the clubs performed. Molly and he talked endlessly about acting and the future of the theatre. He was trying his own hand at writing but when he showed one effort to her, she dismissed it airily, as "too academic". Yet they acted well together and quarrelled their way amicably through several decades in the story of the Scottish theatre.

Molly's first major dramatic club in the late twenties was the St George Players, a group connected with the co-operative move-ment. An amateur actor of note, Guy Muir, had founded this club, and later he introduced her to a man who was to have a great influence on her development as an actress — a moving spirit in the Scottish Community Drama Movement, R.F. Pollock of Balloch who had acquired a reputation as an authority on dramatic technique and production. An extremely well-read and thoughtful man, he brought to the productions he directed a degree of preparation and a high seriousness that gave them a style and finish that certainly was far removed from the honestly prepared but less intensely investigated approach of the average club producer.

He was a great admirer of the productions of Theodor Komisarjevsky (1882-1954), who had been the director of the Imperial and State Theatres in Moscow before coming to England in 1919. There he put into practice Stanislavsky's theories on characterisation and production, perhaps most notably in the Chekhov season at Barnes Repertory in the nineteen-twenties, bringing a humanity and liveliness to relieve the strange, gloomy, elegiac quality that had previously pervaded the English view of these delicate tragi-comedies of people encapsulated within their own indecision.

Pollock made a fair, square statement of his intent in an article published in *The Scottish Stage* (January 1932). He saw the players as recreators of the dramatist's original conception and declared categorically the players' aim was 'to make an audience believe that real things were happening to real people'. He believed that the cast, once selected, should have an ensemble reading and discussion of the whole play, after which the producer should co-ordinate the results. The enormously detailed preparation he demanded can be illustrated by this excerpt from the same article:

> Practical steps in recording the results of this process can best be explained under two headings, mental and physical. This is how they are applied to the dialogue of the play. The mental:
> (1) map out the setting;
> (2) mark off the thought compartments;
> (3) distinguish between minor and major thoughts;
> (4) mark off the force of these thoughts.
> The physical:
> (1) record the actions accompanying the thoughts;
> (2) similarly the movements;
> (3) the facial expressions.
> To render these results easily available, they should be numbered preferably on blank pages, interleaved, and these numbers related to the dialogue to be spoken. The complete record need only be in the hands of the producer; the excerpted directions applicable to each character will suffice for the guidance of the player interpreting the character.
> Reflection will make it clear that, when actual rehearsal begins, the groundwork is already complete. Entrances and exits are understood, positions and cross movements defined, gestures and pauses decided. It only remains to develop the play by practice.

He invited a group of the most outstanding amateur actors of the time to join a new group, the Tron Theatre, so called after the seventeenth century steeple, a well known landmark at Glagow Cross. This kind of thoroughness with long, gruelling rehearsal periods of up to three months certainly was a discipline. The production copies given to each player were precisely annotated, with detailed typed notes inserted at every utterance to be made. The timing of pauses too was preordained, allowing one, two, three or more silent pulses to punctuate the flow of the scene.

John Pollock, (no relation) one of the finest players of the amateur movement Glasgow was to know, described it simply:

> If you had to cross a table, stage left, and come back, he made you cross, and count three silently before moving back. It seemed to work.' The indefinable aspect of this technique was to count one, two or three of what? Some of the actors reverently intoned, "Pollock, Pollock, Pollock".

The general opinion of actors looking back on those rehearsals was that the talented improved but the less able stayed as they were. For the gifted, the time seemed tedious, and yet Molly, an actress who operated by instinct, always held this training time as one of extreme value. Certainly she always used it to prepare and structure the way she would deliver lines, but, in fact, she was recording the niceties of timing and stress that came from her own inbuilt time clock. She still maintained that by using a simplified version of the framework imposed on a role according to the Tron Theatre method, a competently sufficient performance of a supporting part could be obtained from anyone who had the industry and enthusiasm to tackle it thus. In future years she was able to invoke acting from an amazing number of people, some of whom brought little more than willingness to the task.

Their first presentation was Ibsen's *The Master Builder*, presented in the Keir Hardie Institute in Renfrew Street. Four private performances were given. The programme note says:

> *The Master Builder* has been chosen for its suitability for experimentation.
> At the moment there are no Scots plays available for the application of a production technique designed to deal with the unexpressed, but the producer, Mr R.F. Pollock, feels that Ibsen's play offers excellent existent material. If the production be successful in bringing out the undercurrents of thought and feeling then a step will have been made towards providing a medium for the Scots play when it comes along.

One critic remarked of Pollock's 'new methods' of production that '. . . if they have not been much employed in the work of Glasgow amateurs . . . they are the familiar techniques of the stage'. He went on to concede, however, that 'Mr Crawford gave a really brilliant performance as Halvard Solness, revealing the man morbidly tortured by conscience and the artist aroused to battle with himself. For this psychological study no doubt Mr Pollock deserves most credit, but Mr Crawford's sustained acting must be applauded. Miss Edwards caught the wild note of that untamed "bird of prey" Hilda Wengel. Miss Rough contrasted the repressed creature of Duty, Aline Solness, Messrs Macrae, Young and Mace touched in successfully the lesser parts, and there was the right suggestion of the infatuated girl book-keeper in Miss Urquhart's picture of Kaia Fosli.'

The following year, Pollock produced *The Three Sisters*, by Chekhov. E.J.P. Mace, one of the most distinguished actors of the Glasgow amateur stage, recalls being asked to play the part of Kuligen. The degree of involvement and constant endeavour given by R.F. Pollock is perhaps best illustrated by the letter he sent regarding the part during rehearsals:

Drymen Road, Balloch,
15/3/32.

Dear Mr Mace,
    You know, I am sure, that I rely on your valuable aid to bring off THE THREE SISTERS. I have been writing to all the others with some comments as there is so little time at Rehearsals.
    A word or two about my conception of KULIGEN. You are getting just what I want, and have quickly got at the nervous gaucherie of the fellow. He rushes in where angels fear to tread, and then makes it quite evident that he never could be an angel or anything like one.
    If this trait is emphasised, it will help to keep the audience interested in an otherwise queer galaxy of characters, none of whom are likely to be clearly defined, excepting perhaps CHEBUTIKEN and even he is superficial: all because we are rushing into production without getting under the skins of the characters, not only individually but relatively.
    I fancy KULIGEN in the following relationship, although I know the similie is a poor one. He is the ringmaster, constantly moving about, with a toy whip, while turn after turn takes place in

the ring. But he is responsible for keeping it all going while he cracks his whip. There may be one touch of the human that could be expressed. He is a pseudo model husband. He strives hard to make that common knowledge. There is a pathos in his efforts. Latterly, he might be said to realise this, when he seem to suspect MASHA'S affections are growing around VERSHINNAN, although the evidence is only faint. Yet, he catches a sort of definite glimpse at the end, and of course, he has not the strength of character to evince himself.

But let me tell you I think you are giving a clean cut character study and I am indeed indebted to you for coming forward to my aid. I can only thank you, and say that I wish I did not find my efforts so constricted, the result being that the ensemble may not do justice to the sacrifice you are making. Sincerely, I thank you.

Yours

(R.F. POLLOCK)

Molly played the part of Irena, the youngest sister, and she loved the play. The reviews, though guarded, gave her the encouragement she needed:

The history of the three sisters is melancholic, and yet of an utter simplicity which the unmoved might dismiss as tedious were it not that Miss Edwards, Miss MacPherson and Miss Urquhart fill the parts with understanding and grace. Mr Macrae as Captain Soleni gives an immaculate picture of that weird character from which G.B.S. might, even yet, take inspiration.

And again:

. . . Miss Urquhart seemed to respond best to the production and gave an unusually interesting performance.

The family rushed to see her of course, and all her many friends. Jessie Adamson remembers the production as having something special about it, really a professional finish which took the audience to the heart of the play. Mr Mace recalls a moving moment in the young Irena's performance, when in Act I instead of *saying*, in response to Chebutiken's remark on a book he is reading, 'That's worth making a note of. Balzac was married at Berdichev', she continued to play Patience, while *singing* softly, to a haunting little scrap of melody, 'Balzac was married at Berdichev'. That kind of instinctive invention was what gave her acting on so many occasions a touch that lingered on in the memory of those who watched her. Perhaps the most important lesson learned from working with Pollock was an awareness of the importance of movement. In a short article in *The Scottish Stage* Duncan Macrae wrote:

> Stanislavsky . . . was among the eminent producers who spent a great deal of time rehearsing gesture.
> . . . If the shameless amateur can go on without knowing his lines, he'll have no qualms about not knowing his gestures.

So in an age when a kind of restrained naturalism was the favourite mode on the London stage, this small band of Scottish actors had begun to develop the beginnings of the very physical style of acting that was one of the most individual hallmarks of the Scottish contribution to the early productions of the Glasgow Citizens' Theatre founded by James Bridie and a group of like-minded enthusiasts in 1943.

During this time a completely new and ambitious venture, to be named the Curtain Theatre was first envisaged in a basement room of the Keir Hardie Institute. The Tron Theatre Club were rehearsing upstairs, and a small associate group were presenting a series of one act plays in what purported to be a tiny theatre downstairs, called 'The Brown Room'. Grace Ballantine was the producer and Norman Bruce, a journalist, who was one of those wise, resourceful visionaries who often play such an active part in theatrical movements, was a sympathetic listener when she expounded her theory that a new little theatre must be formed, with premises of its own. The Scottish National Players were, in 1932, taking the Athenaeum Theatre in Glasgow, for a series of two-night runs; the Tron Club relied on the hire of the Keir Hardie Institute. Grace Ballantine's idea, which was immediately supported by Molly, was that the only way to create a satisfactory company was to have permanent premises. Norman Bruce had the right kind of inspiring genius to be a director of such a venture, and the ladies approached him for his advice.

Elsie Russell wrote of his reaction in the *The Scottish Field*, July 1968:

> He issued his edict — "Not until you have 100 people willing to hand over a pound each and pledge their support." More toasted muffins and the challenge accepted in true Churchillian fashion by Grace Ballantine. "Right'" she said to Molly, "we'll go out into the highways and byways and get them!"

And that is precisely what they did. One of the very first to give his support was Molly's brother Alasdair, and he brought others who brought others — till 100 supporters were finally gathered together. Norman Bruce was again approached and he agreed to go ahead. The new theatre was under way but as yet without a name or premises.

"We were first of all given some old flats by Harry Hall of The Queen's Theatre," said Molly, "and then Grace received a gift of the most beautiful front curtains. I said to her — there's the name of the theatre — The Curtain Theatre. And so it was." It was the year 1932 — but still no premises. Then they heard of a big drawing room in a large house in Woodside Terrace which was to let. "I was closely connected with the group and because Grace was unwell at the time she asked me to go and have a look at it and report on its possibilities. And so, on a bright sunny morning, I went to number 15 Woodside Terrace and was shown into a fine, large, L-shaped room. I saw the possibilities at once. The longest part of the L could be the stage and wings and the remainder the auditorium. I reported back and the deal was soon clinched. About 70 seats were put into the auditorium and a tiny stage, dressed with those beautiful curtains, was erected. Norman Bruce became its Artistic Director."

The story of the Curtain Theatre is one that would fill a book on its own. Its aim was to present a vigorous season of plays with as many worthwhile new Scottish plays that could be found, their foremost achievement in that vein being surely Robert McLellan's *Jamie the Saxt* with Macrae playing the title role for the first of many times there.

The opening programme in January 1933, however, was a double bill of, first, John Drinkwater's *X = 0*, a bitter, fierce attack on the futility of warfare depicted in scenes from the Trojan War. Douglas Moodie, who later joined the B.B.C., produced this, achieving the illusion of depth and distance by use of skilful lighting and imaginative stage setting, even though as one critic said, 'the smallness of the theatre almost set the stage in the lap of the audience'. The other play was *The Bear* by Chekhov, in which 'Miss Molly Urquhart was spirited in the role of Madame Popov'.

For Molly this was an exciting and impressive venture. She realised just how far determination and clearsighted, practical leadership could take a group, as the many subsequent productions at the

Curtain Theatre maintained the high standard that Grace Ballantine had set. Donald MacKenzie, the playwright, who would have had his first play performed by the company in 1939 had the war not brought their activities to a halt, remembers Molly at that time:

> Her speech was resonant and bell-like with Highland intonation, with the Highland and Western Isles way of speaking as a kind of sub-fugue in her voice.
>
> She was never pretentious, never tended to come across with an intellectualised attitude about a part. She was an intuitive actress, who got it right by feeling her way into a part, thinking about it very deeply then coming across with it in a very strong way because she had an immense vitality that was the characteristic. That enchanted the dramatist in me — the way she could project a part!

Obviously having gained as much experience as the amateur world could provide, she was now searching for any possible openings on the professional stage. There were not many in Glasgow.

She was by now well-established in her Civil Service job, in Govan Telephone Exchange. Her keen sense of concern for those less fortunate than herself had motivated her to begin a drama group, that as well as the few pupils she herself taught on Saturday mornings was made up of some of the children she met in the district through which she walked to the Govan subway. At the first meeting held in a small local hall, the din was such that even her powerful voice could not make any impresssion, so the next week she went along with her father's ship bell in her shopping bag and clanged it continuously till silence reigned. The children became interested, and any further dissidents were told if they did not wish to take part, they need not come back. Most of them remained, and took part in a programme of plays, poems and songs presented successfully in Govan Town Hall, organised by the Y.M.C.A. Literary Society.

Sometimes she would take those youngsters by tram to the edge of the countryside which even today surges invitingly north, south, east and west of Glasgow. From there they would walk and talk, often sitting in a group to read poetry aloud. She had a way with children and they loved her direct, unpatronising manner. Even those who found the poetry sessions demanding would cheerfully go along with what she suggested just to please her.

ACTRESSES HAPPEN . . .

She was always popular, and was never short of escorts, but the young men who sought her company while she was rehearsing or appearing in a play soon found they would have to come along to see the show or better still, give some assistance back stage or front-of-house. Several of them did, but by 1932, her most constant companion was that same William McIntosh from the Black Isle who had noticed her at her first dance in the Highlanders' Institute so many years earlier. Now an established member of the Police Force in Glasgow, he was a well built handsome man, with dark hair and the same mist-grey blue eyes as he admired in her. He had great charm and gentleness of manner and he too spoke the finely enunciated English of the Highlander. They made a handsome pair and were obviously deeply in love but they had to reach a decision. Willie wanted to get engaged but Molly was anxious to fulfil her ambition to become an actress.

So it was in the Howard and Wyndham Scott Centenary season in the Theatre Royal that the professional name she had planned to use finally appeared — Mary St Clair. In the summer of 1932, she auditioned successfully and obtained a small part, where, beautifully gowned as Queen Caroline of England, she listened to the heart-felt plea of Jeanie Deans who begs that her sister Effie's life might be spared. She wrote briefly on this, her first brief professional appearance in a 'drama' that was freely adapted from Scott's *The Heart of Midlothian:*

> The producer was Millard Shevlin, known affectionately as 'Shevvie', and I remember how on my first entrance, as Queen Caroline, he stood in the wings with a handkerchief and at the precise moment I was to enter, he dropped it and I sailed on, literally terrified. Dear Shevvie, he was kindness itself to me; he really taught me how to face an audience.

In the summer season of 1933, Mary St Clair was again a featured player, taking on at various times in the season the parts of Flora in *Guy Mannering*, Helen MacGregor in *Rob Roy*, and notably Effie Deans in the 'Jeanie Deans' production, standing in successfully in an emergency.

These Scott adaptations had appalled the purists and filled the theatres since they had started 'barn-storming' around Scotland in the late nineteenth century. Jack House in his review of the first

39

season in *The Scottish Stage*, July 1932, swithered between laughter and despair:

> People tell me I should not say anything against the production because it is "traditional". That may be — if it is so, then the sooner we forget the tradition the better. My own opinion is that the Edwardian actors of the play had so much personality that their audiences would stand for anything. And most of the people who go to "Jeanie Deans" today will stand for anything.
> Yes, the "Jeanie Deans" audience is a shock to any experienced theatre-goer. They applaud each "patriotic" sentiment — indeed, any sentiment that is sentimental enough gains their approbation. When, for example, the Duke of Argyll, beholding Jeanie Deans in her plaid, remarks, "Jeanie, me gal, me 'eart wahms to the tahtan!" the cheers are as vociferous as when rabid Rob stands upon the bridge and shouts, "Yew have not yet subjewed Arrrrob Arrrrroy"!

W.J.W. of the *Evening Times* helplessly capitulates in his review of *Guy Mannering*:

> Who wouldn't think they got the worth of their money when Julia Mannering, having at midnight just escaped detection by her jealous brother in a secret meeting with her lover, immediately relieves the scarified audience by bursting into song; first with — of all things — "Lo, hear the gentle lark!" and then "Buy my caller herrin'!"

Millard Shevlin was Dandie Dinmont, and briskly dealt with the 'cumbrous literary lingo' by taking 'a comedian's licence' with it. The audiences were 'large and appreciative' and Molly was on the boards of the beautiful Theatre Royal with a professional company at last.

She played with the company till autumn, 1933, then on the first of January 1934, she and Willie became engaged. He loved her very much, and understood her better than anyone else ever did, discussing with his own practical wisdom the way she might continue with her career, should the opportunity arise. For he did agree, with a dimension of understanding rarely found in husbands in the Scotland of those days, that she should continue. He was proud of her acting and knew how much a part of her it was. Though she wanted to go on acting under her own name, between them they decided that the mildly affected 'Mary St Clair' should fade away with the Scott season, and her name for stage purposes should be Mary S. Urquhart, firmly announcing her nationality.

For it was at that time that she became very much aware of the decision that she must take. Either she would have to work incessantly at her voice, so that she could try to sustain a perfect English accent, or she would become known as a Scottish actress. Her sense of nationhood was always strong, and upon entering into a partnership with another Scot, she decided, wisely, to be as she was.

The wedding date was fixed for 1 August, 1934. Lexy and Kit were to be bridesmaids along with Willie's one sister, Jess, and Lexy sewed not only their dresses but Molly's dress also. The bride's head-dress, in a style reminiscent of that worn by Mary, Queen of Scots, Molly designed and made herself.

The service was to be held in Partick, Gardner Street Church. Lily, her cousin and close friend, came to the house in the afternoon of the wedding day to find the bride on her knees scrubbing vigorously at the stairs leading up from the close entry to the house.

"Mary! This is your wedding day!"

She leapt up in panic. "Oh, Lily, what's the time?"

On learning it was only three o'clock, her face relaxed into her usual cheerful smile, "Oh, what a fright you gave me! The wedding's not till five o'clock. We've plenty of time for a cup of tea."

One incident which shattered even Molly's calm, was the fact that the minister, the Reverend Kenneth Gillies, usually the most punctilious of men, had that moment of complete forgetfulness that haunts all men of the cloth, and forgot to turn up for the ceremony. As the bride, now trembling a little, waited in the vestibule with her father, who was magnificent in full Highland dress, the matter was quickly resolved, since Willie's brother Peter, a fully ordained minister stepped in.

Molly wrote his final words to the couple on the back of one of her wedding photographs:

May the love which brought you to this hour
grow with the passing years.

The local newspaper reported the wedding in full:

41

The little Partick church, tastefully decorated with gladioli and lilies, was crowded on the occasion of this popular marriage; and a large number of people were attracted to the church doors on the arrival of the colourful bridal party.

The bride, who was given away by her father, wore an exquisite period gown of ivory satin and a Mary, Queen of Scots headdress with a full, flowing veil. She carried a sheaf of lilies.

Her bridesmaids, the Misses Lexie, Jess and Kit Urquhart, had chosen deep lilac satin, overcast with fine net, with gloves and muffs matching. Miss Lexie Urquhart is a prominent Maryhill Harrier and an ex-Scottish Woman's Sprint Champion.

The bridegroom wore the MacIntosh tartan kilt. His grooms-man, Mr Donald MacIntosh, a brother, and his father, were also dressed in the kilt.

The reception, held in the Belhaven Hotel, then situated in one of the elegant tree-lined terraces that line Great Western Road, is described in a letter that Mrs Urquhart wrote to the couple who were spending their honeymoon on the little island of Gigha off the coast of Argyll, in Gigalum Cottage, belonging to Mrs Duncan, Aunt Effie's sister-in-law.

27 Caird Drive
Glasgow W.1

3rd August '34
My Dear William & Mary

So pleased to get yr letter and hear you were on yr way to the Isle of Gigha, I was afraid you wd miss yr train. What a send off you got, I think the whole thing went A.1. and all comments are great. It was the prettiest wedding ever — everybody was in love with the minister. It was just a pity Ally did not give the names of the people to sit at the tables to yon very polite waiter; it is in these things that I feel how useless I am, but in the whole everyone went away very pleased with themselves. Betty gave her recitations and got a great response. Donald gave the Rose of Tralee and the Cameron Men and it was great.

Dad gave Mrs Neilans, Betty, Annie Andrew and Jenny Watt a dance. We had a nice cup of tea at 10. Peter proposed thanks to Ally. Ally, to someone else and Dad to Harry. Dad was up yesterday to square up and they told him it was a beautiful wedding and the company delightful, they loved the pipes, they were head over ears in love with the kilt. Everything was so reasonable and it was served so dainty — Dad was thinking it wd be a great place for the Gairloch Supper.

We sent a good piece of cake to Govan also all the flowers. I just said 'to all at Govan Exchange' and the complimentary card. I hope you get good weather and that yr holiday does you both good. I must stop now as Kit wants the pen in a hurry.

Love to both from all
Mother

Chapter Four

A Place of our Own

> . . . to give to airy nothing, 'A local habitation and a name.'
> (Shakespeare)

Since Willie's police duties were with the south-eastern division, the couple had bought a flat in Clifford Street in Ibrox. A pleasant, three storey high, grey sandstone street, it ran parallel to Paisley Road West but was tucked away from the noise of traffic.

The door opened into a square hall from which doors led to a good sized lounge and bedroom, kitchen and bathroom. The kitchen was one in the old-fashioned style, with plenty of room for dining table and chairs, and a bed recess, in which a spare bed could be accommodated behind concealing curtains. The proximity to the main road and the easily accessible Kinning Park subway station made the area one of the best served, transport-wise, in the city, and there were plenty of good, small shops.

Molly got busy with paint and wallpaper. Her energetic approach was effective though slapdash. There was nothing she would not tackle, and the flat was soon decorated, the hall being especially remarkable in a dramatic colour scheme of lacquer red, black and white, Chinese lamps giving it a look of the Orient, emphasised with a black and crimson dragon rug which Molly had made herself. With a high-handed disregard for conventional metho's, she made curtains, lampshades and cushion covers working by rule of thumb, her seemingly haphazard approach achieving the effect she sought, despite the sceptical glances of Lexy who often came to help with the sewing.

Though happy enough to be a housewife, she soon was involved in theatrical activity once more. She had planned a more ambitious production that might again include the children who had been her pupils and part of her Govan group. It was to be *Children in Uniform*

A PLACE OF OUR OWN

by Christa Winsloe, a play set in a Prussian boarding school for girls. The fiercely militaristic discipline plays havoc with the sensitive. Manuela, an intelligent, emotional girl, is championed by a humane teacher, Fräulein Von Bernburg, who tries in vain to oppose the relentless authority of the head mistress, Fräulein Von Nordeck, a part which Molly herself played. She also directed and organised the whole group, which she had named the Ross-shire Players, because of the help she received from the Ross and Cromarty Association in funding the project.

Marguerite Black, another very fine amateur actress, from the Transport Players, a well established amateur group, played Fräulein Von Norbeck, and sister Kit had been roped in to play Countess Kernitz. The rest of the all-female cast were very young, many of them beginners. Despite this, the play, presented in the Athenaeum Theatre in February 1936, was the hit of the season, and little Isobel Walls, only fourteen years of age, played Manuela.

> Fräulein Von Bernburg, most difficult part of all, was taken by Marguerite R. Black of the Transport Players, whose splendid performance cannot be praised too highly.
>
> Isobel Walls, as Manuela, the sensitive pupil, met the demands of a highly emotional role with admirable sympathy and restraint. The stark realism and pathos with which she invested the final tragic scene enthralled the audience.
>
> Miss Mary S. Urquhart not only played the leading role of the headmistress and evil genius of the school, but also produced the play and is therefore doubly to be commended. (*Daily Record*).

A more telling tribute came from 'Busker', the critic with the *Evening Citizen*:

> The attempt of the S.C.D.A. to have drama established as part of the curriculum in schools would have met with no opposition had the members of the various education authorities been present at the Ross-shire Players presentation of "Children in Uniform". The acting of the children in this play was remarkable. As a rule I detest child players, and even more the stupid material thrust on them by their elders, but the children in this show had a play of exceptional merit to work on and they made full use of it. The role of Manuela calls for sensitive playing but the 14 year old Isobel Walls, was more than equal to it.

45

If the education authorities would forget their red tape and take this company round the schools it would be the best day's work that had been done in the interest of child education for years. But I suppose by the time the powers that be dream about a move of this sort, little Isobel will be a grandmother.

There is little doubt that Molly was not only a teacher, but a director who could train and exhort her company into that extra effort needed to make a success in what was a highly competitive field. She knew what she wanted, she could make people believe in themselves, and as long as they were prepared to work, she would put every effort into helping them. But if they showed lack of co-operation, or displayed any signs of an overweening confidence, her temper would flair up like a volcano and she would 'tear them off a strip', so that they either survived and mended their ways, or vanished.

The group knew she was fair and saw that she was usually right. Yet the warmly maternal side would take back as many as wanted to come to the flat for tea and talk, where, Marguerite Black recalls with awe, they observed, week by week, the progress of a full-sized rose pink woollen carpet their hostess was making for the lounge.

That carpet's completion was a marathon task. The night it was finished, Molly moved the lounge furniture, rolled the carpet into position, and when Willie came off duty, she proudly showed him the twelve square yards of pink floor covering, which set off the greens of the furnishing. He admired and praised her work, but as they sat together by the fire late that night, he asked her the question she had not liked to frame herself. "You want to go back, don't you?" There was no need for an answer.

An advertisement in *The Stage* announced that the Sheldon Browne Company, a repertory company, was playing at the Cragburn Pavilion, in Gourock, and needed a character actress. Molly decided to apply.

Ewan Roberts, who came from Edinburgh, had trained as a tweed designer but had forsaken textiles for the theatre in 1935 when he made his stage debut as Lord Hastings in *The Scarlet Pimpernel* at Edinburgh's Lyceum Theatre. His crisply defined characterisations have enhanced many a West End production, but in 1936, he was the 'young and very handsome man' who received Molly in the box office when she arrived at the theatre. He continues:

A PLACE OF OUR OWN

I was, in addition to playing, also called Acting Manager, I think
only because I had a typewriter, so I just happened to be in the box
office the day Molly turned up in her musquash coat and a big, blue
off-the-face hat. It is an encounter I have never forgotten. A friend
had brought her down by car from Glasgow and she was hopeful
there might be odd parts she could play during the season. I spoke
fairly broad Scots in those days but I could "put on" a posh accent
when required and so could Molly. We started very formally and
then suddenly my accent slipped, then hers slipped, and we got on
like a house on fire!

Georg (sic) Sheldon, who had toured with his own musicals met
Richard Browne who had been the stage manager of the company
Sheldon ran. He managed to extract from somebody £400 to start
his own repertory company and that's how they went up to
Gourock. To get a theatre, he advertised in *The Stage* and offered
an award — and Greenock Council came up with the Cragburn for
£10 a week. We went up and opened with a play of Ivor Novello's
called "Full House". If we played to £120 a week we were well
away. We really did quite nicely. Salaries were around £3. 10s. 0d.
to £4, digs were cheap, and we were really very well off.

The Cragburn is a large hall of the kind that was a feature of many
Clyde seaside resorts. The stage was adequate, with reasonable
dressing-room accommodation behind, and the rather spartan
seating could be removed, should the hall be required for dancing,
whist drives or other diversions. The company there was a very
distinguished one. 'A picture postcard, price tuppence, showing a
group of the entire company may be obtained by applying to any of
the attendants', the programme announced. 'Members of the
company will be pleased to autograph these on payment of one
shilling, the proceeds to be devoted to the Duncan McPherson
Hospital'. The group included Sheelah Wilcocks and Dorothea
Smith-Wright (now the famed TV director, Dorothea Brooking) as
well as Ewan, Molly and the directors.

Molly's first part was as Mrs McFadyean, the garrulous neighbour
('she talks like a typewriter') in *Hunky Dory*, a Scottish comedy by
MacDonald Watson. Written in the nineteen twenties, this little play
which is a collection of caricatures and running gags, still gets the
audience laughing and has proved an unlikely survivor when many,
many better written dramas have sunk without a bubble. Ewan
played Peter McGuffie, a plumber, who painted incredibly awful

47

pictures as a hobby. One was a terrible explosion of orange, reds and yellow. That one, Peter maintains, has a moral — 'Never look for a leak o' gas wi' a lighted candle'.

But the company performed a good variety of plays each running for a week, including *The Barretts of Wimpole Street*, *White Cargo*, *The Ghost Train*, and Bridie's *Storm in a Teacup*. Molly's notes record the tremendous affection in which 'Uncle Georg' and 'Brownie' were held. The experience she gained there was invaluable. Despite her handsome appearance and good figure, she inevitably played the character parts, because she could handle comedy and dialect; although Ewan Roberts recalls how once in Noel Coward's *Hay Fever*, she looked 'absolutely marvellous' as the vampish Myra, 'that very sophisticated lady, and I always felt that secretly that was how Molly would like to appear'.

With every encouragement from his sister, Alasdair, who was her admirer and disciple, and who had been following in her footsteps, gaining recognition as an actor in the Transport Players and other amateur groups in Glasgow, took the plunge, and successfully auditioned for the Sheldon-Browne company. He proceeded to play competently a series of supporting roles both in Gourock and in Hoylake. The rest of the family sighed with resignation. They had always been interested in Molly's acting, but thought it was something people grew out of. She was absolutely delighted to have her beloved 'Ali' take up a theatrical career. She believed in his ability as fervently as he in hers. Once, for a few weeks in Hoylake, brother and sister shared the same digs with Ewan Roberts and the very pretty young leading lady of the company, Sheelah Wilcocks. Often joined by Norman Holland, now a successful playwright, they were all equally enthusiastic, 'talking', as Mr Holland puts it, 'endlessly about the theatre'.

Endless enthusiasm was an essential ingredient for the actor then, weekly rep. making extraordinary demands on a company, who would be rehearsing a play during the day, playing in another in the evening, while determinedly trying to forget the lines of the play that had ended the week before, in case they intruded in the current work. Though Molly was never a full member of the company, she still got the practical grounding she needed. Gourock was near enough to travel back by bus or train most evenings to Clifford Street. The company enjoyed her presence and acknowledged her playing.

Ewan Roberts remembers her being excellent as 'the stern Arabella' in 'The Barretts of Wimpole Street' and as the landlady Mrs McFie in *The Wind and the Rain.*

In the Gourock company, she found people in whom she could confide her own gradually developing idea of beginning an experimental theatre of her own. Georg Sheldon was a ready listener, who encouraged her, emphasising the necessity of obtaining her own premises, something she had already learned from the Curtain Theatre venture. Only then, he said, was the way clear to further her aim.

Molly wrote, 'He told me how to go about it, what to do, who to contact, but felt that I should widen my own experience by playing in another repertory theatre.' So it was that she applied to Cambridge Festival Theatre in response to an advertisement in *The Stage.* She was engaged as a 'character actress' and joined a company headed by the late Dorothy Reynolds and Basil Lord, with directors Frank Harvey and Alfred Huxley.

Her portrait, taken by the theatre photographer in Cambridge, shows her to be a mature, serene woman of considerable beauty. She was indeed supremely happy. She was fortunate to have a marriage partner who loved her enough to accept this temporary separation; she herself felt so secure that she went off to Cambridge to further her apprenticeship in theatre, full of confidence because Willie believed in her completely. Developing as an actress, becoming more aware of the technique of interpreting and directing a play, she gained much in personal assurance.

Yet despite her appearance, at the age of thirty two she was firmly categorised as a character actress. Among the parts she played at Cambridge were, the Nannie in *While Parents Sleep* by Anthony Kimmins ('Miss Mary S. Urquhart', said *Variety Weekly*, 'looked and acted like Nannies do.'); she gave 'a cheerful and humorous study' as Mrs Bramson's char in *Night Must Fall* by Emlyn Williams; she 'should have been a little sterner' as the wife of a missionary, the Rev Alfred Davidson in *Rain* by Somerset Maugham, and she was 'superb as the common old mother with a weakness for vodka' in *I Lived with You* by Ivor Novello. All these, calling for a variety of accents and character make-up, were received with pleased equanimity by the press. But in a comedy called *The Rotters* by H.F. Maltby, when, as the Strange Lady who comes from the past of the smug Councillor Clugston, she used her own 'Scottish English' voice, the *Cambridge Daily News* was perplexed:

> Mary S. Urquhart did not by her accent appear certain whether she came from Lancashire, the States or Ireland.

In a repertory company of those days, players were engaged to fill a definite niche — character, ingenue or whatever. It was not any more likely that an actor would transfer from one type of part to another within the season than, say, an opera company would place a mezzo in a soprano role. Anyway Molly's own voice, though clear and softly modulated, still had Scottish overtones; therefore, she was not considered suitable, in an English company, to play leading roles either in contemporary dramas or comedies, or in classic plays.

In Cambridge, she was befriended by an elderly lady who was a constant patron of the theatre. Miss Alicia Cameron-Taylor, aware that actors away from home can often be lonely and miss just the simple little events of the pattern of ordinary life, used to invite her for afternoon tea, every week. This lady used to insist that broad comedy was not for Molly and that she should go for more serious dramatic parts. Her visitor listened and was heartened by her appreciation, but even nowadays, although there has been many an American Mark Antony and Hamlet, we have yet to see an Irish Cleopatra or Rosalind nor yet a Scottish Portia or Cordelia.

Molly always wanted to act in Scotland; at that time, however, she made the realistic decision that she was a Scottish actress and would become known in that way, if she were to become known at all in her profession. It was the right decision for her, but not one that would make the going any easier either north or south of the border. The Cambridge experience had been both enjoyable and invaluable in many ways, not least in that it had helped her to decide finally to banish Marie St Clair and settle for being Mary S. Urquhart.

The maintaining of the flat would have been a problem if it had not been for a happy meeting that was to solve the problem and bring her a friend for life at the same time. Having returned to the Cragburn company after her months at Cambridge, she was kept busy learning lines and rehearsing. Her method of coping was to pare housework down to the bare essentials, then go round the place like a tornado whenever she had a spare day or so. But she soon realised that if she were to continue to act some reinforcements were necessary. She got the name of a Mrs Elizabeth Mallen, a young married woman with one son, from Mrs Scott, mother of Joan, a pretty schoolgirl with acting aspirations who had just begun to get a few parts in amateur productions. 'She's marvellous', affirmed Mrs Scott, and indeed a marvel she proved, coming at a time when Molly was involved rehearsing by day and acting at night.

Elizabeth, who lived in Harmony Row, in nearby Govan, made her way to Clifford Street, on Mrs Scott's instruction. The key had been left with a neighbour. Her heart failed her a bit, when she saw that even the brass nameplate and letterbox were dull, for it was a point of pride with Scottish housewives that 'the brasses' must be polished to an almost white gold colour, no matter what else was neglected. Inside, she was confronted with the Oriental hall, with the dragon rug somewhat marred by fluff, and the flat looking the way homes do when housework begins to stockpile over even a few days. Elizabeth got the first impression of the owners from their wedding photograph on the sideboard. She decided immediately she liked them, and set to work with a will. When the mistress of the house came back from rehearsal, the flat was like new again. She met her help, a slim, dark-haired, vigorous little woman about her own age, and took to her immediately. They became friends on the spot. They had the same sense of humour and were both hard workers. Elizabeth became part of the family from then on, coming three times a week to keep the domestic scene in order. She got to love the theatre — especially if her 'Mrs Mac' was playing. 'Elizabeth knows me better than almost anyone else', Molly used to tell me. 'She's one of the closest friends I've ever had'.

And indeed, Elizabeth did constantly berate her for missing meals, for not dressing warmly enough, and for taking her resilient health for granted. She recalls her horror at seeing Molly taking clothes off the kitchen pulley straight into a case before dashing off to catch the London train. "Mrs Mac — they're no' dry! You'll catch your death!"

"They'll be dry by the time I get there", was the cheerful rejoinder, which did little to reassure her worried housekeeper.

Between engagements at Gourock, Molly was involved with a project connected with the 1938 Empire Exhibition, held in Bellahouston Park. The Scottish Pavilion contained a representation of a clachan, or small Scottish village, and it was suggested that a group of short plays, such as might be given by a local club to such a rural community might be presented. Molly, with the Ross and Cromarty Association, planned a programme and assembled a cast, including one John Cameron, a young man who had appeared in a play she had produced for the Former Pupils' Dramatic Club of the local Govan High School. John felt he had contributed enough to the furtherance of the Scottish theatre, but he thought of a substitute, another fellow who, like him, worked in the shipyards and would be really interested. So Archie Duncan takes up the story of how his theatrical career began:

> I was an electric welder and I knew how to fit a fly joint and a pipe. John said, "This polisman's wife, a Mrs McIntosh, wants me to be in a play, acting a plumber. I don't want to be in it. But you like the acting, so on you go. Just chap on the door and say, I'm no gonny dae it but you will. You're daft about acting." Molly opened the door to see 6½ feet of shipyard worker standing there bashfully, with his clean shirt on. I announced, "John Cameron disnae want to be in your play, but I'm gonny be in it." Molly took a look, visibly quailed and backed slightly. Unaware of the niceties of waiting to be invited in, I breenged past her, explaining the while, "I'm a good actor. I'm as very good actor. I've even written plays masel." (He omitted to say his writing had been confined to *The Gipsy's Revenge*, a drama written while he was at primary school. His most extensive audience was his own and Hughie Condron's mammy. There was later a command performance for Mr Condron and Mrs Bissett.) I produced the book and read the part. It was a Glasgow shipyard character. If I canny dae anything else I can dae that.

Their efforts did not meet with much encouragement, for the audiences were small in number, though one reporter stoutly asserted that 'the plays submitted were comparable to any one-act plays in the English language'.

Another theatrical venture, which proved, as it happened to be a kind of full dress rehearsal for Molly's own plans, occurred in the nearby town of Dumbarton. R.F. Pollock had been one of a number of moving spirits who had been working towards the opening of a little community theatre to be run by amateurs. A place had been found, and the local paper, the *Lennox Herald* announced details of the first season; six plays running from two to four days every second week from September to December.

Molly was called upon to rally a company and produce the opening play. She chose Merton Hodge's *The Wind and the Rain*, a contemporary play about student life in Edinburgh, and having gathered a cast that included Marguerite Black, Andrew Crawford and Donald Ross (the two last named from the 'Clarion' Club of Glasgow) she took the small part of the landlady, which she already knew from Gourock.

The hall at Bankhead in Dumbarton had been transformed. Fitted out with cushioned seats, and a reasonably well equipped stage, it let the audience see they were indeed in a theatre, superior to the usual hall accommodation with which amateurs usually had to make do. It was named the Scottish People's Theatre (S.P.T.)

The fund raising committee had worked hard and the townsfolk including the Lord Provost turned out in force to the opening production. The play was enjoyed by the audience, and the local paper said of it:

> The S.P.T. are to be congratulated on selecting this play for the opening of their season. While it does not reflect the highest ideals of the Theatre, as an educative and cultural force, it does provide that entertainment which theatre audiences do, and have a right to, expect on occasions.
>
> The producer, Miss Mary S. Urquhart, is experienced both in production and acting technique and, with the assistance of her little group of Glasgow players, offered to the S.P.T. audiences a show on which only the hyper-critical would comment adversely.

The excitement of the opening week of the theatre was marred by the sudden death of R.F. Pollock. A sombre visionary, he had devoted all his spare time for many years to his theory of a Theatre in Scotland. What he achieved was commemorated in the Scottish People's Theatre and other similar little theatre movements which took their inspiration from Dumbarton. Also many Scottish actors had been inspired by his thoughtful dedication. Their careers too commemorate his work.

Molly was deeply moved by Pollock's death and her work in the first season in Dumbarton became her tribute to him. The next production which she also undertook was Reginald Berkeley's *The*

Lady with the Lamp, a dramatisation of the life of Florence Nightingale in which Edith Evans had appeared in the Arts Theatre in the London season of 1929.

Molly was to play Florence, Andrew Crawford, her suitor Tremayne, a fictional character, while Donald Ross was to be Lord Palmerston and Greta Weir, Mrs Herbert. There is a scene between Florence and Tremayne, set, rather operatically, in a garden by a fountain, in which the young man, in a somewhat sentimental scene, shyly declares his love for Florence, addressing the fountain as a kind of inanimate intermediary — 'Fountain, tell the lady . . .' (This sort of thing did occur in costume plays of the nineteen twenties in so-called romantic scenes.) I may say that the depiction of Florence Nightingale though a bit soft-centred in the early scenes, gains a more convincing strength as the play proceeds.

Molly, who always seemed to infect people with her own enthusiasm, came along in great excitement to a rehearsal saying that a local businessman to whom she had been talking about scenery had offered to lend a fountain. "A real fountain!" she asserted to Andrew Crawford. "And it works".

Any thoughts of the difficulties that this elaborate stage property might present were forgotten during the final rehearsals. It arrived just in time to be set up for the opening performance. Andrew Crawford remembers it, all too vividly. It turned out to be a glass and chrome structure, with coloured lights which would have looked more at home in a fairground or an ice cream parlour than in what purported to be the garden of a stately home. But the curtain went up and there was no chance of altering the situation, even when they discovered too late, that as soon as the power was switched on, the gentle flow of water was accompanied not only by coloured lights flashing but also by a steady insistent mechanical roaring. So the all too fragile dialogue had to be shouted out, as if in a high wind, instead of the discreetly modulated tones which had to some extent masked its inadequacies. The fountain stood silent and unflowing for the rest of the performances. Jack House wrote about it in the *Evening News*:

> My visit to the Scottish People's Theatre in Dumbarton this week left me wondering why a small town like Dumbarton can create its own little theatre while Glasgow can only talk of it.

Molly agreed whole-heartedly, and decided the time was right to put her own plan into operation. She started systematically to search for suitable premises to set up the theatre she resolved to make. Willie realised this was something she had to get out of her system. It meant putting thoughts of her own personal career as an actress aside, but she was intent on bringing her dream into reality — '. . . to give to airy nothing, a local habitation and a name'.

Chapter Five

To Travel Hopefully

'To travel hopefully is a better thing than to arrive, and the true success is to labour'.   (R.L. Stevenson)

In 1938, Britain was aware that the dark shadow of Nazi Germany was beginning to have an effect upon life in these islands. Adolf Hitler had assumed command of Germany's armed forces and their mobilisation threatened Austria and the Sudetenland. Britain's Prime Minister Neville Chamberlain returned from the Munich talks proclaiming, in the words of Shakespeare that seemed more convincing from Hotspur's lips in Henry IV Part 1 '. . . Out of this nettle, danger, we pluck this flower, safety'.

The nation waited. That never was a curtain line.

In London, the West End offered a huge variety of plays, opera, musicals and revue.

In Glasgow, nine theatres had shows ranging from *Rose Marie* to Harry Roy and his Band. London's Leslie Henson was appearing in *Running Riot* while Glasgow's Doris Droy was in *Puss in Boots*. Far from the splendid foyers of these well-established theatres, Molly went on exploring old church halls, disused warehouses, large Edwardian terraces, searching for the right place to house the small experimental theatre she had dreamed of starting in Scotland. She recalled advice 'Uncle Georg' had given her in the Gourock days: 'It's no use hiring a hall here, a hall there. You must have premises where your company can rehearse, where you can build your sets, paint flats, store costumes and above all, create your own atmosphere. Then you'll have a theatre'.

Her travels finally took her to the Gorbals in the south side of Glasgow.

TO TRAVEL HOPEFULLY

After long tribulation, I finally found a suitable hall near Gorbals Cross. It would seat about two hundred, which was ideal for our purpose, it had room for a fair-sized stage and dressing room space. I was all set to go.

She ascertained that the premises were available for a rent within her means and the formidable task of cleaning was begun. What an extraordinary curtain-raiser that would have been to the later establishment of the Glasgow Citizens' Theatre in Gorbals Street only minutes away! But her hopes were dashed, and from a most unexpected quarter Willie was the unwilling stumbling block. A highly regarded detective inspector in Glasgow's Police Force, his integrity and life-style were all his superior officers could wish. No doubt the fact that his wife was an actress had caused a few eyebrows to be raised but Molly was a satisfactory spouse who accompanied her husband frequently on many public occasions, such as the Annual Charity Ball, held in Barrowland by courtesy of Mrs Maggie McIvor. No 31 Clifford Street was, with the combination of Molly's practical talent for interior decoration and the help of the now-essential Elizabeth, as attractive a flat as any couple could wish for.

But the governing body of the Police Force looked askance at the wife of one of its members setting up any kind of business in Glasgow and even an artistic venture such as this did not meet with approval. This was a stunning blow, and Willie returned home, fearful that the news would have a seriously depressing effect on his wife's spirits.

He need not have worried. After the initial disappointment came a burst of towering fury that might have caused the whole Force to retreat in disorder had they encountered it. That out of her system, she thought calmly of a means to get round this new difficulty. It came to her, in a flash of inspiration. With arms linked in the closeness that characterised their marriage, Willie and she sallied forth, undaunted, this time to seek premises within reasonable travelling distance yet just outside the city boundaries!

At that time, the tramcar went to Rutherglen, a little Royal Burgh that had obtained its Charter long before Glasgow, that had always insisted on its seniority, treating with indignation any notion that it was or would become part of Glasgow. Indeed, in the eighteenth century Rutherglen had some claim to distinction in drama, since there is a minute in Glasgow's records forbidding Glasgow inhabitants to travel to Rutherglen to witness stage performances. It was during a visit to Rutherglen that Molly found what she had been looking for after a search that had lasted in total over eighteen months:

> One day my wanderings led me into the Royal Burgh of Rutherglen and there I knew I had found the answer. As I entered the old Congregational Church in Main Street, shafts of sunlight through the stained glass windows on either side of the stairway reached out in welcome. A perfect setting — for did not the drama begin in the Church? The dignity and beauty of it all completely held me in its spell. I had arrived.

Indeed, the church in East Main Street was an exceedingly fine building in which the exigencies of ecclesiastical architecture met those required for a theatre amazingly closely. It had a fine, square-set area without transepts. Rows of pews afforded spartan but adequate accommodation for, at most, about two hundred and fifty people. The pulpit was centrally positioned between the choir stalls, and the aisles led towards two doors that opened on to a staircase which led down to the vestibule, now to be the foyer. There was a room on 'stage' level that would make the women's dressing room, and another below that would accommodate the men. It was full of possibilities.

It was also full of dust and cobwebs, since it had lain disused for some time. Major changes would have to be effected, choir stalls and pulpits giving way to stage, curtains and lighting. But those were aspects she knew she could cope with. First of all, she had to ascertain whether a lease of the building could be obtained for a rent she could afford. Since their marriage, Willie had insisted that his wife should have a separate bank book. Money saved from her Cambridge-Greenock days had been put by towards her constant dream. Molly was a creature of imagination and vision, but she was intensely practical and independent; never for a minute did she expect anyone to help her to fulfil her aim, nor did she under-estimate the nature of her undertaking. As she wrote herself: 'Anyone who wants to found a theatre must be prepared to lose money, not to make any'.

But in addition to that realistic philosophy, she had her solid home background behind her; so with her mother's commonsense household economy as an example, she had a fair grip of the situation. She decided to launch the business with £300, a sum which in those days, could buy a sizeable detached house in a good area. The owner of the building turned out to be John Paterson who had come to Rutherglen many years ago from Roxburgh, and had founded the still famed oatcake firm of J. Paterson & Son Ltd. Mr Paterson was that splendid combination, a good businessman, shrewd as he was successful, and a public benefactor, who had helped the Congregational Church to obtain and maintain this and further buildings.

Molly made an appointment with him, and told him her plans. He listened carefully as she outlined her scheme, observing the basic commonsense that tempered her admittedly infectious enthusiasm. He sensed in her just a little of the kind of business acumen that he respected.

"Do you think that you can make a success of a theatre in Rutherglen?"

She did.

"May I ask how much money you have behind you?"

With some diffidence, she told him of the £300, the immensity of the sum seeming somehow diminished when spoken of aloud in the presence of a successful business man.

"You have more than I had, lassie, when I started. Go right ahead and I'll make it posible."

And so he did. He rented the building at a nominal sum, and stood by like 'a veritable fairy godfather', as Molly said. Whether he had much faith in what must have seemed an incredibly harebrained scheme to bring serious drama to a little town with not only five cinemas but also open country at its back door remains a mystery. But there is no doubt he recognised a kindred spirit in the would-be artistic director, who took her chances in astute Scottish fashion.

Although Molly could say with perfect conviction, 'I had arrived', to others it must have seemed her task was just beginning. Certainly the building was the right shape and had basic seating accommodation. ('Take a pew!' the current Wodehouse-type slang parlance for, 'Have a seat!' suddenly took on a new significance.) The acoustics, naturally, were excellent, and there was sufficient dressing room accommodation and toilet facilities. Heating was coal-fired, with a temperamental brute of a boiler. Entrance and exit were adequate, since the church obviously had been inspected, once upon a time, and deemed suitable to house a congregation. Now it was to house an audience.

Amateur circles were already well aware of her quest to find premises. Now the bush telegraph went round — 'Molly's found her theatre. She'd be pleased to hear from you'. The stalwarts were there immediately. Andrew Crawford, Donald Ross, Joan Scott, Eileen Herlie, (then O'Herlihy) also Margaret Smith and Ella Crichton, who were originally pupils who had played in the Govan Town Hall productions. Amy Malcolm from the School of Art and Tom Masson who wanted to do decor joined with enthusiasm in the discussions at the Clifford Street flat early in 1939.

Most people faced with such a situation would be thinking in terms of architects' plans, costing of the renovations and the drawing-up of a work schedule for full-time tradesmen. I would imagine that such an approach never crossed Molly's mind. All she had needed was to find 'suitable premises'. Those obtained, she saw her way clear.

She did try a committee first of all. 'We began with a committee, but that didn't work out. Too many arguments over unimportant details . . . I hadn't asked anyone to help me with the financial side of the theatre so that if it flopped, I alone would be responsible and I saw my little capital dwindling away. When that was gone, I had no more. The thing to do was to scrap the committee and proclaim a dictatorship, which is the only way a theatre of this nature can be established'.

A dictator? A benevolent despot? Perhaps rather a benevolent matriarch. Molly had been motherly since she was a girl and most of her company were younger than she was. None of them seemed to have any doubt whatsoever that her leadership would bring the little theatre into being. Of course, as a happily married woman, with the steadfast support of a husband whose natural business acumen would take care of book-keeping and other financial matters, she was both secure and mature. Also as a thoroughly professional actress who had worked in companies of considerable reputation she spoke with real authority. But it was her extraordinary energy and personal warmth, her enthusiasm and vitality, the inspiring belief she had in her theatre and her company that made everyone quite

60

certain this venture into drama was going to be something really special.

It was certainly a great adventure to march into battle led by such an amiable Amazon. And battle it was to be with plans, strategies and tactics to overcome the enemies that militate against all theatre-makers: public indifference, critical attack, ways and means to make ends meet financially and devices to sustain interest after the first novelty wears off.

In the first instance, this artistic onslaught was concentrated in the persons of Molly and the faithful Elizabeth who in the early weeks of 1939 set forth on the blue tram to Gorbals Cross, where they changed to the red bus and a tuppenny ride to Rutherglen. The pained expression of the conductor when he saw the panoply of brushes, dusters, mops and pails from Clifford Street that festooned his two passengers soon vanished in the face of that brilliant smile that was never more confident than when its owner was tackling the impossible. The pair of them got 'tore in' and had made considerable inroads by tea time when Elizabeth went back to make dinner for the detective inspector, while Molly, sustained by sandwiches, waited for the 'late squad' arriving, for the company all had full time jobs.

Everyone set to with enthusiasm. Molly was putting her hand to anything that was to be done and so did the whole company. People who had joined out of an interest in acting, decor, lighting or costume — all worked with a will to carve a viable theatre out of the old church. Amy Malcolm who was then teaching in Art School recalls, 'We raced from work to get there. It was such an adventure'.

Willie's friends were there to help too, of course, and Molly's sister Lexy, as always inventive with her needle, this time was making green silk shades to cover the traditional ecclesiastical brass pendant lamps. Cousin David Stewart was helping in the dismantling of the choir stalls, and felt stirrings of unease when, as a fully ordained minister, he found himself uprooting the pulpit ('Doing it Kosher?' someone wisecracked.) A stage supplied by the old established theatrical hire firm, Bambers of Charing Cross, gave way under the constant pounding of youthful feet, but a good Rutherglen firm of joiners built it solid and sure, reinforced with wood from the old choir stall.

The heating was put on to dispel the chill air and dry out the paint. The somewhat recalcitrant boiler broke down. Mr Paterson was contacted to find out which firm had installed and serviced it. With typical generosity, he underwrote the repair bill, offering to wait for repayment until the theatre had become established. Perhaps, secretly, he saw his gesture as one of support to a gallant but futile venture.

Many people saw it as that. John Duncan Macrae was sceptical, and at this stage stood back from proceedings, thinking that his friend of many years had finally bitten off more than she could chew. Even Willie harboured secret doubts, wondering whether the scheme would end in heartbreak. But Molly was resolute so he worked quietly alongside, supporting her in every way, but ready, if need be, to pick up the pieces. He took on the business side, and kept, from the beginning, impeccable and detailed accounts of the finances of the venture, that are unique in themselves.

The people of Rutherglen looked on discreetly. Like Glasgow, the town already had some well established amateur dramatic clubs, and there was a little resentment to the idea that the venue had been chosen because of its proximity to the city and not for its own sake. But the lady behind the enterprise did not intend to keep her distance. Out of inclination as well as necessity, she was her own public relations officer. She went round the shops herself, offering two complimentary tickets to those who agreed to display posters, breezing along Main Street in her usual friendly fashion, in a way that did much to generate enthusiasm and interest in the new theatre that had suddenly mushroomed in the town. On entering a little draper's shop to explain her mission, she apologised for eating a caramel that had been popped into her mouth by the elderly confectioner next door. The draper was amazed. 'That's the only time in my experience he's ever given a sweetie away to anybody!'

On 24 March. 1939, the *Rutherglen Reformer* had the following report:

A CHANCE FOR THE AMATEUR
New Dramatic Movement for Burgh.

Plans for the fostering of Scottish Dramatic Art with Rutherglen as the centre of the movement, were revealed to our representative this week by Miss Mary S. Urquhart, a lady well known in theatrical circles as a producer and an actress.

"I intend renting the old Congregational Church building in East Main Street and to stage plays which I feel the public want.

My idea, too, is to encourage local talent, either in acting or in authorship, and generally fill a gap in the entertainment of the people."

Her company's first production will be Merton Hodges's 'The Wind and the Rain', a story of Scots student life which will be staged in the old Church early in April. The Church has been reconditioned inside and accommodation effected for the seating of about 300 persons.

Miss Urquhart, who herself is a professional actress, played in the Festival Theatre, Cambridge, and at the Q Theatre, London, and for the past two seasons has been a member of the Gourock Repertory Theatre.

'Jingle' of the *Evening News*, now better known as Jack House, journalist and Glasgowphile, gave more information:

There are some weel-kenned faces among the players that have gathered round to support Miss Urquhart. Incidentally, it's hoped to form a stock company, partly professional and partly amateur. The group includes Eileen Herlihy, of the Pantheon, the Scottish National Players and the B.B.C.; Marjorie Richardson, also of Scottish National Players and the wife of my brother critic, "Masque"; Joan Scott, Andrew Crawford, Margaret Smith, Frederic Grant, Donald Ross and Gordon Sayer. The artistic direction is to be by Amy Malcolm, who taught in the School of Art, and Tom Masson.

Rutherglen's new acquisition will hold about 250 people. It has my avuncular blessing — but I hope they'll change the name!

The name? It was to be the MSU Repertory Theatre, taking the name from the initials of the founder. (To be pronounced 'Emm essu'). An ego trip? Perhaps Jack House was hinting sceptically at that possibility. But it was usual enough for theatre companies to be called after their directors, and there never was any notion that this director sought for star vehicles or star treatment for herself. Her theatre was branded with her initials, just as surely as her touch was everywhere, from directing to floor scrubbing. Her intentions were clear: '. . . to found another Little Theatre in Scotland where talented players can be given an opportunity to play in their native country without having to trail south looking for opportunities. The new theatre hopes also to foster Scots playwrights'. And she would do it her own way.

Chapter Six

'Take a Pew' — 1

The Wind and the Rain was a wise choice for the opening play. Most of the cast were familiar with the play; some had appeared in it in the Dumbarton production. It was a play comfortably within their range, yet it afforded them enough scope, particularly in the leads, to be played by Eileen Herlihy and Andrew Crawford. It deals with the relationship between Charles Tritton, a Londoner who is studying medicine in Edinburgh and Ann Hargreaves, a New Zealander, who wants to be a sculptor. There were satisfactory parts for Joan Scott as Jill, the 'brightly decorative' friend, and for Frederic Grant and Bert Gaston, as the flippant student Gilbert and the French Dr Duhamel. Gordon Sayer, Donald Ross and Iain Crawford completed a very competent cast, with Molly, having fielded her young players with skill, taking on the small part of Mrs McFie, the landlady in whose house the students lodged. Having played it twice before, she was familiar enough with it to devote herself to the others during rehearsals. Amy Malcolm and Tom Masson made a fine job of the one set, the students' study, while Donald Ross was beginning to take over his later responsibility for props. The whole piece was a thoughtful, not inaccurate account of student life in the thirties and had been played throughout the country to popular acclaim.

The advertisement finally appeared in the *Reformer* on Friday 28 April.

MSU REPERTORY THEATRE
280 Main Street

'The Wind and the Rain'
— a play in 3 acts by Merton Hodge

From Tues 2nd May to Sat 6th May 1939
Prices 1/6 and 2/-   Seats bookable Tel Ru'glen 1694.

The die was cast. There was an alarming episode when the local Fire Regulation Committee came to inspect the premises, and in a somewhat relentless manner tested the curtains with a blow lamp, immediately announcing emphatically that they were inflammable. So the whole company gave up one evening to spray them with the appropriate solution to remedy the matter. Molly was alternating between 'star and char' as Elizabeth put it, dusting and polishing one minute, trying to compose herself for press photographs the next, and checking all details of staging and production. Indeed on the late afternoon of the opening date, Andrew Crawford and she, enveloped in wrap-round aprons and dust-caps to try to preserve their appearance for the performance, were scrubbing out the foyer, when a group of reporters arrived and enquired of the charladies the whereabouts of Miss Urquhart.

"Haud on there a minute, son, an' I'll see if she's in," said Molly, and went off to the dressing room, changed her clothes and her accent, and gave them their interview!

The time for opening the doors came at last. The foyer, now gleaming, was banked with flowers, a splendid gesture by the Rutherglen parks department. Photographs of stage celebrities past and present decked the walls proclaiming that the MSU Theatre intended to be part of theatrical tradition, and telegrams from families and friends were pinned side by side with those from the theatre, including one from the ever thoughtful Dame Sybil Thorndike, from Sir John Martin Harvey and from the great Matheson Lang, whose farewell performance coincided with the opening of this new venture.

A fair sized audience came in. Fifty seven tickets were sold at one shilling and sixpence, and this made up the number to well over a hundred. The critics from Glasgow were there as well as the faithful Tom Clydesdale of the *Rutherglen Reformer*. All were seated comfortably enough on the pews, which having provided adequate support for the congregations who had listened there to innumerable sermons were surely sufficient to esconce an audience viewing a play. Molly, having rushed from the foyer where she had met the early arrivals, to the shallow wall cupboard without a door in the women's dressing room — this was her only privilege in the theatre since it allowed her to lay her make-up and costume in readiness until she had finished at the box office or front-of-house when they were short-staffed — converted herself from artistic director to Mrs McFie, the landlady, rallied her young team and went on to pitch.

The audience, having been prepared to be indulgent, were pleasantly surprised at being able to receive the play with genuine enthusiasm. D.C.K. of *The Glasgow Herald* said: 'It may be said that this play is not likely to try a company very hard, but it has popular appeal and that is what a young Rep. must aim at until it finds its feet'.

This was a satisfactory endorsement of policy. Eileen Herlie and Andrew Crawford 'played excellently' and as for Mrs McFie, 'in a fat little comedy part, she didn't lose any of the fun by playing it more quietly than most of the Mrs McFies I have seen'.

Paul Vincent Carroll, whose plays had been gaining acclaim in Dublin and New York, spoke at the end to congratulate the company and its director, not only on their performance, but also on achieving such promising accommodation. He revealed to the audience that he and James Bridie had seen similar possibilities in the Church designed by Alexander 'Greek' Thomson in Glasgow's St. Vincent Street, but in this instance, the congregational committee had not approved the return of drama to the church, and the two leading dramatists had to relinquish their plans. He complimented Molly on the success of her negotiations.

And, of course, the whole occasion was a tribute to the strength of her personality. The venture was based on total personal commitment of a practical idealist who was quite prepared to invest it not only with her savings but all her time, her ability, her charm. She always inspired loyalty and her enthusiasm generated like feelings in others. Her company trusted her and had confidence in her. When I asked John Pollock why he and other actors had not given up on those subsequent performances during the first year, where the 'audience' were often outnumbered by the cast on stage, he replied emphatically, 'Molly wouldn't allow it. The only way was ahead'.

Molly often said, 'You can achieve anything you want, if you really make up your mind'. She had said in an interview, "When I was acting with various companies in England . . . I could see then that all Scotland's talent sooner or later finds its way to London and stays there. And the only solution to that, I felt, was to give Scotland a repertory theatre of its own."

So she did.

In Molly's own words, 'The whole town — or so it seemed — came to give us the greatest opening night I have ever experienced.' And indeed, that night Monday 2 May 1939, was the beginning not only of a company, but also of a friendship between the little theatre and the communities of Rutherglen and Burnside, whose people gradually came to support the players with the kind of loyalty that endorses the wisdom of any scheme to develop a love and appreciation of drama through the community theatre movement. People will gain more from regular visits to the little theatre in the main street of their own town than from the occasional appearance of the National Theatre Company; moreover, the one enhances the other. An article in *The Glasgow Herald* (11 September, 1945) noting the opening of the third season of the Glasgow Citizen's Theatre, pays tribute to the interest engendered in theatre throughout Scotland by local repertories. "Mr James Bridie, a moving force behind Glasgow Citizens' Theatre, has envisaged a chain of such theatres linking the various towns in Scotland and the success of the Glasgow Theatre may be the impetus to turn that dream to reality."

The MSU Theatre was the first theatre of its kind to try out this theory in a small-scale practical way. But of course it was also providing the kind of training ground that an aspiring actor needs — the chance to learn his craft *in situ*. And this was to be weekly repertory. At any rate the second play, which was to be another 'known quantity', *The Lady with the Lamp*, had its first night exactly one week after the opening. How the cast managed it is something to ponder upon. Rosina McCulloch who had brought with her a wealth of experience from playing in innumerable amateur groups most notably the Scottish National Players and the Clarion, recalled, 'If you weren't rehearsing, you were helping to clean up the pews or organising a cup of tea. The cameraderie was superb'.

Cameraderie, workers' co-operative, (without the political overtones), or just sheer dogged determination — call it what you like — the curtain went up on Molly as Florence and Andrew Crawford as Tremayne again — this time with a discreet, silent, painted flat for a fountain! 'Jock' Stevenson Lang and Greta Weir added their distinctive skill to the existing team and Archie Duncan loomed in a small part of what he called 'a gey Scots English nob'.

Reginald Berkeley's glossy romanticised treatment of his theme, in the West End house style of the late twenties was acceptable enough to the audience. 'Busker' of the *Evening Citizen* said, 'Mary S. Urquhart gave us a dominant masterful young woman, rather masculine at times as Florence undoubtedly was'.

The single-minded strength of the woman was something Molly could convey, but the English grand manner in which the part was written sat uneasily on her. Donald Ross said that even from his youthful view point, he could not quite believe in her as the English lady, while Iain Crawford recalled bluntly, 'Molly as Florence Nightingale ministering to the sick in a pool of gloom — pretty awful!' Whether the latter remark is a criticism of the play as much as of the player is a moot point, but certainly, of all the varied accents of our mother tongue that of London and the south-east, with its diphthonged vowel sounds, sand-papered smooth consonants and bland melody was the one which sat least easily on Molly. Her warmth was lost in its calm detachment. It was a constant source of wonder to some of the audience and the company that this was the voice she adopted when she spoke at the end of the play on first nights. But perhaps she felt she had broken enough conventions in setting up the MSU and this in her experience was the sound of a curtain speech.

'Jingle's' comments on the play are worth noting. '. . . I thought, however, that the invalid's bed in the final act was badly placed.'

(The placing was dictated by the fact that the director/manager/char/actress had been so hard pressed that she had not quite got the lines of the last act off — and Margaret Smith, the prompt, was tucked *under* the bed.)

And again, about rather overdone make-up: 'This theatre is one of those which give the audience the effect of eaves-dropping, and a line or two too many on the face can be distracting.'

Good advice for an intimate theatre company's technique, but even more apt since on the opening night the number of eaves-droppers was twenty-four — not many more than were in the company. Perhaps it is appropriate here to look at the box office returns for these first two plays. The accounts, impeccably kept by Willie McIntosh and audited regularly, make fascinating reading, and are a unique piece of theatrical history in themselves.

M.S.U. Repertory Theatre,
280 Main Street,
Rutherglen.

Return of Drawings for "The Wind and the Rain"
Tuesday 2nd May 1939 to Saturday 6th May, 1939
(Two houses on Saturday)

		£. s. d.	£. s. d.
Tuesday 2nd May 1939:	57 @ 1/6d	4. 5. 6.	4. 5. 6.
Wednesday 3rd May 1939:	35 @ 2/-.	3. 10. -.	
	29 @ 1/6d.	2. 3. 6.	5. 13. 6.
Thursday 4th May 1939:	13 @ 2/-.	1. 5. -.	
	17 @ 1/6d.	1. 5. 6.	
	6 @ 1/-.	-. 6. -.	2. 17. 6.
Friday 5th May 1939:	24 @ 2/-.	2. 8. -.	
	41 @ 1/6d.	3. 1. 6.	5. 9. 6.
Saturday 6th May 1939:	16 @ 2/-.	1. 12. -.	
(1st House)	21 @ 1/6d.	1. 11. 6.	
	6 @ 1/-.	-. 6. -.	3. 9. 6.
Saturday 6th May 1939:	17 @ 2/-.	1. 14. -.	
(2nd. House)	30 @ 1/6d.	2. 5. -.	
	9 @ 1/-.	-. 9. -.	4. 8. -.
			£26: 3: 6.

Entertainment Tax £1.13 7½.

Rutherglen, 17th August 1939.
I certify that the above is a correct return as shown by the records
and books of account of the MSU Repertory Theatre.

Business Manager.

TRAVELLING HOPEFULLY

MSU Repertory Theatre,
280 Main Street,
Rutherglen.

Return of seating for week from Monday 8th May, 1939 to
Saturday 13th May, 1939 — 7.45 p.m. Nightly.

"THE LADY WITH A LAMP" by Reginald Berkeley.

		£: s: d.	£: s: d.
Monday 8th May 1939:	10 @ 2/-	1: –: –	
	12 @ 1/6d.	–: 18: –	
	2 @ 1/-	–: 2: –	2: –: –
Tuesday 9th May 1939:	12 @ 2/-	1: 4: –	
	19 @ 1/6d.	1: 8: 6	
	1 @ 1/-	–: 1: –	2: 13: 6
Wednesday 10th May 1939:	10 @ 2/-	1: –: –	
	14 @ 1/6d	1: 1: –	
	2 @ 1/-	–: 2: –	2: 3: –
Thursday 11th May 1939:	12 @ 2/-	1: 4: –	
	25 @ 1/6d	1: 17: 6	
	5 @ 1/-	–: 5: –	3: 6: 6
Friday 12th May 1939:	13 @ 2/-	1: 6: –	
	23 @ 1/6d	1: 14: 6	
	5 @ 1/-	–: 5: –	3: 5: 6
Saturday 13th May 1939:	14 @ 2/-	1: 8: –	
	31 @ 1/6d	2: 6: 6	
	20 @ 1/-	1: –: –	4: 14: 6
			£18: 3: –

Entertainment tax paid £1: 3: 0½

8% of £18: 3: –d = £1: 9: –d..

I certify that the above is a correct statement of the returns of the
MSU Repertory Theatre, Rutherglen for the week commencing
Monday 8th May 1939.

Business Manager.
18th May, 1939.

The audience response was not exactly over-powering in quantity although it was heart-warming in quality. Molly's policy for those first weeks was clear; having begun with an enjoyable, middle-of-the-road contemporary play she followed it by a historical piece commemorating a popular heroine. Next she planned to present *Hay Fever* by Noel Coward, then a fairly new play by Paul Vincent Carroll. Approaches to Coward's literary agents met with a polite distant refusal of performing rights, so perhaps fortunately, the domestic scene next to be presented was not the English country house of the theatrical Bliss family, but the room and kitchen up a close in Bridgeton where Ted Lewis, his wife and three grown up children lived, in Carroll's *Green Cars Go East*.

The old colour coding of Glasgow's splendid fleet of tram-cars was the 'Green' referred to in the title of this outspoken play that told of the difficulties children of feckless, dispirited parents have to face when they try to better themselves and to escape from the poverty-stricken slum environment in which they have been brought up. The eldest daughter, Mary, has qualified as a Primary School teacher, and is endeavouring to support her two younger brothers in their attempts to get away from life in the sleazy room and kitchen where their mother ineffectually goes through the motions of keeping house for them and her chronically unemployed, tippling husband Ted. Mary is subsidising Bill, the elder boy, through university and is encouraging young Charlie to find and stick to a steady job. She herself is constantly harassed by demands made on the all too slender salary of a teacher in the thirties, and by the exigencies of teaching children whose deprived background leaves them undernourished in mind and body and therefore insecure and aggressive, while the very inroads these problems make on her personal vitality and self expression are giving her rather complacent teacher boyfriend second thoughts about their future together.

This play dealt with a contemporary problem in a directly realistic way. The theme was in direct antithesis to the popular West End family play such as *Dear Octopus* by Dodie Smith; these tentacles did not draw the members safely into security and love, but rather tried to drag them down into that terrible morass where a stultifying way of life is endured because the effort of coping with and trying to disguise its inadequacies drains its victims of the strength and will to escape.

This was a challenge to both the company and the community. Interest in the theatre was growing; this play would be a measure of its versatility. A gentleman phoned Molly, entranced with the production of *The Lady with the Lamp*. He was delighted to see drama blossoming forth, and indicated that he might be interested in making some money available for expansion. The terms were not made explicit, but Molly, in her best West End voice, was quite charming, and suggested he come round after his next visit.

The company set to with renewed vigour. Molly marshalled her cast of seventeen with a firm hand, and, with her own breadth of understanding and sympathy for the feckless and unfortunate, helped them towards a satisfactory grasp of the characterisation in the two weeks available. Amy Malcolm and Tom Masson created two very convincing sets and a production began to emerge that delighted the playwright himself. His long acquaintanceship with the producer as well as the loyal encouragement he gave to the whole venture made it natural that he should ensconce himself in the stalls during rehearsals. But not even the fact that it was his play that was being rehearsed let him interfere over much. When he put his oar in once too often, with notes after Act I, he was reprimanded by the producer who, with that familiar gesture of the outstretched hand, long fingers curling back in impatient anger, summoned the stage manager: "Ring down the curtain. We'll rehearse this in privacy!"

Paul stomped out in a temper, vowing never to darken the door again. He kept his vow — until 6.30 p.m. the following evening.

Molly herself took on the tragic-comic character of the through-ither Mrs Lewis, while Bert Ross played her tough, recalcitrant boozing workshy husband, Ted. The curtain on Act II rises on the mother, a slatternly woman of about forty-nine, urging her man to rise from a drunken sleep in the concealed bed before Mary and Bill come in at four o' clock. Frowsy, unkempt, with tousie hair and blackened teeth, a dirty makeshift apron slewed round her middle, she was the epitome of down trodden womanhood as she castigated her husband in the authentic whining tones of Glasgow's depressed East End. The years of observation had paid off! One despaired of but could not hate the character. Her performance was a triumph matched by that of Bert Ross as the sullen, irresponsible father. She teeters on the point of despair, and preys on Mary's sense of respectability to save her from the debts that she cannot help incurring. When faced with the gaudy trash offered for sale by:

'Yin o' thae Mohammedan men with the thingmebobs roon their heids' —

she weakens. In answer to Mary's anxious questioning, she confesses:

'I jis' bought a picture o' Saint Michael the Archangel with his fit on the deevil's heid'

(— to pay up, of course!)

The play is very funny, yet the audience constantly glimpses, in mid-laughter, the chasm of despair and lost hope that waits to engulf this family. It was a play that provoked thought, yet was easily accessible to everyone who saw it.

The most difficult part to convey is that of Mary. To convince an audience of steadfastness and unselfishness, without seeming too impossibly virtuous, is always difficult especially beside the deftly drawn tragi-comic characters of her parents. But in Eileen Herlie's performance this was made possible, and the warmth and intelligence that was later to be acclaimed in the West End carried her through.

The play had an unfashionable, up-beat, happy ending. Bill gets his degree, Charlie keeps his job, and Johnny, Mary's fiancé realises her true worth.

But the moments the audience remembered most were perhaps Mrs Lewis returning triumphant from fisticuffs with a neighbour who had been too pass-remarkable about the possibility of her being in the family way:

'A showed him — the auld pansy — wi' yon ee o' his, he could near keek doon your neck and fin' oot whit ye had for breakfast.';

or the indomitable Ted, drunkenly enquiring of the 'shilling-a-week' man, Mr Gongg, who neither 'drinks, smokes nor goes wi' the women'

'Christ! Whit a man! Well, whit the hell dae ye dae?'

This brings the quaking admission that he sang in a choir, whereupon he is forced to give a quavering rendition — a moment of high farce.

The benefactor? He arrived, distinguished, affluent, took his seat and after seeing Molly's brilliantly observed performance of the wilting virago, Mrs Lewis, blackened teeth and all, disappeared, never to be heard of again. Had he waited for her curtain speech, he might have been reassured. On hearing the clear ringing tones in which she thanked the audience and urged them to continue their support, one young girl exclaimed, 'She *can* talk proper!'

The last play before the summer break was a new mystery thriller by T.M. Watson, the Glasgow journalist, *Murder at Blackstone*. Having declared dogmatically during a theatre interval that stage thrillers were simple to write provided you knew the ropes, a fellow writer challenged him, 'Well, go ahead and prove it, Timmy'.

It was a 'Who poisoned Sir John Summerville?' kind of play with heavy stress on cross-examination of suspects who produced a variety of alibis which had to be tested.

It was a rather lengthy, tedious work, and the company were flagging a little. 'Pace was too slow due to an imperfect grip of the text on the part of some of the players' said Masque?. Donald Ross and Andrew Crawford, who were 'sinister' and 'vigorous' each in his own part, confess they never quite solved all the complexities of the mystery themselves. But Tim Watson was to contribute a play that in its superb comic observation should surely have a place in the history of Scottish drama as firmly as plays by Ben Travers are accepted in the National Theatre's canon, *Beneath the wee Red Lums*.

But now, the announcement 'The theatre will reopen the first week of September' gave a breathing space that was gratefully received by all.

For those financially minded, let us record that the gross takings for the period May to June 1939, during which four plays were performed, was £89. 4. 4d. The expenditure was £90. 6. 6d. That amazing start, though not on the right side, Micawber-wise, was enough to prove the feasibility of the enterprise. Molly was involved in the new season's plans already.

Chapter Seven

'Take a Pew' — 2

Apart from visits to their respective parents in Munlochy and Inverasdale, the couple took no holiday. Molly spent the summer evenings reading plays and discussing productions. Brother Alasdair was, as always, the enthusiastic supporter.

From the beginning, an advertising campaign had been launched. People had to be made familiar with the whereabouts and activities of the new theatre. An enquiry addressed to the Central S.M.T. Bus Company about advertising space on the buses going to and from Rutherglen was met with a politely astonished refusal from the manager, but two large posters with information about the current play were prominently displayed as a regular feature on sites at each end of the main road through Rutherglen, at a cost of four shilling per week, and this continued until the paper shortage, later in the war years, caused such devices to be banned as not in accordance with the save-paper campaigns.

The theatre reopening was postponed till 6 October. To allow the necessary precautions in case of air raids made necessary by the outbreak of the Second World War, sandbags and fire buckets were placed discreetly around the building and directives about emergency exits were reinforced. The MSU Theatre had the additional hazard of the huge Church windows. Willie was appalled. "If those come in with blast, the audience will be massacred!" So they were criss-crossed with unnumerable strips of sticky brown paper that would hold the fragments together even after the blast — according to official advice — and bales of black-out curtaining were brought to make drapes large and dense enough to keep even the smallest chink of light from escaping. Rosina McCulloch recalled the announcement made before every play, to the effect that should the sirens sound during the performance the audience were at liberty to go, but it was pointed out that they would be as safe in the theatre as anywhere else. The windows were treated with adhesive paper in the manner prescribed, but Willie was not content until they boarded them up. The performance, of course, was to continue. (Rosina: "Later on we just let the bombs and guns punctuate.")

The end of September saw the company rehearse once more, this time a Scots comedy, *Tullycairn* by Joe Corrie. Preparing the play had now taken a definite pattern. Molly never auditioned, but cast shrewdly, she gave her more experienced players the scope to develop and could assess when a beginner might be coaxed into giving a credible account of a part to his own and the audience's satisfaction. She worked her cast very hard, always instilling confidence by her own cheerful conviction that everyone in the cast was more than competent. This was something she could do superbly. Her judgment was sound and once she believed someone had talent, she could make him or her believe it too.

The cast met at the theatre on a Sunday afternoon. The script was read and Molly with the group discussed the play and the characters. Then, the first act having been rough moved, they all went home to learn that for the Monday evening rehearsal. On Monday, Act I was rehearsed. On Tuesday, they moved Act II, learned it for rehearsal on Wednesday, and on Thursday, the final Act was moved, and committed to memory for the Friday night. If things were going well, the cast had Saturday free. The whole of Sunday, from 10 a.m. sometimes until midnight, was given over to rehearsals, stage setting and costume fitting, culminating in a full dress rehearsal. The scenery in those early days was often hired, and there was one memorable first night when the set arrived at the last minute and the whole cast dressed, ironically, in full evening dress, had to carry it on just minutes before the curtain went up.

Everything was done as economically as possible. Donald Ross recalls going round Glasgow's street markets, the Barrows, picking up bits and pieces for props. He still has to this day two Austrian scent bottles which he got for a few pence on one foray. The few flats they possessed, a gift from Harry McKelvie who owned the Princess Theatre in Glasgow, were painted and repainted. Artists like Amy Malcolm and Isobel Moffat, who later became scene painter at Sadler Wells, supplied their own brushes as well as their expertise. Amy, though an artist of considerable repute, recalls saying she had no experience of stage design, but had come along to learn how. "Just do it, and then you'll know," said Molly cheerfully. And the sets were very effective!

The company, local shops in Ibrox and Rutherglen, and local people interested in the theatre loaned furniture and small items for props. Molly's flat, which was, thoughout her life, festooned with pictures and curios, was a constant quarry. As clothes became scarce in wartime, items of personal wardrobe were cheefully loaned by friends and often also by patrons; this was quite a sacrifice, as a negligée or evening dress could suffer quite a bit of wear and tear during a week's performance. Molly had a silver fox fur, which draped so many shoulders throughout the season that it became almost a mascot.

This combination of backing the venture with all her savings then running the theatre with frugality and care was typical of an imaginative Highland girl, with a practical Lowland upbringing, who had always worked hard for everything she got in life. There never was any question of a grant or any help at all from local authorities nor did Molly look for such. She had made up her mind on a course of action and she gave herself over to it completely.

That was the key to the matter. She attracted loyalty, because always popular, always fair, she was a natural leader and she was great fun to work with. Moreover the motley band of different talents who followed her to Rutherglen were sure of one thing — she was a thoroughly professional actress, always competent, often brilliant; as a director, she had both sufficient drive and flair to get the play on, in spite of everything. The audience liked the company, because it made sense. Andrew Crawford, who, as many others did, went on to be an actor in the West End and films, gratefully acknowledged the fact that Molly gave him his start, and talks of the early Rutherglen days with warmth.

I was so young and arrogant at the time, but even then I saw she had a good overall grasp. Very slapdash — full of enthusiasm, she could sometimes get cross, very cross and tore people off a strip, myself included. But Molly was one of those people that was 'born with it'. Her instinct took us through. That applied absolutely to her direction rather than any preconceived notions, because I don't think she knew sometimes whether she was coming or going. She was so busy, I remember her striding walk — she had very good legs — going down the Main Street in a green coat and one of Willie's hats, a kind of sporty green trilby she'd made squarer, adding a feather and turning the brim up at one side. She looked very dashing in it. Off she would go round all the shops with handbills. Everybody knew her.

The 'free' Saturday afternoons began to be encroached upon by a rallying cry that was sometimes all too necessary. "I'm sorry, but we'll have to sell tickets on Saturday afternoon." That meant that the company literally took two or three streets apiece, knocked on every door, introduced themselves and convinced the astonished householder that within walking distance there was a play worth seeing all the next week. Everyone had his own district — Rosina McCulloch remembers being met by an elderly, bewhiskered gentleman on his doorstep, who, upon hearing her name, berated her soundly, 'How daur a McCulloch hae onything to dae wi' theatrical performances!' But he always ended up by taking a ticket, because, as a McCulloch himself, he wouldn't let down a member of the same clan.

She had to call at doors the whole length of Stonelaw Road. The big house at the top boasted a maid, who opened the door before she had time to ring, saying, "Madam is waiting for you in the drawing room."

Somewhat astonished, Ros went in to be greeted by a genteel elderly lady, presiding over a silver tea service. "My dear, I've watched you going to every door all the way up that long road. There will always be a cup of tea for you here."

She herself eventually did come to the theatre complete with Shetland shawls, cushions and hot water bag. This was a precaution taken by more than just elderly patrons, because although the baleful boiler warmed the pipes to that bare temperature deemed adequate in those days to keep the congregation from actually expiring during the sermon of a winter Sunday morning, the heat was not sufficient to dispel the chill of the evening, especially when the audiences were small.

Audience numbers were a matter for concern. Critical acclaim and a prestigious reputation are not always enough to fill a theatre, and during that first year, although the company never seemed to have been downcast by it, the numbers attending would have been the despair of most Thespians.

The reasons? The first novelty was wearing off. The blackout conditions had made people wary of going out at night, and early support from Glasgow dwindled while Ruglonians had not yet entirely taken the venture to their hearts. Rutherglen did not like to be considered a second choice, and while the theatre was intent on becoming integrated with the community, the community proceeded to 'gang warily'.

The cinema offered considerable competition, and to Molly herself, who, from the Saturday matinees spent at the pictures with Cousin Lily to the end of her life, adored films, it must have been understandable. With four cinemas in Rutherglen itself, the Rio, the Odeon, the Grand Central and Green's, not forgetting the Rhul in Burnside and the Savoy and the Ritz in Cambuslang, all presenting continuous programmes of, mostly, double feature films, with changes of programme mid-week, many people found theatre going, especially in such spartan conditions, a habit they could live without.

The gross box office takings along with programme sales for the first five plays from October to December 1939, worked out, on average at around £19 per production. Since this represented the use of the theatre for two weeks, even with a peppercorn rent of around £40 per year (plus £19 in Burgh rates) and fuel and lighting expenses seeming amazingly low comparing them with today, still the theatre was far from being on secure ground, financially. Indeed the total expenditure for the same four months totalled £139, though this may have included a few non-recurring bills for some new gas and electrical fittings being installed.

'We'll stick to "Box Office", then slip in a good one', Molly had declared. And for the Christmas and New Year Season Jack House, drama critic and journalist, changed rôles and gave them a specially written version of *The Babes in the Wood*. An agreeable romp with a great deal of local reference, it had original songs by Val White, scenery painted by Amy and Tom, a Highland Fairy called Fiona, and a Dame McTrot — Molly herself. Pretty Joan Scott was the boy Babe and John Pollock played Peter Polmadie. Nettie Young and Gillian Rodger, (later senior lecturer in German at the University of Glasgow) were very junior members of the cast — Villagers, Retainers, Robins. Dr Rodger recalls that over the generous run of almost three weeks from Tuesday 19 December to Wednesday 3

January, including performances on Christmas Day, Boxing Day
and New Year's Day, the audiences varied from a handful to a quite
sizeable house on New Year's Day, the traditional day to attend
pantomime in the Scotland of former years. Indeed, the smallest
attendance was eight people on Wednesday 20 December (takings
twelve shillings) and the largest 90 people (takings £7. 4. 6d).
The gross takings came to just over £50, from which the 7½% was the
author's royalty — £3. 15. 9d!

But it was much enjoyed, and Donald Ross, then in the army,
came back on leave — and played the Demon King, a part which had
been written for him, for one performance only, Andrew Crawford,
who'd been unable to take a part for the whole season, was smuggled
on one evening as a woodsman, and did a brief spot — "I'm a Tree!"
(with apologies to the great Douglas Byng!)

Those people in Rutherglen who went along with their children,
all with dim torches and luminous badges to show in the dark like
fading Tinker-Bells, had a thoroughly enjoyable evening out
without travelling into Glasgow, and some of them, having found
their way to the little theatre, did come back as regular supporters.
They learned that the wee theatre along the road was a welcoming
place, with its roaring open fire in the foyer.

The real hazard was something other than the war. Since it was the
policy in wartime to eliminate all weather reports from the media,
lest it might prove helpful to the enemy, it was the beginning of
February when the *Rutherglen Reformer* reported, retrospectively, the
fact that late December and January had seen the Burgh beleagured
by the worst freeze-up in living memory. So badly affected were
domestic water pipes that people had to get supplies from street
hydrants and a picture of the frozen clock on Sir J. Rochead's
Victorian Baronial style Town Hall, that still dominates the street,
was captioned, 'Who says Time never stands still?' The theatre had
not escaped unscathed in the great freeze-up. The antiquated heating
system, never very effective, had burst quite irreparably, and a new
one had to be installed. So the blankets and travelling rugs that
patrons had felt necessary to bring along to the theatre during those
early winter months were now invariably supplemented by hot
water bottles, those of the old stone variety being deemed best to
keep the feet from numbness.

Before the new heating system was installed the company

presented, on the 19 January, *Close Quarters* adapted by Gilbert Lennox from *'Attentat!'* by W.O. Somin. The nature of that dramatic essay can best be captured by quoting in full the review from the *Rutherglen Reformer* of 19 January 1940:

CLOSE QUARTERS:
MSU PLAYERS PERSONAL TRIUMPH

'The continental play, "Close Quarters" at the local MSU Repertory Theatre this week is a personal triumph for the players — Miss Mary S. Urquhart and Mr Andrew Crawford.

It seemed considerably daring to produce a play containing only two characters, but the company had obviously confidence in its members and both Miss Urquhart and Mr Crawford demonstrated that they fully merited that confidence and went forward to score a distinct histrionic success.

A play in three acts, we flash from situation to situation, sense the despair, the thrills, the happiness of the characters, and are altogether carried away; barely conscious, sometimes that it is only a play.

The story concerns the murder of a politician by a woman who had been his mistress and also informer of her husband's political secrets. This play is laid out in a continental capital where political agitators carry revolvers "for protection". It is being repeated tonight and tomorrow night.

The production is cleverly staged and there is not a lagging moment throughout the whole three acts. Particularly well done were the off-stage voices and effects.

Miss Urquhart is again responsible for the production and Mr Masson for the stage managing.

The *Reformer* was published on a Friday. If the critic had been there on Monday or Tuesday evening he would have added one more to the audience of eight on each occasion. On the Wednesday, there were six people, and Andrew Crawford recalls everyone of them coming round at the end to say how much they had enjoyed it, whereupon they were all invited to stay for tea with the company. The takings for the week were £5. 17. 0d, gross. Though the reviews spoke up warmly for the success of the evening, the freezing weather, the failing heating system and the echoing empty auditorium took its toll of Molly, who, finding difficulty with her lines in this long piece, secreted the prompt in the fireplace. She dried up so completely one night that she glided in a dramatic, tragic movement upstage to have a prolonged discusson with the prompt to get her on the right scene again. Andrew was left inventing a kind of Middle-European nostalgic flannel: "Do you remember, Elsa, before the war, those little boats on the river, the songs, the laughter, the beer — Ach so. Then it was that we were so happy . . . (Aside): Molly, for heaven's sake *hurry up!*"

The next play was *A Corner in Hearts* by Winifred Carter. 'A Sparkling Comedy' said the advertisement, desperately. (By this time, there was a regular announcement inserted in the *Reformer* on Page Two every second week, alternating with 'MONUMENTS. James Robertson & Son — Select Stock') Gross takings £6. 11. 0d. A local group, The Rutherglen Players Dramatic Club hired the theatre for a week and drew full houses for their presentation of the farce *Tons of Money.*

During that week, there was a good deal of positive thinking. A feature in the paper made it clear that the new heating system had been installed, and the little theatre was now 'one of the cosiest places in the district'. The play to be presented from 2 March, Joe Corrie's *Cobbler's Luck* was 'one of the funniest comedies ever written' and was 'crammed with good Scots humour.' The box office picked up. No doubt the company had worked harder than usual on the Saturday ticket selling trot. Three hundred and twenty-eight people attended, one hundred and fifty-three of those on the Saturday night, and the gross takings leapt to £19. 2. 0d.

So comedy it was to be. And that comedy should be the preference of the people is understandable when we look at the items of news that were ominously changing the homely texture of life in the little town. The following items are culled from the columns of the local paper during March:

> Rutherglen A.R.P. (Air Raid Precautions) Emergency Committees are considering a Regional Proposal to increase personnel in Air Raid Warden Posts, Rescue Parties and Decontamination Squads.

> War Allotments ('Dig for Victory!') are being cultivated throughout the Burgh and its environs.

> The Burnside Scouts Dance held in their hall last Saturday maintained an atmosphere of cheerful abandon which . . . made

one wonder where Hamburg gets its ideas about the "moral corrosion" of the British People.

SOLD BUTTER WITHOUT COUPONS
First Offence: Grocer warned

Although the issue of babies' gas helmets was originally planned to include all babies up to two years of age, parents should bear in mind that, in general, babies of 18 months are ready to exchange the helmets for small children's respirators.

People needed to laugh, and if laughter helped them to find the way to the theatre, it was a happy means to an end. This was a practical policy to win an audience and to make financial ends meet. Yet the fate of the enterprise hung in the balance, for there was no doubt that the theatre was running at a loss and the strain on the finances of the McIntosh household was becoming excessive.

Yet even during this period, a play be a new Scottish author was given its première. Andrew Crawford, who confessed to being just a little in awe of Molly when she was in her theatre director vein, took her a play, saying, "Would you mind reading this? A friend of mine has written it and I don't think it's bad!" And Molly glanced down the first page, looked at him over her spectacles, and said, "You wrote it, didn't you?"

Andrew confessed that he had. "Well, we've got that week in April we haven't fixed. We'll do it."

Though in retrospect Andrew shudders at the 'creasified characters — a Gaeity girl come into money (Molly), a young composer fellow working a show (Andrew), his girl friend (Joan Scott) — all such a crib, it just wasn't true' — on it went to admiring gasps from the local press. Molly as the ex-Gaiety girl 'absolutely took the show and ironed it out' and one number with music by Val White was delivered with every ounce of her considerable vitality to become a show stopper:

I was one of the beauties of nineteen-ten.
A lot of water has passed under the bridge since then.

Nothing for Noël to worrry about, but an example of how a little aplomb goes a long way.

The company had gathered strength. Kay Plumer, Doreen Johnstone were regularly featured, also the redoubtable Guy Muir, and Jenny Haig, who was to remain a life-long friend, added her distinctive comedy style. Marion Wiseman, who was in another local amateur group, coming in to play the invalid in the wheelchair in *Guests at Glentaggart*, recalls her impressions:

> I was thrilled to be 'in'. Molly was so wonderful to work with. There was never any jealousy, but then her casting was always right.
>
> She'd such a sense of humour. You'd never know what she was going to say next, but she kept the work going; she had a way of drawing it out of us.
>
> Loved it? That wasn't the word. It was wonderful. You'd find that as time went on, by the Wednesday night you knew every line in the play.
>
> She taught us too. From that very first moment my *A*s were too broad. "My p*a*arrot is dangerously ill" But Molly soon put that right.
>
> The Sunday dress rehearsals sometimes went on after midnight. If Molly wasn't pleased she'd announce, 'It's on its bottom. Bring it *up*' And we'd go through the whole thing again.
>
> I never worked with anyone who could produce the way Molly did. When I went on afterwards with others, I found I'd lost this thing I thought I had.

Chapter Eight

'We Never Closed'

Like the famous Windmill Theatre in London, The MSU kept going constantly throughout the worst years of the war.

During the summer break of 1940-41, Willie and some of his friends rebuilt the stage. Some of the scenery had usually been hired from the Sheldon-Browne company, but Rosina McCulloch had a contact with Lord Inverclyde, through a mutual family friend, Tommy Lorne, who had been one of the great comedians of the Glagow variety stage. Inverclyde held a governmental post of some influence during the war and when Molly and Ros went to see him, he requisitioned some scrap timber so that in 1941, with the help of Bill Blakeley, master carpenter of the Wilson Barrett Repertory Company, two permanent sets were built, Donald Ross and others worked all the next summer making scenery that was adaptable and interchangeable so that hiring costs could be cut out. Harry McKelvie of the Royal Princess' Theatre in the Gorbals often gave them discarded flats and cut outs from the pantomime season. A flat of a Cinderalla coach was unloaded: Molly took one look at it and declared, "That could be made into mullioned windows. We'll put on *Cranford*."

In May of 1940, the play to be presented was *The Tinker's Road* another of Joe Corrie's comedies that had proved so popular with the patrons. Corrie, orginally a miner from Fife, wrote a great number of such plays, set in rural Scotland, and because of his considerable talent to amuse, they have given great delight to many an audience. That he was capable of a wider range of subjects and a greater depth of expression is immediately apparent when one reads some of his poetry and the powerful *In Time o' Strife*, a play in which he depicts life in the mining communities that he knew so well. Yet his comedies are neat and workmanlike, with a great deal of humour, the brisk plots and clearly drawn characterisation making them ideal vehicles for the many amateur drama groups that long have flourished throughout Scotland.

This has resulted in a somewhat unfair belittling of his work. James Bridie said he mourned over him, as he did over T.M. Watson, another writer whose comedies were immensely popular, and prayed 'that they may see the light'. Yet in Scotland, since John Knox and the Reformation swept drama out of the theatre and into the pulpit, there has not been a continuous dramatic tradition, and the clubs using the folk comedies of Corrie, Andrew P. Wilson, T.M. Watson and others have done a great deal to bring audiences to the beginnings of theatrical awareness. Corrie, in the nineteen-thirties, suited places like Campbeltown, while even in the forties, a Citizens' Theatre touring company found that Inverness was not quite ready for Ibsen.

Drama is the easiest form of literature for most of us to appreciate. Live dramatic statements can communicate ideas to innumerable people who would not have either the time, the opportunity or the inclination to obtain them from a book. But the theatre must operate on a multitude of levels, because that is how we operate. Cliff Hanley in an article about the Theatre, 'What's It For?' (*Citizens' Theatre Twenty-First Anniversary Conspectus*, 1943) maintains, 'I like good trivial plays in the theatre'. But he goes on to say: 'We live on the surface of ourselves. We need the nudge of the drama to push us deeper into ourselves and discover the curious things that are going on there'.

Excellently said. But first bring in your audience that is then to be nudged.

The Tinker's Road is a three act comedy based on the situation that arises when a very anglified laird, Major Standfast, plans to fence off a long established public right-of-way that traverses his land. This not untypical situation provides the starting point for an innocent good-humoured piece of theatre; with characters such as Gibby Glen, the miller, Andrew Sneckie, the local butcher, and Ronnie Standfast, the Bertie Woosterish son of the laird, it gave a strong cast opportunities for convincing portrayals. The cast assembled at the MSU was certainly strong. Their regular leading man, John Pollock, whose work at the Curtain Theatre has been so outstanding, Guy Muir, a stalwart from the Tron, Joan Scott, Andrew Crawford and

Christopher Page who were to go into the professional theatre, found their playing well matched with that of Tom Masson, Chrissie Spiers, Doreen Johnstone and Sheila Hope. Molly and Alasdair were in it too, so it is not surprising that John Pollock's best friend Jimmy MacKenzie, who on John's invitation came to the first night with Betty his wife, was absolutely entranced with the quality of the performance in this little theatre not a mile from his home in Burnside. Yet, Jimmy recalls, the audience that night was about twenty in number.

When he went round to congratulate John, he met Molly for the first time. "But this is great stuff you are putting on. The theatre should be full."

Molly thanked him but shrugged her shoulders ruefully. Even she had become a bit dispirited. The people who came seemed to enjoy the shows, and the reviews in the *Rutherglen Reformer* were favourable, often glowing; but the paper came out late on Friday, so that it only left the Saturday performance for those whose interest was aroused by the notice.

"I'll fill your theatre for you." Jimmy said. Touched by his obvious sincerity, she thanked him warmly, but felt he too would be defeated.

Willie had been at the theatre that evening and John and Jimmy arranged a meeting with him to plan the strategy.

James MacKenzie is one of the world's enthusiasts, and when he decides a venture is worthy of support, he tranlates his enthusiasm into effective action. A businessman, he brought a practical, down to earth, approach to the situation. He produced a street map of the district and circled the areas which were within striking distance of the theatre, either by a short walk or bus ride. He planned a full onslaught on a scale far beyond that which the hard pressed cast could carry out on their free Saturday. He decided further that the ticket prices should be reduced by 25%, thus making them 1/6d and 1/-, with half price for children.

Enlisting a number of friends with cars, he set forth to find the future audiences, during the week the company was rehearsing and playing Rodney Ackland's *Plot Twenty-one*. This task force knocked on doors, told the people there *was* a theatre in the Main Street, explained what it could offer, and sold innumerable tickets on the spot.

This very simple but effective technique is often neglected when a new theatre venture is being promoted. The public can often have the best of intentions about supporting a theatre but it can be the small insuperable obstacles that keep them away. The people of Rutherglen and Burnside needed to be assured on simple points; whether the theatre season would be too highbrow — or too lowbrow; whether it had something worthwhile to offer; how much the tickets were; where exactly the theatre was. Of course, then as now, the information was in the local paper, where the plays were advertised, reviewed and often featured in the Entertainments column. But the fact remains that a personal contact and recommendation is the most effective form of encouragement.

'Once the people found out what their theatre had to offer, things never looked back'. Jimmy MacKenzie's claim can be substantiated by the Box Office returns. From the £18 gross taken by *The Tinker's Road*, the ticket sales in June realised £26 gross for *Ghosts at Glentaggart*. For a Cinderella-type comedy *Bedtime Story* by Walter Ellis, they were to reach an unprecedented £38.

On the last Saturday night of the season John Pollock had by chance met Willie on the red tram that went to Rutherglen. Arriving about 6.30 p.m. they saw an unwonted crowd of people surging round the front of the theatre. Exchanging grim looks, they broke into a run, Willie shouldering people out of the way till he got in. To his relief he found Molly in the foyer somewhat astonished to be precipitiously embraced by her anxious spouse, who asked if there had been an accident.

"What do you mean?"

"That huge crowd. . ."

"That's the queue for tickets!" she told him triumphantly.

It is worth remembering when looking at the returns for this little theatre that it could take up to twenty patrons to realise £1 at the box office. The record breaking last night of *Bedtime Story* was:

94 seats @ 1/6d	£ 7 1. 0d
132 seats @ 1/-	£ 6. 12. 0d
2 seats @ 9d	1. 6d
7 seats @ 6d	3. 6d
	£13. 18. 0d

Two hundred and thirty five people had crowded into the pews. The theatre had been filled. Molly gave Jimmy a book of Barrie plays inscribed with her favourite R.L. Stevenson quotation, 'To travel hopefully is a better thing than to arrive . . '

As 'Jasmac' he went on, adding programme notes and attending to publicity. But he had already proved his point. The theatre had found its audience, and the books began to balance.

Chapter Nine

'Take a Pew' — 3

The season rolled along steadily with a play presented every second week. The people of Rutherglen were by now developing a proprietary attitude to the little theatre. *The Reformer* began to use such phrases as 'our talented company', 'Mary S. Urquhart now well known to Rutherglen and Burnside audiences'; in the advertisement for *Storm in the Manse*, a Scots comedy in which John Pollock gave a superb character study of 'Auld Nick', the Rev. Nicholas Urquhart, the director was happy to add the following: 'Patrons are kindly requested to apply early for seats, as bookings are heavy especially for Saturday.'

That, of course, was why the theatre could never take off as a money-making venture. Even the most successful productions seldom drew an audience of more than an average fifty for the first night of any run; and occasionally the number could still dwindle to around twenty. On the other hand, the Saturday night performance could and did draw just over the two hundred patrons that was all the little church-into-theatre could comfortably accommodate. Why, then, was the policy not adapted, so that the plays would run for only the last three or four days of the week? We need to refer again to the purpose that Molly held to be at the heart of the whole enterprise: actors were to undergo the whole practical experience of being in an average repertory company, which like the Sheldon-Browne, would be presenting a weekly change of programme. What is really amazing about the MSU theatre's achievement is that in the four years of its existence it presented 97 plays, 15 premieres among them, with in many instances a basic corps of players taking part often throughout a whole season's productions. Molly, herself, directed almost every play, and played in most of them, sometimes the leads, should a play require her kind of strength, often supporting roles to fill in, for instance in *The Drum of Drumdarg*, doubling as Beenie, the maid and Tinkler Jean the 'spaewife'. Her verve and energy was matched by many of the company. The stage manager in the early days was often listed as that theatrical dogsbody, 'Walter Plinge'. As John Pollock said, "When the scene was finished, the curtain would fall on the cast who immediately took the set off." Rosina McCulloch, who perhaps played more than anyone during the theatre's history; says:

> You learned to play everything — you had to. I remember being given a tennis-playing 'ingenue' when I was all of twenty-nine and certainly considered myself too old! Molly said, with her beaming smile, "You're the only person available, Ros, so just get into a wee pair of white shorts and get on with it."
> Paul Vincent Carroll sent me up of course, "Begorra, Ros, ye've got dimples on your knees! But there's far too knowing a look in your eye for any 'ingenue'."
> She was such a bonny woman. To me she didn't play dramatic parts often enough. She was excellent as Mrs Brown in 'Gallows Glorious' and as Maggie in 'What Every Woman Knows'.
> But she was the ideal person for director because she could be like a rock and she was so fair. There was certain parts she had to play but she was delighted when her company's talent developed and the leads could be taken over, leaving her with a supporting role. She had just that gift of leadership.
> We had some supremely happy times.

The production in November was a revival of their first big success *Green Cars Go East*. This played to an unprecedented 890 people. Molly had introduced the custom of allowing a small sum to the company for travelling expenses. This varied, rising from 7/6d by stages 10/-, 15/-, £1, to an occasional £2 depending on whether the player lived at home or was in digs. If a professional actor came to play for them during a 'resting' period, as happened later on, he received a little more. This again, was more than the ordinary drama clubs did, and although the sum was small, it compared not unfavourably with the full time salaries paid in Gourock in 1938, and did represent a quite considerable proportion of the gross takings. Also it gave a status of what might be termed semi-professionalism to the players.

A dramatisation of *Little Women* followed, and then over

Christmas, that irresistable piece of Scottish corn, *Hunky Dory* managed to draw some reasonable houses, despite weeks of thick fog and temperatures of 9°F below freezing.

Gallows Glorious by Ronald Gow was the 'good one' slipped in early in 1941. This story of John Brown, one of the first champions to fight for the abolition of slavery in America, was an ambitious venture which was given an amazingly effective showing, and stands out in the memory of all who saw it. John Pollock gave one of the finest performances of his career as John Brown and Molly as Mrs Brown was equally strong. Miriam Owens, that splendid actress who had graced many plays in the SCDA movement, and little Rita Laurie, a talented performer from the Children's Theatre Group Molly ran on a Saturday morning were two more of a very able cast. Decor was by Donald Ross, who also played Colonel Robert E. Lee, and a male quartet, under the direction of the indefatigable 'Jasmac', who was acting as publicity manager, sang in the play's last moments, 'John Brown's Body' (the famous battle-hymn of the Republic) to great effect. A prestigious success, it was a bit disappointing in that it did not draw the crowds but perhaps the constant grimness of war was in part responsible.

The spring of 1941 was to see the west of Scotland under ever increasing pressure from air raids. They culminated in a fearful week in March when raids on Glasgow and Clydeside, night after night, shattered hundreds of homes and took a heavy toll of lives. In Clydebank alone, a small town where most of the menfolk worked in the shipyards, seven thousand homes were destroyed.

The policy of comedy was therefore not just a matter of financial necessity. If there ever was a time when people needed to laugh this was it. A lively production of J.B. Priestley's *When We are Married*, in the Scottish version by James Woodburn, was a huge success. The Scots idiom brought its own eloquence to this account of the smug countenance of three middle-aged marriages being discomfited into reassessment with the participants' discovery that they had been 'hitched' by an inadequately qualified clergyman.

A double bill of *The Income* by Joe Corrie, an extraordinarily funny one-acter, set in a doctor's waiting room where a Mrs Gummidge of a woman, Mrs McKye, reduces the rest of the patients to the verge of nervous breakdown by her luridly depressing amateur diagnoses, was coupled with a two-acter, *Let Go the Painter* by D. Gordon Wright, in which Molly, as well as directing, played an infatuated Girl Guide and a tea-cup reading neighbour. A bit of a tour de force, especially when she had also played the lugubrious Mrs McKye.

The audience adored it. And why not? A task of the playwright is certainly as Arthur Miller says 'to present us with a viable unveiling of the contrast between past and present, and an awareness of the process by which the present has become what it is'. The little theatre did not avoid defiant and stirring statements about the war which affected the Home Front more than any other in history had done. But that was to come later. When the air-raid sirens sounded, with their wailing, lurching warning that told of German bombers in the area, the audiences who decided to stay in the theatre got the performance *in toto*, despite the extraneous noises-off of the world conflict through which they were living. Raids usually began about nine o'clock, after dark. Sometimes the long level note of the 'all-clear' signal did not sound till well after midnight. On some of those occasions the audience were entertained by the company in an impromptu entertainment of songs, recitations, jokes, till it was safe to make their way home.

On a few such occasions, many of the company, including Molly and Willie, slept on makeshift beds in the pews all night, often wondering, if the bombs had been excessively bad, what, if anything, would be left of their own homes when they returned. Rosina McCulloch, John Pollock and some others who lived in the Dennistoun district of Glasgow could walk home, as they did one night when a particularly deafening series of explosions had made them desperately anxious for their families. Rosina recalls:

> We had to talk our way past all the air raid wardens who naturally tried to prevent us from walking through the devastated areas and the rubble. In Duke Street, all the windows were in and when we passed Katherine Henderson's Corset Shop, we saw a young police constable as pink in the face as the ladies' underwear which, with eyes averted, he was tossing back through the broken plate glass window.

Miraculously, their houses and families were safe, but those days of the blitz, when the soldiers called up to secure the safety of their dear ones were, in a terrible paradox, receiving messages of the casualties on the Home Front, had so enraged Paul Vincent Carroll that he began then to write perhaps his most telling drama of the Clydeside blitz, the epic, *The Strings, my Lord, are False*.

Call-up, of course, was affecting the company. Andrew Crawford had joined the Navy, Iain Crawford, the Merchant Navy, Alasdair Urquhart, the Royal Artillery, Christopher Page, the Army, while James Stuart and Douglas Swanson were in the Royal Air Force. Val White, whose musical talents had provided the songs for the early shows, was working in a Government Department. Donald Ross, who had been called up when the war began, was discharged because of ill health, and after some time recuperating he was able to continue in his multiple role as stage and property manager as well as actor.

Call-up was nearing for some of the girls too, and indeed as the war progressed, Lexy and Kit were both in the women's services, and Molly herself did not know when she too might receive her papers. Having no children nor immediate family responsibilities, in her mid-thirties, she was not considered immune from service in some kind of 'essential work'. Even established commercial theatres had a difficult enough time holding their players in wartime. Hardly commercial, the MSU Theatre, despite its unflagging and successful efforts to provide a community with entertainment throughout the dismal years of war, would not really be enough to keep her at home, should the national crisis escalate.

This highlighted one of the most serious stumbling blocks for Molly and Willie's plans for the future of the theatre. Mr Paterson, 'veritable fairy godfather' of her enterprise had been most impressed by the dogged determination that had brought the venture to success. He had hoped to sell or rent the building, and when he realised Molly was earnestly bent on continuing to present plays in Rutherglen, he offered it to her at, I believe, a very reasonable sum. But already the couple had put all the expenditure they could reasonably afford, and some more, into the venture, and had been faced in the first early months with what seemed the inevitable loss of their investment. The war years were stretching on, with no prospect of peace, and the incidence of air raids in the area made it no unlikely possibility that the theatre could receive a direct hit. No insurance company could offer cover in such a situation. The company was being gradually depleted, the director certainly couldn't be certain of remaining uninvolved in warwork, and the audiences, though indomitably loyal and enthusiastic, did not know what the next week would bring.

Such a climate was not encouraging towards investment. Moreover, Molly's parents in their croft at Gairloch were not getting any younger and visiting them was a problem. Because of naval operations in Loch Ewe and Loch Broom, access to the area was restricted and permits from Whitehall, London, had to be obtained before anyone could visit there, whether they belonged there or not. Since the family found it difficult to obtain the requisite papers in time to allow them to visit their parents during their short periods of leave, their parents began to feel isolated. It was going to be necessary to bring them south sometime, and a suitable house would have to be found.

The caution Molly had acquired during her upbringing was shared by Willie, who could not believe that it was wise to put more money into a venture so beset with possible obstacles. So the offer to buy was regretfully refused and the building was rented during the whole of their tenure of it.

Still, the support which the plays now received took away any gloomy forebodings of failure. The sets were painted and repainted and props and furniture were loaned gladly by all and sundry. The props they had were used again and again, discarded house curtains were used to cover chairs and settees — nothing was wasted. Donald Ross, now working for the Arts Council in London, recalls those days vividly, while shaking his head in sad amazement when he sees the amount of money that is spent on theatre now.

The Town Clerk of Rutherglen, genial Mr Robert Pollock, was someone upon whom Molly called one day in a desperate search to borrow a melodeon. Swept along, as so many people were by her enthusiasm, he found a contact in the local Salvation Army Band and got the instrument for her, before he had time to ponder why a Town Clerk should be engaged in the enterprise at all! "I knew you'd help", she beamed. Just as she was leaving, she turned, "I wonder if you know where I could get a motor bike, for the next play but one?"

Incidents that developed into theatrical anecdotes proliferated at Rutherglen. One originated during the run of *Gallows Glorious* when Molly, in a very moving moment, receives, as Mrs John Brown, the message telling of her husband's death. With trembling hands she opened the envelope to read, "Now that you're a widow — anytime, you're welcome!" — an irreverent borrowing from *Hunky Dory*. Back to the audience, her shoulders wracked with sobs, she muttered to the cast, "Wait till I get John Pollock — I'll murder him!"

On another occasion in *Guests at Glentaggart*, Donald Ross decided to mark his twenty-first birthday evening by substituting real sherry for the customary cold tea that filled the on-stage decanter from which drinks were to be provided in Act II. Everyone was enjoying the surreptitious tipple until Molly came on. The young people did not know that she simply could not cope with even the smallest amount of alcohol, and were horrified to find that she almost passed out on them! Their joke certainly misfired, for later she did not hesitate to tell them all off in no uncertain terms. She would not allow drinking of any kind before a show. And indeed, even at the end of show parties, the beverage was tea, with perhaps an occasional beer brought in by the men. No-one had a great deal of money, and in any case, in those days, drink was not always so fashionable among younger people. The whisky bottle was, on the whole, considered a consolation for the older generation.

One incident occurred during the run of Tim Watson's comedy, *Beneath the Wee Red Lums* which he wrote especially for Rutherglen in February 1942. This was an enormously successful comedy, and Guy Muir and Bert Ross, as Archie MacLean and Gilbert Dalgleish, were enjoying one particular scene on stage as much as the audience. There was a prop half bottle of whisky, from which they each had to take a dram. Molly, as Martha Love, was waiting for her cue, when she noticed new dialogue: "Tak another drop. Dae ye guid! Man, that's awfu' guid."

"How about yourself? It'll dae ye no harm."

The audience roared. They, and Molly, realised it was the real stuff. But although it made a memorable evening, it would not do, and Willie, who was in the theatre, reinforced the director's dictum, the two 'naughty boys' apologised and the whole incident ended in laughter. Guy and Bert were such genial figures as well as being character actors of deserved repute. In the theatre notes accompanying the programmes, tribute is paid both to the range of their experience and their kindly natures. Guy was, of course, the founder of the St George Players and had been a friend of Molly's since then, and Bert Ross had been one of the Scottish National Players, leading character actors, as well as being in many productions with the Curtain Theatre.

My favourite story of the MSU days was about McAuslane, the stagestruck hen. The company put on Philip King's, *Without the Prince*, a comedy about an actor who, suffering from a kind of amnesia which made him imagine he was Hamlet, appeared in a farmer's house one dark night. Molly had rewritten the rural scenes in Scots, and Donald Ross was well cast as the noble-voiced 'Hamlet'. The play was set in the farmhouse kitchen, and a stage direction required that a character come on with a live hen under his arm which, when he put it down, was to make its way out into the yard — not the easiest effect to achieve. However, Molly and Willie went to visit Aunt Effie at her Luss cottage and she assured them that one quite tame hen named McAuslane would cope with this.

McAuslane was rehearsed, and trained to make her exit upstage left by following a few grains of corn leading in that direction. The rehearsals went well, her first night debut was perfect, but thereafter, either through lack of application or excess of footlight fever, she refused to go off! Wheeling nimbly downstage again, giving experimental little clucks and flutters, she extended her appearance each night to the exasperation of Iain Crawford whose job it was to grab her and lock her in the men's dressing room downstairs. The audience loved her, and the cast grew fond of her too, drawing lots for the egg she invariably laid overnight, which wartime rationing had made a delicacy.

Came the end of the week, and a somewhat troubled director announced to the cast that Aunt Effie had offered their feathered fellow-Thespian as a present, saying a good chicken dinner would help out the meat ration. "So," said Molly, with forced brightness, "anyone who likes can have her." The cast thought *she* should, but she demurred hastily. A gloom fell over the party. Then Mrs Mary McGuiness, one of the stalwarts of the theatre who had sustained the enterprise from the beginning with cups of tea, and by then was doing the cleaning, cast scorn upon them. "What keeping you all back? Sure I'll take the creature and thraw its neck. It'll make a fine pot of soup for the family." So, it would seem, McAuslane's fate was sealed.

When Molly went to the theatre on the Monday following, there was Mrs McGuinness — and McAuslane. "Mother o' God. I couldn't do it! The way the poor thing looked up at me . . . " So McAuslane was taken back to Loch Lomondside, where she lived happily for the rest of her days.

Mrs Mary McGuinness was another of those characters who is remembered fondly by all who worked at the MSU. When Molly's Elizabeth, as a widow, had to work full-time in the Rolls Royce factory, she could no longer help at the theatre, though of course she always remained as loyal friend and mainstay of the McIntosh household, Mrs McGuinness got the job as cleaner, and her two bright sparks of children, Bunty and Tony, became fascinated by the comings and goings of the company. They were among the first to be involved in the Children's Theatre group which Molly ran on a Saturday morning. Bunty, an especially talented and enthusiastic young performer, later gave some outstanding performances in the adult company.

Mary, their mother, became a compulsive playgoer. She saw everything, and, later on, she came to take part in the productions. She had a bright personality, vigorous Scots speech, and as Molly was quick to realise, if she was well cast she could, with a little coaching, turn in a creditable performance. She had the knack of listening to what was being said to her on stage, unlike so many beginners who simply stand through other people's lines till it is time to blurt out their own. She did very well in later seasons and thoroughly enjoyed her theatrical life. She fondly recalls Willie's name for her, 'Star by night, char by day!'

The Children's Theatre was run on similar lines to the one in Govan Town Hall. Well over thirty children would crowd into the theatre of a Saturday morning, and enjoyed drama work which led, in time, to performances in the theatre of a varied bill, from short plays and sketches to choral verse speaking and solo items. Rita Laurie, another very talented young performer who could dance and sing, also graduated along with Bunty to the adult company. But other children who did not go on acting remember the experience with great pleasure. One, Kay MacMillan, recalls the excitement of going by underground railway in one of a series of small groups to have tea in the Clifford Street flat. "It was great fun, and Miss Urquhart always made each of us feel so important", was her recollection, and this was re-echoed by several others.

Elizabeth McKay, now chairman of the International Association of Physiotherapists in London, also was drawn into the theatre. In *Green Cars Go East*, a 'back-court' singer is to be heard off stage, in Act I, giving vent to 'Rock of Ages' to her own accompaniment on the melodeon. Molly was going to do the singing, but they were short of an instrument to accompany her. Miss McKay remembered:

> My mother had a little draper's shop in the Main Street. Miss Urquhart came in and asked if we'd put up a bill. We got two complimentary tickets and went to see "Storm in the Manse".
> She came round every fortnight, part of her public relations campaign. I happened to come into the shop from school. I thought she looked very glamorous. I piped up that I could play the mouth organ. "That's useful. I'm doing a play where we need a melodeon. Come and see me after the show on Monday."
> I went round. "Rock of Ages" was to be heard from off-stage in the next play. I contributed each night and from that I got involved in another play, "The Rising Generation", pulling the string to dislodge two ornaments on the mantelpiece someone took a pot shot at. I was by then enjoying being around the place. Miss Urquhart told me about the Children's Theatre, which was by then in its second season. There was a mixed bill — "Rip Van Winkle", and the court scene from "Jeanie Deans" where she pleads for Effie's life. Miss Urquhart gave some readings including "Getting Up". That was a kind of revelation to hear her natural delivery compared with the usual "elocutionist".
> There was no payment to join the Children's Theatre. Bunty McGuinness and Rita Laurie were both star players.

Betty McKay took on front of house duties, and shared box office work with Ella Crichton, so a new generation was being nurtured to bring their special strengths to the company.

The 1940-41 season ended in June with a production of O'Casey's *Juno and the Paycock* that was acclaimed both by those who saw the play for the first time and by those among the audience who knew and loved it. Among the latter group were indeed, two Rutherglen ladies, Miss Nora McGown and her sister Mrs Frances Slaven, who were first cousins to Sarah Allgood, who was the original Juno. Mrs Slaven's daughter Frances, then only six years old, saw almost every play, grew up to be an actress of real promise, but took a post in the academic world. However, now Frances Collins, she is permanent producer in the Lanarkshire Little Theatre in her spare time. The Theatre continued under Molly's direction from May 1939 to June 1944, just under four years. Of the fourteen new plays premièred under her direction, perhaps the most notable were the comedy by T.M. Watson, *Beneath the Wee Red Lums* and Paul Vincent Carroll's, *The Strings, My Lord, are False.*

There was a local tongue-twister that went, 'Ru'glen's roon red lums reek briskly' — one of these tricky verbal tests of sobriety similar to that made famous by Harry Lauder in his music hall song 'Just a wee Deoch and Doris:

> If ye can say "it's a braw bricht munelicht nicht
> Ye'll be a' richt, ye ken.

Tim Watson, the well known Glasgow journalist, had written drama before, including a number of successful one-act plays and material for broadcasting. Always an ally of the MSU, he was now to give them one of their biggest successes in this comedy of Scottish small town life. There is a central romantic theme of a romance with mild complications between an aspiring musician and his more down-to-earth girl friend, but the real delight is in the humorously drawn older characters, a kindly but conniving elderly bachelor, (witten for Guy Muir), a lugubrious Scots undertaker giving scope for the black humour which is so characteristic of Scots comedy, Martha, a brusque, brisk but benign housekeeper for Molly and a flamboyant and flirtatious widow, Maggie Buchanan, for Marion Wiseman.

The play was a natural for the comedy style that the company had evolved, and it was a hit from the start. Although set in Rutherglen in the nineteen-thirties, it takes a swipe at town councils, the magistrates, the police force and the gossipy side of small town life that was relevant to any small burgh in Scotland. *The Reformer* proudly announced that the piece was 'dedicated specially to our own Little Theatre in East Main Street and its charming talented director, Miss Mary S. Urquhart'. The audiences totalled 885 for the week, the gross drawings were £46. Of this, printing accounted for around £4. 5. 0d, Royalties and Entertainment Tax £8. 6. 0d, cleaning of the theatre and costumes £2. 15. 0d, firewatching (in case of air raids) 5. 0d, extra stagehand assistance £1, and expenses to cast

£9. Thus there was about £19 over to cope with continuing expenses, such as lighting and heating, general maintenance and the rent. Not what one would call much of a commercial success, but for this management it was enough to keep the theatre going.

In March, her friend, John Duncan Macrae, joined to play opposite Molly in *Robert's Wife*, the controversial play by St John Ervine in which a vicar's wife, who is a qualified doctor, tries to continue with her career and provide a birth control clinic for the town. For its time it was a challenging play, and one which Molly had seen Edith Evans and Owen Nares perform at the Globe Theatre in London. It did pose questions about religious and social traditions and the patrons thoroughly enjoyed this modern play. There was critical acclaim for 'the superb acting of Miss Urquhart as the vicar's wife and Mr J.D. Macrae as the vicar'.

That was followed by two plays, one a première by a Paisley business man, Matthew Service, a descendant of the poet Robert W. Service. Then *I lived with you* that piece of escapism by Ivor Novello in which Molly had played at Cambridge was slipped in before yet another première by an aspiring Scots author John Titterington *See the Holly Bush*. Macrae again scored a success and was ready to stay on for the rest of the season. Such a strong addition to the company helped Molly to realise plans for productions that she had before only dreamed of. Duncan Macrae was already in full possession of the skills that were to make him one of the oustanding players the Scottish theatre had ever known, and Rutherglen theatre-goers were privileged to enjoy watching him and Molly in a theatrical partnership, surrounded by a company who were learning more and more about acting in the best and only way — by acting.

A Joe Corrie première, *A Touch of Nature*, with Macrae as a Highland gardener and Molly 'perfectly charming as an ex-Gaiety Girl' (*Reformer*) playing supporting roles to Jack Stewart, another professional actor who often played at the MSU, and Rosina McCulloch, having the time of their lives playing a pukka sahib and his 'awfy refined' lady wife, returned from India.

Finally in June, Paul Vincent Carroll's play *Things That are Caesar's* ended on a high dramatic note in which a dying ex-schoolmaster (Macrae) struggles to ensure the intellectual freedom of his daughter despite the mercenary matrimonial plans his ambitious wife has for her. It is a strong dramatic piece, laced of course, with Irish humour, and was 'well received by our now thoroughly critical playgoers'. (*Reformer*)

Another aim had been achieved. A real audience had been created, not just from among the converted, some of whom would travel far to see the best of the season's plays, but new enthusiasts from the very community in which the theatre had been established.

The MSU was now truly a theatre.

Chapter Ten

New plays, new players

The 'Show Newsreel' column of the Glasgow Evening Citizen, September 1942, contained the headline: 'RUTHERGLEN TO SEE PLAY THAT STIRRED BROADWAY'.

This was to be the British première of Paul Vincent Carroll's latest play, *The Strings, My Lord Are False*.

He had watched with interest the productions at the MSU with their gradual gain in style and assurance. His other plays had been given more than competent showings and had been received well by both public and press. So although it might seem, in one way, a great honour that a dramatist who had been recognised as an important talent in Ireland and America should entrust the first British production of what he knew was one of his major works to Molly, Paul was quite secure in the knowledge that if his old friend had said she could cast and present his play, she could. She was too shrewd to hazard either his play or her company in an over-ambitious venture.

Inspired by the heroism of the people who lived in the many small towns that had grown up around the Firth of Clyde, then a centre of shipbuilding, Carroll created such a place which he named Port Monica, peopling it with characters who were not only typical of a cross-section of West of Scotland small town society but also have an almost universal quality, like characters from a morality play.

The action takes place in the Church of St Bride's, where Canon Courteney has provided a refuge room where people beset or made homeless by air raids can come for food and warmth, and even a bed. Scene III is in the crypt under the church which is used as an underground shelter during the raids.

The Canon, to be played by Macrae, is a practical saint, who strives to succour all those damaged in mind and spirit as well as the shell-shocked and wounded. Authority, both responsible and corrupt, is represented by Councillor Bill Randall, Head Warden of the A.R.P., and Councillor McPearkie, the official who abuses his position for his own ends, by obtaining a contract for a building firm to build shelters which were inadequate for the purpose, and by selling food supplies to hotels at black market prices. Ted Bogle, 'a small undersized scarecrow of the streets' was the ne'er-do-well who blamed 'the system' for everything and had put out his wife because, as daily help to Councillor McPearkie, she was 'having it off' with him. Sadie O'Neill a 'woman of the streets' was looking after their little daughter Madge, who is one of the most convincingly written children to have been created in a play. Louis Liebens, a Jew who was maimed at Dunkirk, is a bizarre, tragi-comic character who adds another dimension to the play, while Sarah, the Canon's Irish housekeeper is the essence of hospitality, her brusque tongue concealing a warm maternal nature.

It is a big, warm, sprawling, dramatic, humorous emotional play, with sincerity and compassion in every line. It condemns war, and makes a plea for humanity and tolerance not only in the universal but also in the particular situation, where all Scottish, Irish and Jewish people, with varying degrees of faith, unite against the war in which the world, torn by conflict for reasons often remote and incomprehensible to the man in the street, demands sacrifices of fearful dimensions of the innocent. It is a play that deserves a revival both as an effective piece of drama and as one of the few dramatic memorials to the heroism of so many nameless victims of such indiscriminate bombardments.

The play had been first staged on Broadway, where such fierce controversy resulted that the American management took it off after only a short run. In Dublin, scheduled to run for one week, it played to packed houses for nine. Then it was Rutherglen's turn.

The cast were stalwarts, tried and true, and it was by chance that this play was to bring to the company a talented male juvenile who would act there for many months. Jimmy Speirs had been cast as Louis Liebens, but he was not able to play the part for the first nights of the run. It so happened that a young English student of engineering at Glasgow University had been giving a good account of himself in student dramatic productions. A mutual friend advised Molly of this and she made contact and asked him to come to Rutherglen. Here is Nicholas Parsons' own account of that first meeting:

NEW PLAYS, NEW PLAYERS

When I was at University doing the Engineering course, also serving my time in Drysdales, I had a 'phone call — about Rutherglen and Molly Urquhart — all new names to me. They were doing a new play by Paul Vincent Carroll — 'The Strings, my Lord, are False' — and they were stuck for another actor. It wasn't a case of "Come down and we'll see if you're right!" The conversation was much more to the point.

"Would you be interested in playing in it?"

"What would it entail?" I asked guardedly.

"Rehearsing every evening for the rest of this week and playing through the following fornight."

(It was to open the following Monday and it was now Thursday.)

"Can you learn quickly?"

I said I did have a good memory but secretly wondered if it could cope with this.

"Right. Come down to Rutherglen right away!"

So I went down and saw Molly Urquhart for the first time and was met by that beaming welcoming smile, that tremendous natural warmth and charm. I thought she was lovely. I met John Macrae and the brilliant little gnome-like author, Paul Vincent Carroll, who was Molly's great buddy and with whom she argued almost constantly.

I arrived and they gave me my part. I was cast as a half-crazed, middle-aged mid-European, half-Glaswegian Jew called Louis Liebens, who had become injured and shell-shocked from the blitz. I was all of seventeen at the time!

Well, I played it — and didn't actually disgrace myself. I suppose, at that age, I must have had some kind of instinct and certainly had no real notion of the difficulties involved — this helped carry me through!

Paul started giving me some notes. Molly, realising I was trying hard to get my words off, and also thanking the stars she'd found an actor of any age and experience at such notice, stopped him. An argument ensued in the stalls, and ended with Paul stalking out, after giving himself a splendid exit line — "I've had plays presented on Broadway and I've come to Rutherglen to be insulted by one of my old friends!" Molly said, "Forget about it — let's get on with the play." Somewhat worried, I asked her afterwards about it. "I know Paul. He'll be back, don't worry. I'm not going to have him upset people. He's not an actor. He doesn't understand."

This was Molly's great thing, the way she could handle people. She'd managed to persuade this distinguished, successful dramatist to let her put on this play for its British première.

Louis Liebens' entrance is described in a stage direction as follows:

(. . . His hair is disordered and his mind is a little unbalanced. He speaks in short, quick stabs. He holds a cup containing an egg against his breast with the stump of his arm, and eats with a spoon in the other hand.)

I had my arm in a sling because the character had been injured and shell-shocked in the blitz and had come to the crypt for shelter. Someone gave me an egg to eat but no spoon. Since we hadn't rehearsed with props, I was nonplussed as how to deal with it, so I started eating the egg with my thumb. This act of sheer desperation was commented on later by someone, as "a brilliant bit of business!"

And I remember dear Mrs McGuinness to whom the theatre gave a new lease of life. She came round afterwards and exclaimed, as a genuine Irish woman responding to theatre, about how the performance had moved her — "My Goad, I was blinded wi' tears and snotters at yon bit. Oh my, it was lovely!"

Molly gave her love to all — to Mrs McGuinness and everyone around. She was devoted to Willie — but her affection reached out to us all. John Macrae — ('Isn't he a smasher?') and Guy Muir — ('Don't you just want to hug him') Bert ('He's a wee terror') and dear George Nimmo — she loved them all in different ways for what they were — this was a unique quality. She had a great devotion and affection for all the people who worked for and with her at Rutherglen. It was the same with every company she was in — everybody loved Molly'.

That this play was one of the most popular ever put on in the MSU is a tribute to author, director, full company and audience alike. It was far from the rather trivial 'hate the Germans' kind of statement made in popular war films at the time. It was a thrilling experience that 'involved the spectators completely' the more so when there had to be included the following programme note:

PLEASE NOTE

Part of the effects in this play include siren "Alert" and "All Clear". In the advent of a real "Alert" the play will stop and an announcement will be made. The play will then continue.

So it was that while Glasgow had a theatrical choice of Bobby

NEW PLAYS, NEW PLAYERS

Howes and Pat Kirkwood in Cole Porter's *Let's Face It*, a musical comedy about three grass widows and three U.S. soldiers, in the Alhambra; Carroll Levis's discoveries, and local comedy revues at the King's, the Pavilion, the Metropole, the Queen's and the Empress theatres, the MSU was packing them in with what 'D. McN' the critic in the Glasgow Evening Citizen described as 'a fine piece of theatrical craftmanship which demands acting and effects of the very highest order'. He continued:

> It is difficult to understand why this play should have aroused such fierce controversy on Broadway in the pre-Pearl Harbour days. To the British wartime playgoer the theme is simply understandable and all too familiar. Port Monica, a Scots town, is being blitzed. The house of Canon Courteney, the parish priest becomes the shelter for the wounded and a sort of spiritual cleaning and cleansing station.
>
> From the outside hell of the blitz the ordinary and extraordinary wartime folk troop in and depart, some heroic, some cringing. In the midst of all this the Canon is a tower of strength built on faith.
>
> All the MSU players did well, notably J.D.G. Macrae as the Canon, Rosina McCulloch as the Canon's servant; Mary S. Urquhart as the woman of the streets and little Bunty McGuinness as the 10 year old child.

Bunty did play amazingly well. The child Madge is blinded as a result of the blast. No one who witnessed the performance has ever forgotten the last scene, when she enters with bandaged eyes, her hands stretched out to seek the Canon, and asks:

> Are ye there, Canon? I jist slipped oot o' bed to see ye. My head's no sae bad noo, but ma eyes won't cry. Are ye no' there, Canon?
> . . .

Macrae, as Canon Courtney, lifts her in his arms, his tall robed figure caught in a shaft of light from the window as dawn breaks through the terrors of the night.

> For even this one crime alone, Man all over the world stands indicted. No one can escape. No one can go out like Pilate and wash his hands. To your awful challenge we must all answer — the dead and the living, the future and the past . . .'

And so the curtain fell. What was happening in Rutherglen began to be noticed in the following months. During the run of Carroll's play, Felix Edwardes, the London producer, came to see it and bought it with a view to presenting it in London.

The next presentation was a double bill: *Distinguished Company*, a one act play, one of the early works of dramatist Ena Lamont Stewart, who was to write *Starched Aprons*, the play about nursing which Glasgow's Unity Players were later to present in the Garrick in London, and *Patricia* another première, this time by a new writer, James Oswald Hunter, who worked as a whisky blender in a city bond, and wrote in the evenings. A family man with four children, living in Knowetop Street, Maryhill, he had problems finding peace and quiet to write but had struggled on and was delighted to get a production. "*Patricia* is exceedingly funny and reveals a sound sense of theatre", Molly had pronounced. The audiences agreed. Elsie Russell, daughter of Grace Ballantine of Curtain Theatre fame, joined the company for this production and played in several others, before journalism and broadcasting took up all her time.

Macrae as John Shand and Molly as Maggie in Barrie's *What Every Woman Knows* was another gem in a season that would satisfy even the most jaded theatre goer. The famous lines about charm, 'It's a sort of bloom on a woman. If you have it, you don't need to have anything else; and if you don't have it, it doesn't much matter what else you have,' draw from Maggie the reply, 'I've no charm'. There was a murmur of dissent in the audience every night. One young theatregoer of the time told how it took great control not to jump up and say, "You have, you have!"

But there was a tough fighting streak too. After giving E. Martin Browne's Pilgrim Players the use of the theatre for their presentation of Bridie's *The Niece of the Hermit Abraham* and Andre Obey's *Noah* (Denis Carey playing 'Noah') Molly successfully revived *Beneath the Wee Red Lums* in response to public demand, before putting into rehearsal a new three-act war play by Joe Corrie called *Dawn*.

But the licence from the Lord Chamberlain's office was withheld. Molly was staggered, and reasonably so, for the play's story seemed straightforward enough, following the histories, in alternate scenes, of two families, one English, one German. Both fathers had been soldiers in the First World War; both sons were architects and neither wanted to fight in 1939. The German boy's fiancée was English.

The Strings, my Lord, Are False which stated boldly that the victims of war are needless sacrifices in a power struggle had obtained its licence. But *Dawn* was banned, though it was, as Joe Corrie himself claimed 'a domestic drama set against the background of war'. Official intimation of the ban came in a brief letter from the Lord Chamberlain confirming an earlier telegram received just before the play was to open. In a statement to the press Molly defended the play vigorously, probably pin-pointing the area about which officialdom was most sensitive. '. . . The story comes back to the mother in each case, and I think the theme may be summed up as suggesting that all mothers feel the same way about war. Mr Corrie does not spare the Nazis. Hitler, the Gestapo and all their works are ruthlessly dealt with. But *'Dawn'* suggests there are good Germans still living.'

It is difficult to understand why such a play should have been banned, but the question of public morale in wartime is always a vexed one. The seriousness of the country's plight in the autumn of 1942 was illustrated by an item appearing in a current issue of the local paper pointing out that women were registering as fire watchers and were undertaking such jobs as delivering mail because call-up had summoned so many men to the forces.

A story earlier in the year had been headlined: BOY STEALS KEYS FOR SALVAGE and went on to explain how a youngster, fired by the campaign that urged to collection of everything made of metal, from old pots to rusty railings, for salvage, had to be resmelted and used for arms factories and munitions, had taken the keys, that, in those innocent days, were left outside house doors.

'. . . The keys, stated the Fiscal, were of trivial value, and had only a use value to the occupants of the house.

The boy on being questioned, admitted "I took them for salvage".

The Fiscal's comment was "Patriotism run riot."'

Stories like that perhaps illustrate the strange atmosphere of the home front. The government employed every propaganda weapon available to band people in a common front of relentless condemnation of 'the enemy'. There could be no mitigation of that depersonalised view. So *Dawn* with its more sensitive investigation of human attitudes towards the prospect of world conflict was considered too much of a risk. Whether it would have diminished the war effort of the MSU patrons or not is debatable. Joe Corrie, having produced the kind of serious drama that his critics were always urging that he should, was disappointed and a few months later when asked what he had done with his own copies of the play, replied, with a weary shrug, "I kindled the fire with them".

Third Party Risk, by Gilbert Lennox and Gisela Ashley, was brought forward to fill the gap. Then by way of compensation both to audience and author, *In Time of Strife*, another Corrie play which the Fife Miners' Dramatic Club had presented in the Empress Theatre in Glasgow twenty years earlier, was produced. This was Corrie at his serious best, depicting a mining community in the throes of industrial upheaval, the basic theme being 'A strike never pays the miner'. The audience rallied round and supported the play well. The statutory author's royalty at that time was 7½% of the gross takings which were £32 for the week. That meant Joe Corrie received about £2. 10. 0d. Since the MSU was the only theatre to present his work consistently, one realises the problems facing a dramatist who came from a working class background. Bridie and others mourned over a talent that was, in their eyes, dissipated in the creation of those one-act comedies that were so successful with the amateur clubs and their audiences, but the professional theatre in Scotland paid but little attention to his serious plays until Bridie himself established the Glasgow Citizens' Theatre. There were no Arts Council grants to help a writer in those days, and Joe Corrie had to keep writing the kind of play that brought him a small regular income. His comedies are workmanlike and have considerable verve. There are at least two of his full length plays that deserve a place in the repertoire of a Scottish national theatre. When *Master of Men* was presented in the Citizens' Theatre in 1944, A.S. Walkeley of *The Observer* described it as having 'a balanced sympathy that recalls Galsworthy' and summed it up as 'work that realises well the aim of a Citizens' Theatre'.

Molly in the MSU days did what she could to present as many new Scottish plays as possible, and to give productions to some of the plays that had been acclaimed both in the provincial theatres and in the West End. The month of January, in 1943, saw the company in sufficient strength to present James Bridie's *A Sleeping Clergyman*. A success at Malvern and the West End in the early nineteen-thirties, this play had also been warmly received by Glasgow audiences, often the most disdainful towards their native literary men; "Him? Ah kent his feyther!" was a traditional dismissal for any unwary

110

NEW PLAYS, NEW PLAYERS

Glaswegian venturing to make an artistic or literary statement. But this play dealing with three generations of a family whose doctor sons fight their way through the decades with ever-growing creative energy until the third generation genius, Sir Charles Cameron, discovers a cure for a mortal disease of world epidemic dimensions, had always been a favourite with Scottish audiences. Mrs Winifred Bannister in her excellent book, *James Bridie and his Theatre*, gives a useful assessment of the major productions of this play, and says, speaking in the first instance of the London première:

> The play had 230 performances and at this distance it seems that a fine play inspired first rate acting. Mr Robert Donat considerably enhanced his reputation in the part of the two Camerons. His acting was highly praised in every review. There were those who thought he did better than the play, but this is nonsense. I have no doubt that Mr Donat's playing was of the highest standard, but I have seen the dual role played by actors known and unknown, by professionals and amateurs, and the gale force of Bridie's inspiration has lifted the player to the required level or at least blown through acting deficiencies to electrify the audience. The same thing is true of the other leading parts. The dialogue is there, sometimes brilliant, always rewarding for the player. I cherish the memory of a wartime performance of this play at the "MSU Theatre", Rutherglen, on the outskirts of Glasgow, when Nicholas Parsons, then about twenty, played the Cameron parts very well indeed, and when John Duncan Macrae, still a young school teacher but an amateur actor who had already created an impression, played Dr Marshall, giving an admirable performance professional in every detail, to an audience of about twelve souls, in a bitterly cold one-time chapel on a January night. Molly Urquhart also distinguished herself as Harriet, Wilhelmina and Hope. (*James Bridie and his Theatre*; Rockliff 1955)

Once again, while the theatres in the neighbouring metropolis were offering an unmitigated diet of pantomime and revue, the good people of Rutherglen, by the end of a cold week in January, were braving the elements in sufficient number to crowd the theatre almost to capacity to see a work by one of Scotland's major dramatists.

Macrae's continued support opened new possibilities. Determined to make acting his full-time profession, he planned his every move with necessary caution, and had not cast his lot with the MSU

111

until it was more securely established and had earned a reputation of being, at the least, semi-professional. His strongly characteristic portrayals of John Shand in *What Every Woman Knows* by J.M. Barrie and as *The Admirable Crichton* by the same author, as John Hannah in *The Sleeping Clergyman*, and later in Bridie's *The Anatomist*, as Dr Knox, the part created by Henry Ainley, made for a memorable season, and in return, he had the chance to play a series of parts that delighted and challenged him. One major production followed fast on the heels of another, in a sequence which included a revival of Corrie's deservedly popular *Robert Burns*; Keith Winter's *The Shining Hour*; *The Shawlie*, a play of Glasgow life by Robins Millar, playwright and drama critic; and *When We are Married* by J.B. Priestley. Stalwarts like Clifford Ash, Rosina McCulloch, John Maggs, Miriam Owens, Archie Pearston, Bert Ross, Jean Ross, Elsie Russell, James Speirs, Rob Wilkie, Marion Wiseman and others made a formidable group of players from which to cast.

The theatre was in good heart. The audiences were turning out in sufficient numbers to justify the more ambitious choice of plays and to keep finances on an even keel that allowed the enterprise to continue in some security, modest though the profits were.

Members of the company who have been consulted find it difficult to pinpoint exactly when it was that Molly's apparently super-abundant energy began to diminish. She always had been such a strength to them all, as was Willie, that clever kindly man who had taken on the businesss side of the theatre, and whose growing enthusiasm for drama was evident as his spare time was by then almost entirely spent in the theatre. From the beginning, of course, he was always at first nights whenever he could manage, to see his wife's work as actor-director. He had a keen critical sense, and his assessment of a play was measured and sound, and Molly always discussed her work with him first and foremost. The pair of them acted as advisers and friends to the company. Though the Clifford Street flat was not large there was always room for guests, no matter how unexpected, and the spare bedroom and the couch in the lounge often were made ready for members of the company who were stranded because of late rehearsals, or who perhaps needed a bit of looking after because of illness or loneliness.

Nicholas Parsons, who was one of the youngest members, recalls a typical salvage job by the McIntoshes:

One Saturday when the play finished, I'd a bad attack of blinding migraine, probably due to overdoing things — shipyard — playing every night — and playing rugby for Glasgow University on the Saturday afternoon. I was almost blacking out, so Molly said I was to go back to Clifford Street. Little Ella Crichton was with us and we got the red tram to Argyle Street only to find we'd missed the last subway to Ibrox. The streets were in near darkness, due to blackout conditions. There were a great number of American gum-chewing Servicemen strutting about, somewhat interested in the comely matron with a pretty young girl hanging on one arm and supporting a pale collapsing youth on the other! There wasn't a taxi to be got, and she got a 'phone box and got through to Willie on duty. "It's all right — I've spoken to Willie. He's taking care of the whole thing. We've just got to stand here and not move. Ella! Hold on to my arm. Nicky! Put your head on my shoulder — and just stare ahead and don't take any notice!"

In about ten minutes, a police car with sirens blaring came along and transported us back to Clifford Street.

That indomitable quality, shown in so many ways, had made Molly appear invincible in the eyes of her company. But now even they began to notice how drained she looked at the end of a production. Never having been ill since childhood, she had no connection with a doctor, finding all remedies for sore throats and any minor upsets at the good old fashioned family chemist near her home in Paisley Road West. Yet she felt so ill that she had to seek medical advice, and, accompanied by the ever faithful Elizabeth, she visited a nearby doctor's surgery. When she emerged she was strangely quiet and it was not until she was back home drinking tea brewed by her solicitous housekeeper-friend that she was able to repeat his diagnosis of a large abdominal tumour that meant surgery as soon as possible.

"He wants me to go to hospital next Tuesday. How can I break it to Willie? And what about the theatre?"

Molly was stricken. Ill-health had never been anything she experienced or contemplated, let alone major surgery, and she was terrified at the prospect. Looking at her pale face and grief-stricken expression, Elizabeth's heart sank, but with truly Glasgow optimism, she urged, "Never heed what he says, Mrs Mac. Come on and we'll try another doctor."

Ready to clutch at any sort of straw, Molly agreed, and went to see

Dr Agnes Warden in Burnside, near the theatre.

The company had been rehearsing *The Far-off Hills* by Lennox Robinson, trying with a forced gaiety to disguise their looks of concern when they saw her listlessness. Ros, knowing Molly had gone for the 'second opinion', had found some pretext to come to the theatre early, so that she was there when the ashen-faced director came in and leaned back on the door.

"Molly! For goodness sake, tell me what it is!"

"Ros — she says my tumour's got legs!"

"What?"

"And it's about five months!"

The pair of them collapsed in near hysterical laughter.

"Don't worry about the theatre. We'll give you a couple of months off!" said the perceptive Rosina, who went home that night and entered in her diary under 26 May 1943: 'Molly definitely pregnant'.

Indeed, the company had had their suspicions about the nature of the illness, which Molly, who in many ways was one of the most naïve people who ever walked the earth, had not shared for a moment. Indeed, Doctor Warden had difficulty in convincing her. She had looked at her bonny new patient, and after a brief examination pronounced her to be about 'five months' gone'.

"But I've been married nine years!" said the mother-to-be incredulously.

The doctor, with a twinkle, assured her that, at thirty-six, she was still young enough to conceive successfully and made her agree to give the theatre a rest for a bit. "I'll stop at the end of the season" was the concession given. Since this was only a month ahead, the doctor, who was also a shrewd judge of character, agreed.

In Lennox Robinson's *The Far-off Hills* she appeared in the small role of Ellen Nolan. 'Miss Urquhart does not figure so prominently,' said the *Rutherglen Reformer* critic innocently, giving rise to a great deal of mirth from the company. In a third revival of Carroll's *Green Cars go East* she again played Mrs Lewis, whose tatty apron and baggy dress concealed any noticeable difference in her figure, which was actually still fairly trim.

Then came the summer and a resting period for all, especially for Molly who was, according to the irreverent young company, getting ready for her greatest production.

The theatre's strength was such that the new season started promptly with *The Ghost Train* produced by Bert Ross. The 'En Passant' chat columnist in the *Reformer* made the comment: 'While hardly mellowed with age, the theatre has very successfully surmounted its 'growing pains', and is now regarded as one of Rutherglen's most acceptable cultural institutions.'

A delightful production of *Mary Rose* by J.M. Barrie followed, with Nicholas Parsons, Miriam Owens and J.D. Macrae playing under the skilled direction of Grace Ballantine of Curtain Theatre fame, who cast a very beautiful and talented young university student, Jean Findlay, as Mary Rose, a taxing part which she performed amazingly well.

Percy Owens, brother of Miriam, directed *The Whiteheaded Boy* and it was during this time that Molly went into the nursing home. The company were almost as anxious as Willie, and someone got the job of phoning to enquire how she was every night. Mrs McGuinness, in sepulchral Celtic intonation, told the young nurse who answered the phone to take great care of Mrs McIntosh, since hers was to be 'No Ordinary Baby', this last proclaimed with such oracular intensity that the girl, who was Irish also, cast a quick glance at the night sky to see if there could be any sign of an extra star.

In the next bed, was Mrs Marie Dorman, wife of Harry Dorman, the well known music teacher and composer. A superb pianist also, Marie and Molly found much in common and formed an instant friendship that was to be lifelong. In a profession where friendships tend to be ephemeral, lasting only the length of a play's run, one finds often at the end of a career that has been full of people, an actor sometimes can be a lonely solitary figure. Molly had the gift of friendship, and valued her friends, both those of the profession, and those outside it. Because of the nature of her work, it was not always easy to keep up with friends regularly. But her constancy was such that, on meeting with her even after a period of years, one would find exactly the same warmth, steadfastness and interest.

Mrs Dorman and Mrs McIntosh produced healthy baby boys on subsequent days. James Urquhart McIntosh made his entrance at the end of September. Considering she was in her late thirties, his mother 'did very well', as Elizabeth put it.

The nursing home had somewhat old-fashioned rules, even for the time. Only husband and family were permitted as visitors for the first few days, but various members of the company, desperate to see the baby called on their histrionic ability and appeared as a series of extraordinary relatives, George Nimmo, Rosina and Nicholas among those who successfully talked themselves past the watch-dog nurses. One afternoon Molly was taken by surprise by a very grand lady swathed in furs, descending upon her, till a "God bless you both, Mrs Mac!" announced it was none other than Elizabeth, who had borrowed her finery from a better-off relative. "I couldn't come to see Molly Urquhart's baby in my old tweed coat," declared her 'dear Elizabeth'.

The proud parents held the formal christening party in the Clifford Street flat, with Elizabeth as godmother. Then a few weeks later, there was a second celebration in the theatre. There had always been a 'no-presents' rule at the MSU, but Molly's baby was something special, so the company arranged a party and got a christening mug for the young James, who was then bedded down in a drawer in the ladies' dressing room, sleeping peacefully through the after-show party that went on till the 'wee sma' hours'.

Because rehearsals took place in the evenings, it was possible, having organised a host of willing babysitters, for the couple to resume their theatre activities. Jim was an equable, placid infant and being the first baby in the family was immediately adored by all. Molly's parents had come south from Gairloch, and were living in a picturesque little house called the Swiss Cottage near Hamilton, just seven miles from Rutherglen. Since her mother's health was failing a little, her second daughter Kit had obtained a compassionate discharge from the women's services to look after her. The delight of the parents over the baby was equalled by the pleasure his Urquhart grandparents and aunt found in him, and Kit looked after him frequently in the early years, a close bond developing between aunt and nephew from that time.

Molly and Willie, despite their surprise when their blessed event had been drawn to their attention, were utterly charmed with their little son. Nevertheless, the theatre had this mother in thrall, and as soon as it was possible she was back at work with renewed vigour.

Her reappearance in December was as Mrs Lucy Baxley in Prestley's *Laburnum Grove* directed by Alex Silverleaf, with decor yet again superbly realised by George Nimmo and Marjory Croll.

Miss Urquhart, who in private life is Mrs McIntosh, made a welcome reappearance after her "happy event". She plays the part of Mrs Baxley, the sponging sister, and has a fine co-partner in Nicholas Parsons as the penniless brother-in-law who finds in George Redfern (Guy Muir) good game for his borrowing propensities. (*Rutherglen Reformer*).

After this, the Christmas production was to be *Marigold* by L. Allen Harker and F.R. Pryor. A popular Scots comedy set in the nineteenth century, it deals with a romance between Marigold, daughter of Major Andrew Sellar, late of the 53rd and young Archie Forsyth of that same regiment. The young man playing Archie was appearing for the second time with the company, his first role having been as Dudley in *George and Margaret* earlier that November. He had appeared in films, notably *The Foreman went to France*, starring Tommy Trinder, and *San Demetrio, London*. In an article in the nineteen-fifties, Gordon Jackson recalled his introduction to the MSU Theatre:

> I played in two MSU productions. The first was "George and Margaret", shortly after I had my first go at filming in "The Foreman went to France". The second was "Marigold", I think three films later. My stage experience was strictly limited and though I now recall these plays with what the song calls "fond affection" I also remember that at the time there were embarrassing moments, particularly in connection with "Marigold".
>
> One day I was caught at work — I was still an apprentice draughtsman then — learning my lines under my blotter. Nor shall I forget Molly Urquhart's despairing efforts to teach me the foursome reel for the Edinburgh Castle scene. I'm certain she never thought I'd be able to get through it on the opening night.
>
> Still, "Marigold" did go on, successfully and fairly smoothly, thanks to Molly, with no more obvious technical faults on my part than being stranded twice during the week on the wrong side of the stage. Since there was no space to get round back of the scenery, I had to make an unexpected entrance through some French windows — from which a reasonable audience could only conclude that, in the character and time sequence of the play, I had spent the preceding night on the balcony!

This production in December of what was to be the last full season of the MSU Theatre perhaps typifies in so many ways what Molly wanted to achieve that it should be documented in some detail. The critic in the *Rutherglen Reformer* said:

TRAVELLING HOPEFULLY

Each player contributes immensely to the success of the play. Gordon Jackson, the popular young film actor, giving his services to the MSU comes well up to expectation in the role of Archie, a dashing young soldier, whose charming love affair with Marigold (Jean Ross) is one of the highlights of the play. The big things predicted for Gordon are certainly not exaggerated.

Mary McGuinness has until now played smaller parts, but her performance in "Marigold" as a pawky Scots servant certainly marks her as one with a histrionic feeling.

The cast assembled for this production was an interesting one:

Programme

CHARACTERS
(in order of appearance)

Robina MacFarraline (servant at the manse)	....	Mary McGuinness
Mrs Pringle (wife of the minister)	....	Miriam Owens
Miss Valencia Dunlop	⎧ Aunts of Archie ⎫	...... Elsie Russell
	⎨ and neighbours ⎬	
Miss Sarita Dunlop	⎩ of Mrs Pringle ⎭	.... Anna Welsh
Marigold (Andrew's daughter)	....	Jean Ross
Peter Cloag (Divinity student at the manse)	....	Bill Orr
Madame Marly (Andrew's wife)	....	Margaret Gourlay
James Payton (Laird of Ketinfoot)	....	Bert Ross
Archie Forsyth (53rd Regiment)	....	Gordon Jackson
Major Andrew Sellar (late of the 53rd)	....	John Macdonald
Mordan (Archie's soldier servant)	....	James McGinty
Nigel Lumsden (79th Highland Regiment)	....	Nicholas Parsons
Bobble Townsend (Inniskilling Dragoons)	....	Jack Woods

The Play produced by MARY S. URQUHART.
Decor by GEORGE NIMMO and MARJORIE CROLL.

NEW PLAYS, NEW PLAYERS

That group of players epitomises one of the theatre's major achievements. There was Mary McGuinness, who first came to the theatre to make tea, proving that given guidance and opportunity, she could turn in a performance that was more than competent. Miriam Owens was a mature player of great personal charm, much beloved by the public and professional in everything but name. Nicholas Parsons and Gordon Jackson were two extremely talented aspiring actors, who were finding the best possible way of obtaining a basic training for their subsequent careers that were to take them to the West End stage. Elsie Russell, who became well known both as a radio actress and as a journalist, later held a key position as announcer for Woman's Hour from B.B.C. Scotland. There are also names that have figured from the earliest days of the MSU and a few new ones. Molly had a cast in which she had complete confidence and was able to indulge in the comparative luxury of directing without having to play herself.

It must be remembered too that in running the MSU Theatre Molly was providing a practical training in acting, at a time when there was no drama school available in the west of Scotland. The only possibility of training for an acting career was to go to one of the London schools; since in those days there was no grant structure for students, that made the possibility of taking a formal course dependent on the family income bracket. There was always the possibility of getting a job in a repertory company, but that could mean living in digs, which was a considerable drain on the small salaries paid. Moreover wartime conditions had diminished the numbers of repertory theatres because of shortage of materials and also the difficulty of maintaining a company of actors in face of call-up for military service.

The MSU provided an equal opportunity to all, the only requirements being that a player had sufficient enthusiasm, application and staying power to meet the considerable demands made. If he could cope, he received a training that no other group could provide. And it was available to all classes of society. Rosina McCulloch recalls:

> It was the best way of learning. People came to the MSU just because they wanted to act, half of them not knowing how. And it was amazing how they came on, after a couple of seasons through

the grind, the sheer grind of doing it, of having to remember your words. Not only that, there was a corps of about twelve people, six or eight of us in every other play so that we knew what each other was thinking, so that if you dried, it didn't make a blind bit of difference — you just talked on, ad libbed in character. We worked so well together. You don't get that at drama school.

To return to *Marigold*, the financial statement for the show is interesting in that it exemplifies what a seasonal production staged with appropriate detail would cost:

MSU Repertory Theatre
Rutherglen.
Statement of gross drawings in the above Theatre during the week commencing Monday 20th December, 1943.

Production:— "Marigold" by L. Allen Harker and F.R. Pryor.

		£ s d	
Mon. 20th	16 seats @ 1/6	1 4	
	12 seats @ 1/–	12	
	10 seats @ 9d	7 6	
	16 seats @ 6d	8 6	£ 2 11 6
Tues. 21st	24 seats @ 1/6	1 16	
	22 seats @ 1/–	1 2	
	4 seats @ 9d	3	
	6 seats @ 6d	3	£ 3 4
Wed. 22nd	16 seats @ 1/6	1 4	
	12 seats @ 1/–	12	
	24 seats @ 9d	18	
	4 seats @ 6d	2	£ 2 16
Thurs. 23rd	26 seats @ 1/6	1 19	
	36 seats @ 1/–	1 16	£ 3 15
Frid. 24th	56 seats @ 1/6	4 4	
	24 seats @ 1/–	1 4	£ 5 8
Sat. 25th	95 seats @ 1/6	7 2 6	
	105 seats @ 1/–	5 5	£12 7 6
		Total £30 2	

Royalty fee 10% of total.

Certified Correct ————————————————

Director

Royalty Fee £3   Tax £3   Programme £1 6 6

It is difficult to extract every item of expenditure that relates to *Marigold*. The books were kept impeccably by Willie, but some of the ongoing costs, for heating, lighting, cleaning, printing, rent and rates, were carried proportionately over the season by the income from every production, so the following does not include those costs but only those relating particularly to this production:

Setting	£ 4	5	0d
H.S. Davie			
(Stage dresses)	£11	5	0d
Books		16	6d
Stagehand	£ 1	0	0d
Expenses to Cast	£ 9	7	6d
Royalty fee	£ 3	0	0d
Entertainment Tax	£ 3	0	0d

So the basic costs of this production were at least £2 in excess of the takings grossed.

Over the season, which was to be the last, the seventeen plays each took, on average, just under £34, that is the income covering one week rehearsing, one week playing. Some of the costs were less than those incurred by *Marigold* so it was possible, with those marginal but sufficient profits, to keep the theatre ticking over.

Molly ran the business like a Highland housewife who had to exercise every frugality in order to keep her domestic budget balanced and no more. Every possible economy was exercised, and with the willing help received from the people in the neighbourhood who took a practical interest in the theatre she was able to keep it going. From the local authorities nothing more tangible than benign approval was given. In those days the idea of receiving any kind of financial help from public bodies was seldom thought of by anyone, let alone an independent spirit such as Molly. One of the last in the tradition of actor-managers, she was also running a pioneer version of the civic theatre. Governments have come to see this as an important part of the life of the community, which deserves to have financial aid channelled to it both from national and local funds, administered on the one hand by the Arts Council and on the other by the local authority. The perils of the early months, when it seemed the theatre would not only sink but would drain their own savings, had been overcome by the whole-hearted devotion of both husband and wife.

Her own life and commitment were given over entirely to this venture. That a talent so extraordinary should be the centre of the achievement was its strength and attraction, not only to audiences but to the people working there who gave their loyalty to her as both leader and friend. The theatre in the West of Scotland, it would seem, from the few theatrical histories of the period, disappeared from the moment the amazingly strong amateur movement was dealt a crushing blow by the advent of war in 1939 until the inauguration of the Glasgow Citizens' Theatre in 1943. In fact it was the little theatre movement that kept Scottish drama alive; and in Rutherglen there was maintained for five years a little theatre that was more professional both in attainment and status than any other in the area.

A thoughtful assessment of the extent of her influence is contributed by Nicholas Parsons, who played in over fifteen productions at the MSU before he entered a full time repertory company and thereby began a successful career spanning television, variety, long running popular West End comedies like *Boeing-boeing* and critical successes in the Arts Theatre in Bridie's *Dr Angelus* and Turgenev's *Fathers and Sons.* He recalls:

> She made actors out of people — railway workers, students, teachers, housewives, children.
> I can't visualise her as a teacher at a dramatic academy — though I don't know — she might have been marvellous. But certainly for raw people who hadn't got much experience, in giving them some understanding of what they had to do she was magnificent. I think it was the knack of conveying enough but not too much, enough to help you and not confuse you. And she could move her actors across the stage very well indeed in the limitations of that little theatre.
> She was very good at coaching. She helped me with the part of Cameron in 'The Sleeping Clergyman'. I did exactly what she told me. I knew Molly knew what she was talking about.
> When I went into Rep. later at Bromley with Ronnie Carr who used to teach at R.A.D.A., I had learned enough about acting to follow his direction which was brilliant. He too had a genius for getting a lot out of actors and plays in a week's rehearsal.
> Of course, that was a week of rehearsing all day. Molly never had a reasonable amount of time to get the plays on, but she got them on and delighted the public.
> She gave us the real experience of walking the boards, learning

one's job the hard, the only way. She was a producer who knew what it was about, who gave you enough, who could stage the play in a week — which was unique — exceptional.

There are different kinds of producers — some give too much — some give too little. Some good producers only want to work with talented people because they have a lot to give and want to create something outstanding. But there is another kind of producer who can take people of limited talent or limited experience and give them something — and part of that is giving them confidence to think they can do it; help them develop their own potential. That is great direction, sensing what someone has to give and getting it out of them. In this sense she was a good producer. There's no knowing how she'd have been with a professional company and sufficient time.

Chapter Eleven

'The Wind of Change'

On 11 October 1943, a performance of *Holy Isle* by James Bridie in the Athenaeum Theatre in Buchanan Street, Glasgow, marked the opening of the Glasgow Citizens' Theatre. This venture had been one that Bridie had been working towards for years. To quote from the compilation *Citizens' Theatre: its Story from the beginning to the Present Day* by Tony Paterson:

> Bridie was already, of course, a dramatist of international stature, and it was one of his ambitions to see the establishment of a fully professional Scottish National Theatre which would show the wares of his fellow Scottish playwrights side by side with the pick of world drama. Supported by a loyal band of partners, prominent among them Dr Honeyman himself and George Singleton, founder of that other precious Glasgow amenity, the Cosmo Cinema, now the Glasgow Film Theatre, he set about turning the dream into a reality.
> . . . The main initial problem was to find a suitable home: wartime building restrictions ruled out any kind of new construction, and eventually the Athenaeum, in Buchanan Street, proved to be the only practical proposition. This was a far from ideal solution: stage facilities were, to put it mildly, limited and backstage accommodation inadequate; furthermore, the Athenaeum was irrevocably associated with amateur performances, and, although Bridie appreciated the worth of the amateur movement — indeed the Citizens' in its early stages owed an incalculable debt to it — he wished his new Theatre to be stamped through and through, like lettering on a stick of rock with the word "professional".

Molly had always insisted on professional standards at the MSU. The complete seasons of plays presented meant rigorous rehearsal schedules that called for the absolute commitment of all the spare time her actors had. The expenses given to the cast again made this something more than an amateur set-up, and as well as a professional player as director, the company were occasionally joined by a full time actor such as Gordon Jackson and Molly's brother Alasdair. She was providing real theatre, and the public had responded to it, with ever-increasing awareness.

William Grant Campbell had acknowledged the sound thinking behind her effort in the *Scots Independent* as early as March 1942, in an article entitled *Balmorals Off to Rutherglen:*

> Various people have at various times attempted to start something approaching a civic theatre in our twin Babylons, Glasgow and Edinburgh. They have not succeeded. When they had money, they had no policy. When they had actors, they had no money. At any rate, there is no civic theatre in Glasgow.
>
> (After itemising several examples, he continued: . . .)
>
> Amid this welter of attempts, I give you the one success, the MSU Theatre of Rutherglen. MSU stands for Mary S. Urquhart, a professional actress in Glasgow, whose aim has been the creation of a local theatre.
>
> Mary Urquhart wanted to start a theatre in Glasgow, but she could not get a theatre building. She was clever enough to know that you can't have a theatre without a building. This is the chief drawback which has faced such amateur attempts as the Scottish National Players and the Curtain Theatre in Glasgow.
>
> Two wildly enthusiastic amateurs of the drama, James Bridie and Paul Vincent Carroll, thought of starting a theatre in Glasgow and had a look at 'Greek' Thomson's Kirk in St. Vincent Street. But James and Paul could not agree on certain points, and the Kirk was bought by some Spiritualists. Glasgow is farther off than ever from having a civic theatre.
>
> Mary Urquhart, practical and wise as playwrights are brilliant and illogical, heard there was a kirk to let in Main Street, Rutherglen. She had not much money, but she had enough. She took the kirk, formed a company and started to present plays. . .

In the nineteen-forties, it was still possible for amateur and professional actors to appear together in professional productions. Equity regulations were not so strict, and entry into the acting profession was simpler. When the Citizens' directors began to assemble their first company, they certainly displayed a keen awareness of the talent that was around. Duncan Macrae was invited to join, as was a very young theatre enthusiast, Kenneth Miles.

For the opening production *Holy Isle*, James Arnott, who later became the first Professor of Drama at Glasgow University, but who was then a student at the same institution, was offered, as an accomplished amateur actor, a small supporting role. He decided not to accept, and Nicholas Parsons got the chance of playing on this historic occasion. He acquitted himself very well, and then came back to Rutherglen for the rest of the season. The inception of the Citizens' pin-pointed the fact that the situation for actors and theatre in Scotland would never be the same again. The fact that the civic authorities and C.E.M.A. or the Council for Encouragement of Music and the Arts (later to become the Arts Council of Great Britain) was intending to subsidise the Citizens' and other theatres, brought about vast changes in the theatre, since the prospect of employment on contract was at last offered to the semi-professional actor who, hitherto, had hovered on the brink of total commitment.

The future of the MSU was very much tied up with these developments. Molly, although philosophical in the face of all the ups and downs of the MSU's history, had cherished a secret hope that her theatre might somehow be recognised and linked in some way with the new upsurge of dramatic activity in Scotland.

James Bridie knew and admired her work. It seems unlikely that, in his constant enthusiasm for drama, he did not at some time slip unobtrusively into the pews, particularly when two of his plays, *The Sleeping Clergyman* and *The Anatomist*, were presented within weeks of each other in 1943. His distant cousin, the novelist Guy McCrone, who lived in Burnside, had attended performances there: and his own *Alex goes to Amulree* was given in May of 1944.

The directors of the Citizens' first season were Jennifer Sounes and Eric Capon, a vigorous, intellectual, enthusiastic producer who believed very much in the development of a theatre that had Scottish significance. It was he, when casting Lennox Robinson's Irish comedy *Drama at Inish* or *Is Life Worth Living?* invited Molly to appear as Mrs Annie Twohig, the wife of a hotel proprietor in the little seaside town of Inish, which is submerged in despondency and introspective gloom because of the visiting De La Mare Repertory Company presenting a season of plays by Ibsen and Strindberg. The *Glasgow Herald* said of it:

The people of the town began to look into their hearts and souls, and an outbreak of attempted suicides, suicide pacts and even murder was the result. The players 'with a mission' certainly brought it off.

If that description of "Is Life Worth Living?" by Lennox Robinson — presented by the Citizen's Theatre Company in the Athenaeum — suggests gloom and tragedy, it gives a false impression. This is an uproariously funny play, in which the higher drama is delighfully guyed: a play that has a kick in it, and is at the same time first-class entertainment.

There is a richly Sara Allgoodish performance by Mary S. Urquhart as the hotel proprietor's wife and so good is her brogue that she might have been playing at the Abbey Theatre for years. Duncan Macrae's Hector de la Mare is the "ham" actor to the last degree; and Yvonne Coulette as his wife, achieves the same "ham" standard.

Molly certainly made her mark. Other papers were equally enthusiastic:

'Mary S. Urquhart's Mrs Twohig is a thing of fruity richness' *Bulletin*.

'. . . a clever study of a humorous and homely landlady. . . '
Evening Times.

'Mary S. Urquhart (welcome visitor) *Evening News*.

'The guest star from Rutherglen's MSU Theatre shared top acting honours — with Duncan Macrae. . .' *Evening Citizen*.

Robins Millar in the *Daily Express* paid her quite a tribute: 'that clever Scots actress Mary S. Urquhart is worthy of the Abbey Theatre, her brogue ripples and authentic warmth springs from her'.

The Glasgow public, as well as the critics, warmed to her from the word go. This first guest appearance at the Citizens' left them in no doubt that the lady from Ibrox was a player after their own hearts. She liked working with Eric Capon, and enjoyed the three weeks in the Athenaeum. Though she might perhaps have glanced back a little wistfully over her shoulder at the company which Macrae had been able to join full time, she took up cudgels again at Rutherglen, confirming her statement made to the press, prior to her guest appearance at Citizens', that she was not deserting Rutherglen, nor was she thinking of giving up, 'despite the difficulties with which we are faced at the present time. My decision to play this role with the Citizens' Theatre is rather a gesture of friendship between our two theatres'.

The difficulties she mentioned concerned her tenure of the theatre building. Mr Paterson, senior, having died at the end of 1941, the family, quite reasonably, wished to sell the property, which was bringing in only a small rent. A business company was interested in acquiring it. The value was around £2000, which in 1944 was a vast sum. For the McIntoshes to acquire the property would have meant a mortgage and a complete commitment to Rutherglen. For Molly this was an emotional quandary: to her sensible husband, the idea of buying was out of the question. They did not have that kind of money, the theatre though successful as an artistic enterprise, had been only a modest success financially and profits had been very slender in the last year.

Molly was insistent that the MSU had a status similar to that held by the Citizens'. In this, she was less realistic. Admittedly, some plays and actors from the little theatre were to become, in several instances, part of the future of the Citizens', but in face of new developments of civic-based theatres, her gallant enterprise would have found it almost impossible to survive even if the former terms of tenure had held good. Although it had been a unique pioneering venture that had proved a lifeline for Scottish actors and plays throughout the war years, the concept of Molly's theatre was, in face of changing conditions, outmoded. Moreover, it had been sustained by an extraordinary dedication on her part, her inspiring leadership having rallied her band of players through those dispiriting early months to a period when there had been presented, quietly and effectively, a series of productions of which any company could be proud. It was all an amazing achievement and, of course, it has been successfully emulated. But never again in quite the same gallant, endearing, tight-rope walking way.

It had been while she was at the Citizens' that a chance, throwaway remark from Bridie himself had given her a last glimmer of hope. "That's a wee tuppence-hapny theatre you've got. Maybe someday it could be a thruppence-hapny theatre." A joke? Or something more? Certainly a 'Bridie-ism' which only someone hoping against hope would take as the basis of a serious suggestion about the future of what had been her greatest preoccupation for five of the most exciting, work-filled years of her life. She saw in that 'thruppence-hapny theatre' a vague hint that someday, somehow, there might be a possible tie-up with the Glasgow theatre, the MSU in Rutherglen being used as a possible try-out experimental studio-theatre.

But the Citizens' first year in the somewhat inadequate accommodation of the Athenaeum Theatre, situated within the Royal Scottish Academy of Music, its auditorium reverberating regularly to the rhythmic chuntering of the Glasgow Underground trains whose Buchanan Street to St Enoch station link was just under the buildings foundations, was fraught with enough difficulties, without any further plans for expansion. A theatre that was completely their own was their greatest need.

Molly returned to direct and play in *Mrs Mulligan's Millions* by Edward McNulty, an Irish comedy, in which she appeared as an old tramp who had come into a fortune.

'Miss Urquhart adds to her reputation as a fine character actress,' said the critic in the *Reformer*, well aware that the Glasgow critics had at last been able to endorse heartily his enthusiasm for her playing.

Willie was in no doubt about what should happen. The situation had reached the stage when, in a favourite phrase of his, "Enough is enough", and he had not been slow to notice her success at the Citizens'. Vincent Carroll was on Bridie's board of directors and Bert Ross and James Beirne, as well as Molly and Nicholas, were guest players from the MSU during that first season at Citizens'. But in March it was Molly who was again invited by Eric Capon, this time to appear in a part that might have been tailor-made for her, that of Molly Cudden, a Midlands hotel chambermaid who becomes a millionairess, in J.B. Priestley's *Bull Market*.

This was the last play to be presented in Citizens' first season and apart from Bridie's *Holy Isle*, set in Orkney, was the only play to feature Scots dialect. The original version had Molly Cudden speaking in Yorkshire, but Molly, with Eric Capon's enthusiastic approval, translated the lines into vigorous, contemporary Glasgow-Scots dialect.

In a strong cast that included Denis Carey, Yvonne Coulette,

Duncan Macrae and Sam Hankin, (from the Jewish Institute Players) she simply ran away with the play. The audiences were ecstatic, as were the critics. J. McNair Reid of the *Evening Times* said:

> A chambermaid in the Bull Market Hotel hands over to the night porter a heap of papers left by a defunct uncle. The night porter is an ex-financier of parts and of prison and he discovers a paper that, entitles the chambermaid, rightly negotiated . . . to fabulous wealth. The wealth accrues under the expert guidance of the ex-financier. The servants become bosses in the hotel. The tables are turned.
>
> Well, it is an uproarious farce that you must see for yourself. It is a shrewd and searching commentary on contemporary life. It is Priestley in his most discursive mood. Be sure you see it if only to enjoy Mary S. Urquhart as the chambermaid. She speaks in the dialect of our district, while round about her are the evocations of Yorkshire. She dominates every scene with a natural delight in acting that vitalises all her lines, and the rich quality of her speech brings a new distinction to our native tongue.

And what of the author's reaction? With typical enthusiasm for the new theatre being launched by his friend Bridie, he was present in the audience. When calls of "Author!" brought him on to the stage, he went straight to Molly and shook her hand, and most of his short speech was devoted to thanking her for a performance that was 'truly magnificent and vital'.

Every critic acclaimed her performance in the play. Indeed, *The Glasgow Herald* critic ventured to suggest that: 'Mr Priestley might well have doubts if this "created" part should not remain Scottish'.

It did not, of course, because a Scottish provincial dialect would not be easily accepted in the West End, and when the play went out, renamed *The Golden Fleece*, the chambermaid was played in the original Yorkshire by Betty Warren. But the point had been made well and truly that for the audiences in the Athenaeum, Scots, according to Molly Urquhart, was a language that provided a superb vehicle for comedy.

During the run of *Bull Market* the expected word came of notice to quit the theatre building in Rutherglen.

Although she had reluctantly come to the conclusion that an attempt for them to purchase would be unwise, she did decide, despite her husband's silent disapproval, to approach Rutherglen

Molly and Kit: a childhood portrait

Age 18, first grown-up dance dress

The wedding day, Mr and Mrs William McIntosh

Molly, Cambridge, 1935

Molly, Rutherglen, 1939

The only surviving picture of the original MSU company

Andrew Crawford and Molly in
Lady with a Lamp, Dumbarton

Party at Clifford Street, Gordon Jackson and Eric Capon centre of front row

Molly, ENSA, 1946

"I seem to have this Chinese vase."
An early study of Molly

William McIntosh, manager of the
Citizens' Theatre

"Nae flittings on ma caur!" Molly
warns Ian McNaughton (r.) and
Abe Barker

Fulton Mackay, George Cole, Molly and Mary Wylie in **The Anatomist**

"Swordid dance", Molly and Stanley Baxter in the **Five Past Eight Show**

Molly, Ian Wallace, Lucille Steven and Frith Banbury in **The Government Inspector**

"Ye canny beat the powder blue". Molly, Roddy Macmillan, Stanley Baxter and
Marillyn Gray

Molly and Andrew Keir in **Voyage Ashore** *by Alex Reid*

Jane Aird and Molly in Bridie's **Dr Angelus**

Molly and Bryden Murdoch in Guthrie's 1949 production of **The Three Estates**

Molly and Duncan Macrae in **The Tintock Cup**

Molly as Bonnie Prince Charlie in **The Tintock Cup**

*Renee and Fred Zinnemann with Molly on location for **The Sundowners***
Boat trip in the Congo. Peggy Ashcroft sculls, Molly admires the view

Molly, Mildred Dunnock and Omar Sharif in **Behold a Pale Horse**, *1964*

Molly with Alec Heggie in **You're a good boy, son**, *her last TV play*

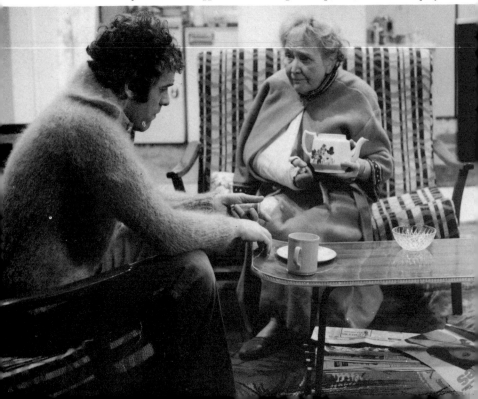

Town Council to see if she could have the use of the Town Hall from Thursday to Saturday on alternate weeks, as temporary premises. The season was drawing to a close. Its last two productions were Guy McCrone's *Alex goes to Amulree* directed by Molly, and then *Juno and the Paycock* deftly directed by Bert Ross with Anna Welsh as an impressive Juno.

Molly's application to the Burgh Lands sub-committee had been presented in May. In August they decided not to grant the use of the hall.

> After careful consideration the sub-committee . . . while sympathetic to Miss Urquhart's desire to run a theatre in Rutherglen, agreed to recommend that the Town Hall be not used for the purpose as they felt the adaptations required to make the hall suitable would not justify the expenditure required.
>
> Andrew Mann, the Provost of the Burgh, moved an amendment to consider further the granting of the let.

The Council's attitude was understandable. It would have caused considerable inconvenience to have dramatic performances held regularly in the Hall, and although it had provided a public service of some magnitude, the MSU, by definition, was a private enterprise, no matter how marginal any profits had been.

Molly had always, in her own words, 'played a lone hand' and had never sought any outside financial investment at the beginning of the enterprise. But her way of proceeding had become anomalous. The next chapter in the story of the Scottish theatre was beginning and it was natural the Mary S. Urquhart who had played so distinguished a role in chapter one should be involved in the consequences. She was asked to become a full-time member at the beginning of the second season of Bridie's theatre.

It says much for Rutherglen that when the theatre building remained on the market the following year, the plan evolved by a group of the actors who had decided, for various reasons, to retain their amateur status, to purchase the building as a community enterprise, was well supported by the town and the Council. After a year's closure, therefore, it opened its doors again, and ran successfully for a further fifteen years. The interior was refurbished, as money and Arts Council grants became more plentiful in the post-war period; it was only in the nineteen-sixties, when costs

131

escalated beyond control that it was sold and became in succession, a gas board showroom, a carpet shop and finally the club premises for supporters of Clyde Football team. But that is another story.

Let the spirit of the pioneers of the MSU be summed up in the words of Eileen Herlie, one of the first band:

> I remember 1½d tram rides to Rutherglen with a bun in one hand and a script in the other. On arrival, these were exchanged for a duster and a paint brush. Soon the duster and the paint brush gave way to the dignity and never-ceasing joy of grease-paint and make-up — and the curtain went up on the first production. In other words, I remember the beginning of the Rutherglen Repertory Theatre — to us at that time the MSU. These were good, glad days, with plenty of work and the satisfaction of building.

And so Molly joined in the work that was so dear to her heart, the first full scale attempt made by the Citizens' Theatre — the challenge was proclaimed in its charter — 'to present plays of didactic and artistic merit, to establish a stage for Scottish dramatists and actors, to found a Scottish drama school'. The Citizens' company worked hard, putting on in the restricted accommodation of the little Athenaeum Theatre ten plays in each of the first two seasons. Stage facilities were very limited, the size of the acting area was barely adequate while the sparse dressing room and back stage accommodation was cramped. The actors had for company the odd rat glimpsed in the deeper, darker recesses of the building.

To Molly, this new life was blissful. The theatre was only a few minutes by underground train from her home, she had more time to spend at home with her husband and little son, and if night duties and theatre work coincided, her sister Kit, now living with her parents in Hamilton, was only too willing to take charge of her nephew. From having to be 'Lord-High-Everything-Else' at Rutherglen she could now enjoy a variety of parts, under the direction of the man she admired most of all the series of directors she worked with at Citizens', Eric Capon.

A vigorous, slightly built English director from the Midlands he had very strong feelings about the importance of developing theatres in centres other than London. He had been enthusiastic about including as many Scots as possible in the company, and was anxious to include plays by Scottish writers in the season.

Another member of the company was Ian Wallace, who is now an opera singer of international reputation. He joined the Citizens' after having been invalided out of the army, and also recalls Eric Capon warmly as: '. . . a highly intelligent man with a curious staccato way of speaking, He was very, very articulate, although you never thought he was going to be, for he stuttered and stammered and then out poured the most marvellous exposition of what one was expected to do. He was one of those directors who approach the actor more from the point of view of intellect than instinct, and gave a general picture of how he saw the part and how he saw the play and then left the actor, to some extent, to put his own interpretation on it. An extremely nice person, he showed a real sympathy and understanding of the Scots actor and gave great encouragement to the 'local products', in the way of actors and writers, to present their own work'.

Capon was keenly aware of the possibility of the emergence of a Citizens' style of acting. From Curtain Theatre days, movement and gesture had always been held as a vital part of the approach to a part, and in some of the Scottish players, he discerned a vigorous, larger than life kind of bodily expression, that was far from the more restrained realism of an actor trained in the West End style. He, more than any other, was aware of the amazing range of parts Molly had encompassed at Rutherglen. His complete confidence in her versatility was shown when he gave her the part of Mrs Minnie Williams in *A Comedy of Good and Evil* by Richard Hughes. The wife of the Rev John Williams, Rector of Cytfat, she is described by the playwright: ' . . . a repressed face — protruding eyes. An astonishing capacity for putting speech into a dramatic form, regardless of its content: a tendency accentuated by extreme difficulty with the English language. Manner abstracted. She thinks as a grasshopper jumps. No education. A wooden leg'.

This extraordinary play, which is a comically bizarre debate on Good versus Evil, shows the home of a poor Welsh preacher invaded by an emissary of the devil in the form of a precocious little girl (played by Gillian Maude). She replaces Mrs Williams' missing limb with a new one, 'elegant, seductive: in silk stockings and Paris shoe, altogether à la Vie Parisienne'. And it behaves as if it had an exotic life of its own refusing to be hidden, flaunting itself under the nose of the amazed populace, to the embarrassment of its owner.

133

"There's legs and there's legs", she comments wryly.
Molly used to recall the part with a mild kind of surprise. "It was quite difficult to play". The critics applauded her performance as well as that of Gillian Maude, in a play which most of them described as 'unusual'. The *Glasgow Observer* commented, 'What a grand performer is Miss Urquhart. The first native Scottish actress who is Abbey standard'.

The Treasure Ship by John Brandane came next, followed by two premières, Corrie's *A Master of Men* and a new James Bridie comedy, *The Forrigan Reel.*

From an owner of an unruly 'limb of Satan', she was cast in this Scottish extravaganza set in the Speyside in 1740, as Mrs Grant of Forrigan, wife of the Laird, who was to be played by Jameson Clark. A good wife who runs her household with consummate skill, she is so bored with the monotony of her existence that she falls ill of a strange malady that makes her behave as if she were a clock.

In a talk given at the Citizens' Theatre Society over thirty years later, she was asked by a young lady how on earth one could play a woman who believed she was a clock. Stepping sideways rhythmically, her head moving automatically into the 'tick-tock' rhythm that had punctuated her performance she said, with an unconscious humour, "Well, you've just got to take your time!"

The solution to Mrs Grant's problem is in the wild fiddle music played by Old MacAlpin, a creature of 'infinite eld', who lives with his son Donald, a half-fey, half-daft shepherd, who dances a Strathspey all night through with the Laird's wife when her mad meanderings have brought her to their bothy. Her maid Mairi, who has run in alarm from the strange encounter, brings the Laird and his search party to the scene as dawn is breaking and Mrs Grant, who has danced herself well, greets her husband with exuberance, whereupon the exhausted Donald is hailed as a healer. His aged father, quick to recognise a good thing, exploits the situation and he and his son using the same method go on to cure a young English Lady, Clarinda, daughter of a Yorkshire baronet, of her melancholic disposition.

It was a glorious mélange of comedy, music and dance, and had all the uninhibited vitality of a family Hogmany party, when the wild Celtic strain breaks through the calm introverted everyday Scot. The tick-tocking and wild dancing of Mrs Grant gave full bent to Molly's enormous energy and vitality, while Duncan Macrae, his long comic lankiness accentuated by a brief kilt and a large balmoral, gave for the first time a display of his tremendous comic ability that later made him one of the great pantomime drolls. James Gibson was Old MacAlpin; wily and fly, as dressed in the tattered remains of old decency, he assumed the air of a seer.

It was a glorious romp with all the immediacy of myth and legend, and became a huge success, the kind of theatrical event that makes people laugh even when the mention of it years after recalls the insouciant charm of its humour. The critics applauded and the public flocked to the Athenaeum, so that for a month the theatre was packed.

Eric Capon had brought it to life vividly, saying in his gurgling, enthusiastic way more than once during the rehearsal period, "I'm not sure what it means, but it's awfully, awfully funny."

Some critics have later tried to read deep significance into this endearing Scottish farce, but Bridie himself thought of it as a romp, the lightsome spirit of which was most successfully revived in recent years in the 1976 production in the Pitlochry Festival Theatre, where it was warmly received by audiences of holidaymakers who wisely chose that beautiful part of Scotland where they can enjoy the scenic delights of Perthshire by day, and by night visit a theatre which proudly has, as its motto, 'Stay six days and see six plays!'

During rehearsals of the play the Urquhart family had received a telegram that Alisdair, who was in Germany in the Lovat Scouts was 'Missing'. The terrible uncertainty cast despair on the whole family. Molly was going through rehearsals like an automaton, waiting for further news.

It was Ian Wallace who brought in the second telegram. His father, Sir John Wallace, through a connection with the War Office, had managed to get a more up-to-date report. He wired, 'Your friend's brother is safe' to Ian who came rushing in late to rehearsal, waving the telegram. That kindly man Eric Capon said, "That's enough rehearsing today, Molly. Off you go and tell you parents."

The company were to go on a Scottish tour with the backing of C.E.M.A. They planned to visit Inverness and several smaller towns that had for a number of years been starved of theatre. At first the plan was to take out two productions. *The Forrigan Reel* and Ibsen's *Hedda Gabler* of which the company had given a competent enough account, considering it was only their second season. When it was discovered that funds would not permit two touring plays, it was decided that the Ibsen tragedy should go forth to the Highlands. An article in *The Bulletin* commented briskly:

> . . . it is not enough to send exquisitely trained concert parties from London to the backlands of Scotland. One cannot live upon an imported diet of strawberries and Devonshire cream.
>
> And this, one rather fears, is the big idea hatched by the Arts Coucil; an idea in whose light Scotland is seen chiefly as a handy colony to give longer seasons for a London élite.
>
> Perhaps the one notable Scottish achievement under the auspices of C.E.M.A. was the Citizens' Theatre production of James Bridie's "The Forrigan Reel". That is a truly Scots play, and an excellent play; moreover, a play that one feels it is very unlikely that the author would ever have written had he not had a company and a theatre for its production in Scotland.
>
> Thus far, C.E.M.A. gave a free hand to the Scottish venture. Yet is is said that when the Citizens' Theatre proposed to take "The Forrigan Reel" on a Scottish tour, London forbade this and insisted that the company should take "Hedda Gabler" instead — a play that the company was manifestly unable to act.

One cannot but agree that a truly native product of some liveliness might have been a better introduction to the work of the company, as well as being a more persuasive means of converting people to the habit of theatre-going.

However, the 'Forrigan Reel' company was to be far travelled, because in June, after playing a week in Bristol, it was to go on an E.N.S.A. tour to Europe. The company were duly inoculated and put into uniform, and set off for their first appearance furth of Scotland.

Audiences in Bristol gave them a splendid reception. The show, of course, had great visual appeal, and the infectious gaiety of the music was irresistible. A local paper said, with an engaging gallantry: 'We understood a lot of it. Not all, Mr Bridie, but that is our misfortune for being born English'.

Alistair Sim came to see it with a view, it was rumoured, to a West End production. The servicemen came to see it in great numbers. Much encouraged by the lively reception, the Scots joined the

English company with whom they were to share the tour which was to visit Paris, Hamburg and Lubeck. Their offering was a production of *Peer Gynt* with a starry cast that included Laurence Olivier and Margaret Leighton. The presentation of *Peer Gynt* showed all that was finest in British theatre. Yet it is not unreasonable to point out that in the mood of the moment, just after victory celebrations had marked the end of the long conflict, the Scottish extravaganza had more popular appeal. In Paris, the many French civilians who thronged to the Opéra Comique responded to the liveliness of the piece. In fact one evening, after the performance, a Corporal Macbain of Leslie in Fife, took off his heavy army boots to give a demonstration of the sword dance and the Highland Fling, to the piping of James McNeill who was providing the music for the play. The skirl of the pipes attracted hundreds of people, who, after a demonstration of the eightsome reel by the company, went wild with enthusiasm, clapping and dancing until the piper was finally exhausted.

Molly's legs, which had been such an asset in pantomime at Cambridge, gained the informed approval of the dresser at the Opéra Comique. This lady had once looked after Mistinguette, the French musical star, whose famous limbs had been insured for a colossal sum. "Madame, she would 'ave loved zis play of ze legs," she sighed, looking not only at Molly's, but at those incredibly long angular appendages that seemed to stretch for ever from the miniscule kilt worn by Macrae.

An incident that spoke uncannily of the magical power of the dance-cure occurred in Hamburg. Molly had picked up some kind of flu germ, and became thoroughly unwell, shortly before curtain up. There was no understudy ready, so dizzy, with aching head and a fiercely high temperature, she staggered on, much to the disapproval of the German doctor who had advised her to go straight to bed. She could recall little of the first scene which she got through somehow, but when it came to the Strathspey which lasted a good two minutes, she felt she would never see it through. To her surprise, as she danced, she began to feel better, and although she was bathed in perspiration, the fever quite amazingly was gone. So there might be something in the old legend after all.

Her Mrs Grant was a splendid creation, and the dialogue is written with the underlying rhythms of the Highland voice speaking

English. It has, in some ways, the quality of Synge's Irish speech in a work like *The Playboy of the Western World*. Every line has the essential intonation of Scots, yet there are very few dialect words. The epilogue, spoken by Mrs Grant, perhaps illustrates the warm pleasant charm of the piece and also lets Bridie have a gentle dig at those members of the audience who, having often criticised him for being too highbrow, were now rather reproving of his antic disposition:

> Well, there you are. By way of aftermath
> I bring soft answers to the righteous wrath
> Of those who feel this kind of Lowland Fling
> Crude and impertiment and no' the thing.
> We have no wish to set the heath on fire
> From far Loch Eirebo to near Kintyre.
> Nor do we seek to boil the simmering pots
> Of dour, pragmatical, sermon-tasting Scots.
> The most ingenious of them can't but fail
> To point a moral to our crazy tale:
> Unless it be that every now and then
> Women go daft from dullness — like their men.
> The dreary seconds go, "Tick-tock, tick-tock,"
> Till they grow skeerie and run up the clock.
>
> So cheer us up whenever you've a mind.
> Kiss us or skelp us as you feel inclined;
> But keep in mind that half of our camsteeriness
> Is just pure, simple, undiluted weariness.
>
> The author chose, tonight, to light his Stage.
> With simple humours of a by-gone age.
> You find his capers creak, his tapers dim?
> Don't boo the actors — lay the blame on him.
> To cheer you up a bit was all he meant.
> If he has done it, he is well content.
> Go out, then, to the throughfare and say:
> "In parts, amusing; not what I call a play."
> But say of us (and we can stand the test)
> "They're decent poor souls; and they did their best."

Towards the end of the second season, James Bridie got a

marvellous break from another much respected Glasgow man of the theatre, Mr Harry McKelvie who owned the Princess' Theatre, a neat Victorian playhouse which had opened in 1879 in the heart of the Gorbals district on the south side of the River Clyde. An admirer of all that Bridie was doing for the theatre in Scotland, Harry McKelvie offered him his theatre on a ten year lease at the moderate rent of £1000 per annum. Moreover, he offered to pay the first year's rental himself if the Board of Directors could get a ten years' guarantee of rental. The building could not be sold outright because of a trust deed on the property which said it should eventually pass to the Victoria Infirmary, where, incidentally, Bridie, in his persona of Dr Osborne Henry Mavor, had been a consultant for several years.

The Princess' Theatre had opened as 'Her Majesty's' in 1878, and after a faltering beginning had been the platform for a glorious variety of entertainments ranging from music hall to melodrama, 'Scotch' comedy to Shakespeare. Its most memorable contribution to the Glasgow scene was the series of enchantingly home-grown pantomimes, all of them with thirteen letters in their titles, that, as presented by the enthusiastic impresario Harry McKelvie, ran from autumn until early summer. Families from far and near axiomatically included an outing to the Princess' panto as part of their seasonal festivities, enjoying the splendid unlikely stories of *Tammie Twister* and *Jinglin' Geordy* (or *Let Glasgow Flourish*). Brilliant comedy with a strong local flavour featured not only the great dame Tommy Lorne, and later the rubicund comic George West with his elegant 'feed', Jack Raymond, but also some rumbustious ladies, the superb Jeanette Adie, as Principal Boy, and two Glasgow comediennes, the buxom Jean Kennedy and a tiny, dainty woman named Sylvia Watt.

The shows were as far from the elegant chocolate box presentations of the larger Scottish theatres as plain bread is from pan; admittedly there were great comedians in all the Scottish shows in those days, Will Fyffe, Harry Gordon, Dave Willis and Jack Anthony all bringing their own special brand of humour to spice the spectacularly staged, traditional stories such as Cinderella and Aladdin. But the Princess' Theatre, as the Metropole and the Queen's did likewise, had their characters journeying 'On board the Kleptomania' to 'The Land of Hokey Pokey' the whole sequence lit by the humour and dialogue that were peculiarly Glaswegian. And the regular patrons came in their thousands, year after year after year.

It was the final performance of *Hi, Johnnie Cope* starring George West and Jack Raymond (who featured in their final spot, for no particular reason, a brilliant burlesque of Shirley Temple and Freddie Bartholemew in the accents of Glasgow Green) that marked the end and the beginning of two remarkable chapters in the theatrical history of Glasgow.

"I've leased the theatre to a creditable company," said the genial proprietor, who in some ways was one of the greatest benefactors that Scottish drama has known.

Bridie, in his speech of acceptance, paid sincere tribute to the Princess' pantomime tradition, which had given Glasgow over sixty years of light hearted fun, every bit of it as clean as a whistle. This was not the end of the pantomime, he declared, for it would live in the hearts of Glasgow people.

In a heart-warming welter of goodwill, the theatre changed hands and the Citizens' had a home at last. As Bridie said to the audience that night, "The Citizens' Theatre will be yours, the same as this pantomime is yours. We're proud to follow pantomime". He led the audience in a rousing chorus of 'For He's a Jolly Good Fellow' to which the beaming Harry McKelvie replied "I've been here a long time. But I'm no' leaving. I'll still be living in the building."

As indeed he was, in body as well as in spirit, for he and his wife did remain for some time in the flat within the building that had been their home for many years. His presence was a link with a very substantial past tradition.

It was then full steam ahead for the new season. Unfortunately Eric Capon had gone to pastures new, without Glasgow ever having had the chance to see his skill as a producer given full range on a stage of reasonable dimensions. But he was succeeded by Matthew Forsyth, recently demobbed from the R.A.F. to take up once more a career in the theatre from where he had left off at Malvern Festival Theatre. He tackled the play chosen, J.B. Priestley's *Johnson over Jordan*, with an energy which was emulated by a company in which six out of the seven women and seven out of the ten men were Scots.

In an interview conducted by Colin Milne, an eminent drama critic, for the *Scottish Field*, James Bridie gave his answers to the most frequent criticism that had been made of the theatre, its comparative neglect of Scottish drama:

Yes, there has been such criticism, but the Citizens' Theatre did
not set out to present purely Scottish plays. Its object was to stage
plays of quality that were not likely to be seen in other theatres in
Glasgow. From the success of our first two seasons, it is obvious
that there is a public for such plays. And we did not neglect the
work of Scottish playwrights as you know.

Make no mistake about this, however — we are willing to
encourage Scottish playwrights and Scottish plays . . .

Speaking of the company, he refers to the number of Scottish
players engaged, adding, "We hope to reinforce the company from
time to time, by professional artists well-known in Scotland. There
is no doubt that we shall be able to tackle native plays as they arrive."

The theatre opened on Tuesday 11 September 1945. The *Daily
Record* reported the occasion:

The Princess' Theatre, new home of the "Citizens' " is blushing
in all the glory of new paint and decoration. It is resplendent like a
bride now that it has been wedded to the high art of theatre.

The journalist's prose is straining to cope with the importance of
the unique occasion. And an occasion it was, with the foyer
thronged, statesmen, professors, business executives, a scattering of
titled personages, mingling with the patrons, who were a mixture of
invited guests, those who were already supporters of the company
and those who had been for many years 'regulars' at their local
playhouse, which, according to some of the press, had been elevated
to a prominence hitherto undreamed of. The portico of the theatre
was designed by the nineteenth century architect David Hamilton,
its six doric pillars surmounted by statues of four of the Muses,
Thalia, Melpomene, Euterpe and Clio, alongside Shakespeare and
Robert Burns. Perhaps only the last named would have found the
atmosphere slightly alien.

The play was an adventurous choice, carried out with efficiency.
The critics were approving but in a guarded sort of way:

That Priestley's "Johnston over Jordan" does not stage quite so
well as it reads does not detract from its importance. (*Evening
Times*)

To present a drama of this calibre in opening a new venture takes courage. That the experiment was so successful is a tribute both to the quality of the company and the resourcefulness of the new producer, Matthew Forsyth.

Priestley visualises a dream state which is supposed by the Tibetans to occur immediately after death, and filled with visions symbolising events in the life just ended.

There are fantastic episodes, such as the inquisitorial reception office on the "other side" and a night club peopled by harpies in revolting masks.

It lacks humour, but ends in a happier "Inn at the End of the World", from which Johnson, in bowler hat and overcoat, departs disconsolately, presumably in search of further purgatories along an endless white corridor.

The general effect is macabre, yet it is a play that should be seen and closely followed.

In the large and highly competent company, outstanding performances are given by John Roderick as Johnson, Joan Matheson as his wife, Michael Golden as a celestial guide, James Gibson, Mary S. Urquhart, Jane Cain and Richmond Nairne. W.C.G. (*Evening News*)

The performances were generally praised, in particular that of John Roderick as Johnson, though the *Glasgow Herald* commented in quizzical manner, ' . . . even from behind a grotesque mask one could not mistake the Molly Urquhart voice'.

Rona Mavor, wife of Dr O.H. Mavor (James Bridie) had the right idea. When asked by a society columnist what dress should be worn at the Citizens', she replied, firmly, "Battledress!"

She was right, of course. The battle had begun, the battle against the theatrically barren years, the battle to win an audience from a city that had grown indifferent about native dramatic offerings, mostly because it is difficult to sustain an enthusiasm for something that is not, in fact, proffered by the local theatres.

That is why, in retrospect, *Johnson over Jordan* still seems a strange choice. Admittedly, it was a contemporary and controversial work by Priestley, one of the most exciting and stimulating writers of his time. But it was not a 'natural' vehicle for a new, raw Scottish company. Would it have been unacceptable to go for *When We are Married*, Priestley's classic comedy that had been so successful at the MSU? Might it not have been a happy marriage of cultures to have presented it in the James Woodburn Scots translation? The play chosen must have given many of the 'regulars' of the old Princess's season the fright of their lives; it took a long time before the local were persuaded to return. George Singleton ('Mr Cosmo' to Glaswegians) tells a lovely story of how Mrs McKelvie who, along with her husband, was one of the honoured guests on that occasion, commented to her husband, after watching Johnson's rather harrowing journey in Act I, "It's no' very cheery, Harry." One cannot but agree.

Alan Dent, that lad o' pairts from Maybole, who was then associate critic to James Agate, agreed in *The Sunday Times* of 16 September 1945 in forceful terms and at a greater length:

> With an impishness amounting almost to the appearance of perversity Mr Bridie and his committee chose for the housewarming — and for the great occasion of setting up their two year old Citizens' Theatre in a professional house of its own — a revival of Mr Priestley's modern morality, "Johnson over Jordan". Why? Can thrawn nationalism be extended to the point of choosing a play because it has the seal of London disapproval? Or was the choice dictated by the desire for a "difficult" play which should show the new venture's impressive paces in stagecraft, lighting, contrivance, and virtuosity of production in general?
>
> One was impressed. Mr Matthew Forsyth's producing was inventive. Mr John Roderick as Johnson — a part that overtops the rest as much as Everyman does in that rather similar and rather better play "Everyman" — is an interesting and new young actor. But one kept on saying "Why?" in the intervals and at the end — and heard the question around one, too. It was all the more vexing to be told that Mr Bridie has a delightful new play of his own on the stocks called "The Forrigan Reel". Surely that was the dance to open with rather than Mr Priestley's uncertain sarabande?
>
> Meanwhile the repertory is to be supplemented within the next fortnight by a sixteenth-century Scottish comedy, Mr Robert McLellan's "Toom Byres", and by Mr Paul Vincent Carroll's "The White Steed". We were assured by one of the speakers at the first night that we were assisting at "the birth of a great effort in adult education through a chain of Citizens' Theatres". This miracle in the Gorbals may come to pass; and one fervently hopes it will (with the active sympathy of the Arts Council). But let not progress ever again be endangered by the choice of a pretentious failure that has already been given every conceivable chance in the South.

TRAVELLING HOPEFULLY

The tolerance that, for the most part, greeted the opening play was the tolerance of an audience of seasoned theatre-goers, who were prepared to be indulgent over their new theatre. But something more was needed, something that journalist Kevin Carroll highlighted in an article in the *Daily Record* under the heading 'Lesson of the Abbey':

> What then does the drama movement in Scotland need? Strange as it may seem, it is an audience . . . a virile and lively audience who will demand the best and get it. In short, we want an "Abbey Theatre" audience, who give an author, especially a new author, exactly 15 minutes to prove himself. If he doesn't, he soon hears about it.

The difficulties were the same, on a larger scale, as those the MSU Theatre had faced and overcome. It seems, in retrospect, a little puzzling that the Citizens' management did not seek, in some way or another, a discussion with the lady who had sought and won an audience for her theatre in the Royall Burgh not five miles away. There is no doubt that she was still enjoying the luxury of being a mere player, and it was absolutely outwith her nature to proffer any advice unsought. But it is interesting to speculate upon the reasons that the powers that be in the theatre did not take advantage of the practical, experienced advice Molly might have brought to policy planning meetings.

Molly was one of the gang at the Citizens'. Never one to be anything other than friendly and down-to-earth, she most certainly did not come to Citizens' trailing clouds of glory from her past achievement. She was always concerned with the immediate present; she had tied up the ends in Rutherglen and was intent upon her new work. She thought of herself as a very ordinary woman, and unless she was putting on the style for a special occasion, she dressed in comfortable anonymous clothes, wearing for many years a favourite fur fabric coat to rehearsals because it was warm, and had been of good lasting quality. She wore easy-fitting flat-heeled shoes, or even carpet slippers, her wavy hair dressed any old how; she was the epitome of a motherly Glasgow 'body', friendly towards everyone, and extraordinarily un-selfconscious and unassuming. She found herself in the company of old friends — Macrae, Archie

Duncan, young Gordon Jackson, and later Roddy MacMillan, Andrew Keir and Fulton MacKay — working as most of the actors did in the first years for £6 a week. It is too sweeping to divide the company according to a superficial social strata; let it suffice that the group she found herself in was, on the whole, made up of native Scots, who had come to the theatre, not through a formal training, but through the amateur movement, and from the left wing of that.

She did not expect special treatment or recognition of herself as having been an actor-manager. Indeed, it was around this time that on being invited to open a sale of work at Tarbet, she was delighted to see beside her name on the posters announcing the event the bracketed explanatory phrase, 'Ann McCallum's daughter'.

Certainly, she did not present herself as an authority on theatre management and production, and, since the world tends to accept one at the face value one puts upon oneself, no-one sought her advice. Indeed, some of the company looked at this cheerful, easy-going lady and mentally dismissed the rumour that she had run her own theatre. She had innate good judgment and an acute awareness of what made good theatre, but she kept her own counsel and never chose to quarrel with her director. Too well aware of the demands of the role, she accepted for herself the discipline she had expected from her own company.

If her help was sought, as indeed it was by Matthew Forsyth who acknowledged in a programme note her assistance with the 'Doric Dialogue', she gave it willingly and without fuss. She was always the first to welcome a newcomer and make him feel at home, as Ian Wallace and many others acknowledge.

In fact, just as in Rutherglen and in almost every company in which she ever found herself, she became the mother figure. As Lea Ashton, later to be stage director for several seasons, remarked, "I always found the company enjoyed having her about. There was always such a fondness crept into people's voices when they spoke of Molly. She had a deep love and concern for others."

As an actress she was completely professional, but what so many of her associates recall is the tremendous enjoyment she found in her work. Not that she was over confident; she still needed reassurance, but by then it was that which came as a result of long deliberation and painstaking preparation. She was ill at ease only if she felt she was not up to standard. She tackled a role with vigour and added gradually the details that made her performance alive with the dimension of truth.

However, the season's plans were made and *Toom Byres*, a Scots comedy by Robert McLellan set in reiving times in the Borders in the sixteenth century, was to begin the following Monday, thence to alternate with the first production in true repertory fashion. The 'Pertinent and Otherwise' column of *The Bulletin* commented on the fact that this comedy was: 'Very Scots in its language. But it turns out that there wasn't too much to worry about, for only four of the cast of eleven are non-Scots. In fact, it looks as if the Citizens' really is equipping itself for a bit of Scottish pioneering. We hope'.

The Scotsman said of 'Toom Byres': '. . . Robert McLellan's richly amusing comedy has neither the weight nor the provocation of J.B. Priestley's 'Johnson over Jordan' and for that reason it may prove more popular.

'. . . A Doric play cannot be hurried, and it was more than coincident that the clearest and most effective of last night's players were 'resident' Scots Mary S. Urquhart and James Gibson'.

The question of popularity had already been raised. That lively writer James Barke, whose trilogy of novels based on the life of Robert Burns had enjoyed some considerable success, flung down the gauntlet in the columns of the *Evening News*: 'Now there are two main schools of thought concerning the theatre.

'One school takes its tally from the box office; the other clings to the criterion of "artistry". And, strangely enough, the two are held to be incompatible.'

Bridie wrote in defence of 'Johnson' as the opening play, asserting in words taken from Mr Barke's article that the job of the Citizens' Theatre is to produce such plays as the theatre-going public does not ordinarily see on the boards of the commercial theatre.

While this little discussion was proceeding, the play that the Glasgow public had flocked to see had been taken up by Alistair Sim who had written to ask the Board if they would release Molly to play her old role of Mrs Grant in a production that was to open in Sadler's Wells theatre on 22 October, with the possibility of moving into a West End theatre later.

Ian Wallace was to play 'Forrigan', and Duncan Macrae as young McAlpin was to leap forth on an unsuspecting London. Alistair Sim was the producer, and he also took over the role of Old

McAlpin. In a manner that recalled a mother buying new clothes for her child so that he might appear more impressive in the eyes of the elegant relations he was to visit, Bridie revised the play, putting in a new opening scene, set in Bath from whence the ailing Clarinda and party were to make their journey north in search of a cure, and adding a new set of songs with lyrics by himself, set with considerable style by Cedric Thorpe Davie.

It was to be Molly's first London appearance and the first time she was to work with Alistair Sim, one of the few Scots to have become an established West End actor. In a career that began at the University of Edinburgh when he taught phonetics, he had played in the Old Vic and films, as well as appearing in the première productions of Bridie's *What Say They?* at Malvern in 1939, where he played Professor Hayman, a baleful student-hating Clerk of Senate, and in *Mr Bolfry* in 1943 in the Westminster Theatre, in London where he played the Calvinistic Reverend Mr McCrimmon to great effect. A friend and admirer of Bridie's, he had been deeply interested in the progress of the Citizens' and had followed the fortunes of *The Forrigan Reel* from its opening. He had liked the performances of the original cast, and was shrewd enough to bring three of them to London.

In its new and elaborate form, the play came to Sadlers Wells. Molly's dressing room was bedecked with greetings telegrams, from Willie, from friends in and out of the profession including Joe Corrie and his wife. Two were especially prominent, one from her father and one from her mother, both having decided to send their best wishes to their daughter, but fearing the other might think it was making too much of a fuss of a mere London opening!

Cousin Lily and her husband Dan had organised their holiday from Inverness to coincide with the opening, and indeed a great number of exiled Scots were present at the first night.

London was staggered, 'We Reel, Too, Mr Bridie' said Stephen Williams of the *Evening News*. Other verdicts were 'rather a pretentious trifle', 'an oddly graced tarradiddle with music which I somehow feel should not have come south of Finsbury Park'.

Even Alan Dent's first notice declared that 'this haggis of an entertainment shouts aloud — if a haggis can shout — for later and longer consideration'. And indeed in an extended article he did, in his ineffable way, illuminate the darkness in which the play seemed to have left the English audience, in an exposition worded, as he put it, 'in plain Saxon'. He concluded:

> In a rhymed epilogue, Mr Bridie tells us not to be daft enough to look for any moral in his daftness. But I for one am not going to pretend that there is not a moral strongly implied — the moral that dull or ailing ladies are none the worse for a Forrigan Reel (which is whatever your delicate imagination suggests it may be). If this is not the meaning of the piece, then this piece is entirely meaningless — and I'm a Gomeril!
>
> But then, many of us will be content to shut one eye and take it all as meaningless, since there is a certain odd wayward charm about Mr Bridie's daftness.

The critics did pay somewhat grudging tribute to the players. Stephen Potter said: 'Whatever else it is, it's not a play. Disarming words — especially when spoken in a bored-critic voice by a charming actress in the bold exculpation of a piece, delivered at the end of 'The Forrigan Reel' in heroic couplets. The art of Epilogue should be revised.' But he goes on to point out that 'private jokes in general lose their point if they have to be bellowed across the waste spaces of Sadler's Wells.' And indeed, this was something else that diminished the effect of the play — it was really designed for a much more intimate theatre. Mr Potter goes on to reflect just how well his friend's comic gift was understood by Bridie who could 'fire off the subterranean mines of Alistair Sim's humour with sudden reflections on the theme of sudden death: "That it's a terrible thing. It would kill a horse".'

Macrae's performance was hailed as outstanding by some and incredible by others and Beverley Nichols expressed somewhat waspishly, his 'sincere sympathies to Miss Molly Urquhart, who tick-tocked with a verve that was worthy of a better cause'.

Molly loved London and its people. She enjoyed Cockney humour and in fact, as she always did, found her way very quickly to the real people of the neighbourhood.

The play did not run long. The songs, though fine enough in themselves, did tend to slow the rumbustious pace of the original, and perhaps bamboozled the critics into thinking it was intended to be somewhat loftier than it was, a kind of ballad opera.

Alistair Sim, that most polished and meticulous of actors,

steadfastly refused to sing the song that had been written for Old McAlpin. Using a melody from balladry with somewhat bawdy associations, Bridie had written a lively 'Wraggle taggle gypsy' kind of narrative about a handsome tinker who caught the eye of a fine lady:

> A lady she was dressing, a-dressing for the ball,
> When she saw a great big tinkler leaning up against the wall,
> With his kilt and his flea-bit sporran,
> An' his whiskers flying free
> An' his bonny ragged bonnet hanging low upon his bree

Ian Wallace recalls the cast absolutely falling about with laughter when Alistair tried it at rehearsals. 'There were several verses. I recall another line: "I'm six foot ten of tinkler, and I think I might as well . . . !" Alistair took fright and wouldn't do it in the opening performance. He loved to hear people laugh, but he was always afraid of "going over the top". To sing a number — that was something he'd never done. Molly and I implored upon him. "Alistair, you must do it! It will be a sensation!" But nothing any of us could say would persuade him.'

An incident that occurred one night perhaps justified his reservations. As he struck up the melody of the song on his fiddle and Molly as Mrs Grant swung into the reel with Macrae, there was a start of recognition from one part of the house where a large group of soldiers from north of the border, had come to get a 'drop of Scotch'. With unerring ear, they pinpointed the original piece of bawdry which still has a currency in the less self-conscious folk-scene, and the 'waste spaces of Sadlers Wells' resounded to the sixteen verses that were sung at the top of their voices. Molly and Macrae were almost helpless with mirth, the English audience feared another Bannockburn, the orchestra, who had finished the set score, sat all unheeded, and the back stage crew 'looked at each other in a wild surmise'. The curtain was due to fall to denote the passing of the night, but it was obvious the soldiers' chorus had the bit between their teeth and would sing their ballad to the bitter end. So on went the dance, with Alistair's face getting more and more suffused with crimson at this turn of events. "Molly! Molly!" he hissed to the dancing figure, "what can we *do*?"

"Do? Do nothing. Keep going. They're having a ball," whispered

Mrs Grant, in full Strathspey step, through her benign smile. As the much elongated scene ended in cheers and tumultuous applause, it was obvious that the spirit of the piece was still a potent one for any Celt who wandered in to Sadlers Wells during the run! For once, despite a lifetime's expertise in the dances of her country, Molly collapsed breathless as the curtain fell.

After the London run, it was home again to her family and the Citizens'. As always, Molly came home to Scotland with a joy in her heart. Very much a Scottish lady, she became even more intensely so, the minute she crossed the border. Gordon Jackson and Rona Anderson recall how, at a cheerful singalong evening in their London home. Molly, having just arrived from Glasgow that day began to sing in her strong vibrant contralto, 'The Rowan Tree', with lyrics by Lady Nairne.

She just got as far as that, and burst into tears. Jimmy Gilbert, who was accompanying her collapsed with laughter, as did the others. "But Molly — you can't be homesick already. You're only just off the train!"

But she was. And for all that she enjoyed travelling, she never went furth of Scotland unless to visit relatives or if her work in plays or films necessitated it. Once, years later, having played at the Arts Theatre in Galsworthy's *In Chancery*, there was a chance she might get a part in the next play. An English actor asked her if she would try for the part.

"No. I'm going home, then my husband and I are motoring up to Wester Ross to visit our relations."

"But it's a play by Christopher Fry."

Thinking he hadn't understood, she told of her plans again.

"But . . . Christopher Fry."

She gave up. There was no possible way of making him understand.

She joined the Citizens' again for their Christmas extravaganza, *The Pyrate's Den*, in which she was to play Mrs Thom, the wife of an eighteenth century Glasgow Bailie who has been making an impressive fortune out of the tobacco trade with Virginia. With the amazing double standard so many of his kind employed, he chides his son for having the reek of tobacco about him, adding: "If it has pleased the Lord to prosper us by the sale of that vegetable, it is none of his intention that we should ourselves be transformed into fiery lums or chimbleys in the employment thereof."

Happy enough to have been admitted 'to the fellowship of the Lords of the Tobacco Trade who walk the plainstanes to the Glory of God and the dignity of this City', he resolves, in an unprecedented moment of daring, to take a trip on one of the trading vessels to the Carolinas. His wife, quite unjustifiably accusing him of deserting her and the three grown-up children, resolves that the whole family will go, and with dramatic development of an enviable pace, after only a short space at sea, the whole ship load is captured by the pirate Captain Teach, the notorious 'Blackbeard'.

The playwright, one A.P. Kellock, wrote of the sources of his story in the note prefacing the typescript copies. (It is a sad reflection that this, among other plays premièred at the theatre, have not yet been published.)

THE PYRATE'S DEN
An adapation for the Theatre
of 'THE LIFE OF CAPTAIN TEACH'
by
Captain Charles Johnson
(London 1724)

There is reason for supposing that 'Captain Charles Johnson' was none other than Daniel Defoe. This possibility has been advanced by William Roughead in an Essay in the Juridical Review. Be that as it may, an attempt has been made in this adaptation to preserve the lively picture of the lawless times so brilliantly created by the original author.

The 1945 adaptor wishes, for the present, to remain anonymous; but he is a professional dramatist of repute whose work is well known in London and New York.

The mild irony of the last sentence indicated clearly to all who knew him that the author was, of course, James Bridie. He was again writing for his company and with James Gibson, ideal as the canny shrewd Bailie Thom, Molly as his motherly body of a wife, and the lovely Rona Anderson as their eldest daughter, he had a good Scots team, with a pleasing variety of parts for the English actors in the company, notably as Blackbeard. The Scots dialogue was well written, with a fine awareness of the lexical and syntactical features of the period, combined with Bridie's innate instinct for the appropriate rhythm of Scottish speech. This is one of this playwright's major contributions to Scottish drama, and an area of his work that has not received either due critical tribute or appropriate academic attention.

That the company — and some of the audience — had found difficulty with the doric Scots of McLellan's *Toom Byres* was something that concerned Bridie. The assumption of an accent and vocabulary foreign to the actor presents problems, not the least of which is that the speaker's lack of ease and comprehension is mirrored in the audience. One can compare the situation with a performance of a Shakespeare play directed by someone like Trevor Nunn, and played by a company of actors who through weeks of thought and study are fully aware of the characters they are playing and of the significance of every line they utter. Such a performance will elicit complete response from audiences all over the country, with no problems about the difficulty of the language level. As Winifred Bannister says of this period in the theatre's history:

> Although he wished to see the folk-play in the doric take an honoured place eventually, as indeed it must to supply a stage with national pretensions with a sufficiency of red corpuscles, Bridie shrank from exposing the weakness of his company's Anglo-Scottish composition, by putting a difficult form of Scots into the mouths of the English actors, but agitation for national drama was increasing at a rate that he had not expected. As Bridie saw it (most people did not agree with him here) there were not yet enough good Scottish actors who were also capable of polished acting in English.

Bridie had lashed out, in a letter to *The Glasgow Herald*, at those he called 'lovers of the drama' who had not supported those three plays, out of the twenty-five performed so far by the Citizens', that had been 'disastrous flops from the box office point of view'. These were *The Good Natur'd Man* by Goldsmith, *A New Way to Pay Old Debts* by Massinger, and *The House of Regrets* by Peter Ustinov, whom he hailed, with commendable prescience, as the leader of the younger school of British dramatists.

He insisted that 'these three plays should have attracted lovers of the drama purely as a matter of interest. Whether they would have

enjoyed the plays when they saw them is beside this particular point
. . . ' 'Have we got,' he cried, 'an educated audience in Glasgow?
Of course we had, but certainly not enough to fill a repertory
theatre for every performance of every play. As for the rest of the
citizens, they were, in their cautious way, just trying to get
acquainted with this new aspect of their city's life. And as has been
proved time and time again, in the beginning of any theatre
movement, it is the player who is the intermediary, not only by
interpreting the dramatist's intention for the audience but by
drawing the audience into the theatre because of the trust and
affection that can develop between particular players and their
followers. As Tony Paterson says in his resumé of the theatre's
history, '. . . players like Molly Urquhart, Duncan Macrae and
James Gibson were in the process of becoming household names'.

So *The Pyrate's Den*, the Christmas extravaganza with the thirteen
letters in its title as a fond acknowledgement to the great series of
pantomimes devised by Harry McKelvie, was launched and became
a huge success. The company's first seasonal show in the Princess'
Theatre, it drew in a great number of the pantomime regulars, many
of whom had perhaps not yet realised that a change of management
had taken place. But the show was delightfully funny. There is a
scene on the island where the pirates entertain their prisoners to a
barbecue, where Molly, as Mrs Thom, was called upon to sing to the
drunken ruffians. Her rendering of:

> Be kind to auld Granny, for noo she is frail,
> Like a wind-swept tree bowin' low in the gale.

had them dissolve into maudlin tears, and her encore, a music hall
ballad, 'The Miner's Dream of Home' had them reduced to wistful
homesick nostalgia and the audience reduced to helpless mirth. The
chorus of this last:

> The moon was shining brightly,
> Twas a night that would banish all sin.
> The bells were ringing the Old Year out
> And the New Year in.

she did with actions, bell-ringing and the lot. Years later, I heard
how she nightly convulsed the on-stage company, with a deftly

153

concealed two fingered gesture on the phrase 'banish all sin'; At the time, sitting round-eyed between my father and mother, seeing for the first time a play instead of a pantomime, and a play that was in Scots and not in the posh English accents with which in my mind drama was inevitably associated, I thought she was the greatest thing since sliced bread.

Chapter Twelve

'A Citizens' Person'

"Matthew Forsyth", reminisced Archie Duncan with a chuckle, "used to say she was like an untamed horse. Of course," he added in mitigation, in case I might have thought this an ungallant sentiment, "it's common knowledge that I was nuts about her."

And indeed Archie throughout his life had maintained something of the affection and admiration that he had first felt for the 'beautiful lady who came to the door' all those years ago when he went to ask for 'John Cameron's part'. He rejoiced in her success at the Citizens' and he enjoyed his work there as her colleague. In those days arriving at the Citizens' seemed like the end of the journey to Archie, as it did to Molly and the other Scots who had struggled so long to create this kind of theatre. Archie, who for many years acted in the West End and in films, recalled with affection, "The great things in my life always seemed to happen at the Citizens. I got £6 a week for the first year, with an option for £9 for the second year, — with a verbal option on my further services." A character actor of considerable versatility, Archie's towering height and strength took him later into a series of parts ranging from Little John on the long-running television serial *Robin Hood* with Richard Greene in the title role, to supporting roles in American Westerns. In one of these, he was to drive a stagecoach with a team of horses that bolted. The close-up shots of this were to be taken with Archie holding the reins with all his strength, while out of camera a Mr Universe-type stunt man known as the 'wrangler' was to hold the other end. "Pull back them horses as hard as you can!" shouted the director. Archie did, with all the strength of a Clydesider, and for the first time in living memory, the wrangler was whipped off his feet into the air.

Archie's proudest memory was of the time dramatist Arthur Miller saw the 1957 Citizens' Company production of his play, *A*

155

View from the Bridge and said at a luncheon the following week, "This is the fourth production of my play I have seen, including the West End and Broadway, and I think that big guy, who is incidentally, a magnificent actor, came closer to what I had in mind when I wrote the part of Eddie than anyone so far."

While he, along with Molly and Duncan Macrae, was obviously essential to the company in the early days, there is no doubt at all that when the play presented was one that demanded a restrained naturalistic style in the high English manner, their physical, larger than life approach would need to be modified. The company, was on the whole, of a modest size, and in the fashion of those times, was signed up for a year. So that casting a play was like finding an occupant for the Procrustean bed; sometimes an actor had to be made to fit. This resulted in such anomalies as the English actor who got thoroughly tangled in the Lallans lines of *Toom Byres* and Molly's vigorous but unconventional performance as Lady Binnacle in *Cornelia*, a comedy by Elizabeth Mackintosh of Inverness who wrote many superb plays under the nom-de-plume of Gordon Daviot, as well as a series of near classic detective stories as Josephine Tey.

The Glasgow Herald said: '. . . In this play, our old friend Molly Urquhart forsakes her familiar working class roles to become the fashionable dowager Lady Binnacle, in magnificent silver fox fur cape. Unfortunately her humour remains local and her accent rather broad to have been so long removed from her native heath!'

Her ladyship had been in the theatre, and, the plot claimed, had appeared as the Principal Boy at the Princess' Theatre itself. The critic's remarks are not entirely fair comment either on Matthew Forsyth's casting, or on Molly's performances, since she had that season played a woman in the French Resistance movement in Robert Kemp's *Victory Square*, Mrs Gilbey in *Fanny's First Play* by Shaw, an Irish 'virago, tearing and tempestuous and singing like a rather rowdy angel' in a new play *A Babble of Green Fields* by Anne Louise Romoff. She had delighted the critics of *The Highland News* and the *Inverness Chronicle* with her performance in Bridie's *Mr Bolfry* which made a superb impression when the company toured in it:

> Mrs MacCrimmon, the minister's wife, finely conceived by the playwright, is gloriously portrayed by Mary S. Urquhart. She is one of those who, at an early age, accept the principles for guidance

in his life as they have been taught them, and find them sufficient
for every emergency. Nothing disturbs their serenity. For her all
that is to be known about election, free will, predestination, even
about heaven and hell, has been settled long ago, so why get hot
about them? — while her huusband at her side wrestles with his
alter ego, she can turn her back and get on with knitting cheerily.
Duncan Macrae was excellent as MacCrimmon. *Northern
Chronicle.*

It was in the part of Lady Binnacle that Molly created a bit of
theatrical lore that has re-echoed down many seasons. Peter Mac-
Donell, then one of the company, remembered its origin:

> Molly seldom did anything by halves. Her entrances were always
> twice as big as life. I remember one particular example. She made
> her entrance as usual through the large double doors — as Lady this
> or that — and swung off her cloak. She usually threw it over the
> back of a chair and joined the general action. This time, for some
> reason she was slightly out of position, there was no chair avail-
> able. She solved the problem by trying to hang it over the top of
> her umbrella and then prop the whole thing against the fireplace. It
> fell several times; in the meantime the play came to a full stop.
> Somebody on stage waiting for the uproar to die down, turned up
> stage and said to Jimmy Gibson who was also waiting patiently,
> "What in the hell is she doing?" Jimmy replied, "I'm not sure. I
> think she's building a tent." "Building a tent" became part of our
> language at the Citizens' to describe any business that might creep
> in unannounced during a run and halt the progress of a play.

Of Molly's skill and versatility there was no doubt whatsoever,
but the very strength of her playing did seem to perplex Matthew
Forsyth and a few of his successors. Not that she was in any sense
'difficult'. Lea Ashton recalls how she always listened courteously to
suggestions from almost anybody, and had an open almost childlike
ability to take even the most insignificant part and make something
of it.

> She had a sense of total gaiety, slightly alien to the rest of the
> company who had a sense of keenness to get on. She worked a part
> at a time, played everything show after show after show, giving of
> her best all the time. She didn't seem to have a desire to get
> anywhere, in fact, she always seemed slightly surprised she ever

157

had got anywhere. She enjoyed being on the stage; that was her great beauty, her great charm — she enjoyed being on the stage, for on the stage she was supreme. She always surprised me by her dramatic ability in more serious parts. She didn't seem to work on it; she just switched on, by instinct became the person.

He speaks also of her tremendous sang-froid and resource, instancing one performance in a later season, when playing an Irish mother where a country cottage setting called for a suitable but incessant sound effect of hens clucking in the background. The actor who was to enter and deliver the speech necessary to the exposition of the play sallied forth with a lurching gait and a glazed expression in his eye that had more to do with an unfortunate over-indulgence in our national beverage than a characterisation assumed for the occasion. Not a line did he utter, except for a re-iteration of the one phrase that indicated he knew where he was at all:

"The chickens . . ." he gulped, unhelpfully. "The chickens . . ." Molly grasped the situation immediately. "Sure and I thought it was me ye was comin' to see, instead of those blasted chickens. Well, off you go and have a look at them and see if you think I've been after feeding them right."

And she propelled the fellow off into the arms of the A.S.M. who proceeded to do his best to sober him up, while Molly turned to the others on stage, and delivered every significant piece of information that should have been imparted, so that the action could proceed, the audience sitting happily unaware through all this little drama. Five years of meeting every contingency in Rutherglen had rendered her an expert in resolving such dilemmas.

However, she was always delighted to tackle whatever was asked of her, whether it was one of Rob Roy MacGregor's daughters, leading her sisters in a high-kicking chorus line (— 'Molly "Legs" Urquhart' commented the press —) in Eric Linklater's romp *To Meet the MacGregors* which was a wild musical version of Walter Scott's Rob Roy even more extravagant than that *Jeanie Deans* of 1934 in which she had made her professional debut; or as the mother in an elaborately staged version of S.I. Hsiung's *Lady Precious Stream* that was the sumptuous but unpopular Christmas offering in 1946. (It didn't have a thirteen letter title!)

Earlier in 1946, the Citizens' lost their able manager, Miss Winifred Savile, who came of a family of theatre managers. She resigned mainly because she felt not enough attention was being paid to box office appeal. Being one of those practical theatre people who thought it a good thing when a play 'washed its face' and was even more delighted when it made a comfortable profit, she could not agree to a policy that was open to supporting some inevitable artistic failures. Mr Colin White succeeded her.

However it was the spring of 1947 that saw both Molly and Archie Duncan going off to London on Alistair Sim's invitation to appear in a new Bridie play at the Phoenix Threatre. *Dr Angelus* was based on the story of Dr E.W. Pritchard, a Glasgow general practitioner who in 1865 was the last murderer to be hanged publicly in Jail Square outside the Courts of Justice in Glasgow. The play, updated to the 1920s, is one of the best in the Bridie canon. Its theme allows the shrewd analytical mind of Dr O.H. Mavor to give convincing substance to his dramatically gripping psychological study of a man whom A.E. Wilson of *The Star* described as 'a Jekyll and Hyde. Having betrayed a foolish servant girl he murders his mother-in-law and his wife and induces his too trusting assistant to sign their death certificates'.

It was a superb part for Alistair Sim, and with his extraordinary gift for casting, he had chosen a company that not only had the young George Cole as Dr Johnson, his assistant, but Jane Aird, who also had worked at Citizens', as Mrs Angelus, Molly as Jeanie the servant girl, with Archie Duncan as the Glasgow Police Inspector, a little cameo part with some of the best lines, appearing only in the last twenty minutes of the play. As Archie put it, "The beauty of having a part written for you is that they put in all the stuff you can do. So it gives you a wonderful chance to show off. But they omit all the stuff you can't do, and the end product of that is that you get the reputation of being a helluva lot better than you are!"

Sim was a great director and he got a tremendous response from Molly. Her performance as Jeanie, the sly, sensuous, impertinent servant girl, who is so sure of the master's affection that she almost openly derides poor, failing Mrs Angelus, dying from the judiciously administered antimony, prescribed by her husband, was a thoughtfully realised study of a part that has often been underestimated and misread.

Jeanie has to be convincing as a domestic engaged to work in a professional household, yet her dress and behaviour have become noticeably less appropriate to her position. She is clever enough to have ensnared Dr Angelus, but not so clever as to realise that he had not the slightest intention of including her in any permanent way in his grandiloquent plans for the future. Her knowledge of the situation between him and his wife forces him to placate her, and thus it is no punishment for him to do so since she is a comely complaisant lass. The touches that remain in the memory are of the doctor's arch little hints of intimacy when, on her first exit in their first scene together, he tweaks her apron strings loose.

Then there is the splendid moment where poor, pathetic, genteel Mrs Angelus tries to rebuke her flouncing servant about the neglected state of the house:

> Mrs Angelus: 'This room's filthy. I can write my name on the dust, look.'
> Jeanie: 'A great thing, education.'

When Angelus, seeing the danger in which her enmity could place him, reassures her of his honourable intentions and undying love, Sim, while fondling her into quiescence with one hand has the other stretched out the while to check the time on his wrist watch. (For this bit of business alone it was worth up-dating the piece!) And her drunk scene, when in answer to the doctor's query about the state of the whisky bottle allowed her to retort, with an intoxicated giggle, "S'empty!" gave the Mavor household at least, a family joke for years after. Yet with Angelus' arrest in the dénouement of the play, when the shallow, stupid girl realises that she has been used and is about to be left, pregnant, alone, her foolish dream in fragments, she could still the audience into awareness of her as a tragicomic figure. To quote Archie once more:

> Her best performance? In "Angelus" — it's got to be Jeanie in "Angelus". She had a thing that the great clowns have — pathos — and into that tarty hoorie maid-servant she injected pathos. Half the time I couldn't see her performance in the last act for the tears in my eyes.

The play was well received on tour and throughout its run of several months. Queen Mary, the Queen Mother, came to see it, and met the cast at the interval. Well-informed as always, she knew about Molly's theatre and her work in the beginning of Citizens'.

Molly was dazzled by this tiny figure of immense be-diamond dignity, silencing with a look the equerry who had the temerity to attempt to answer the Royal rhetorical question, "I wonder what will happen at the end?" As she bowed falteringly away from the first monarch she had met, she heard a wickedly hissed chuckling whisper from her director who was next in line, "That's right, Molly. Arse backwards!"

One night in Leeds during the prior to London tour, Alistair Sim and George Cole invited Molly to have supper after the show. Her sense of direction was never her strong point, and when they were running her home, she remembered the road and the house number, but not the name of the out-of town suburb where her digs were. "Och, it's easy to find," she assured Alistair airily. "You go straight along from the theatre and turn left at the tartan dyke."

"What in heaven's name does the woman mean?" said Alistair.

What indeed? Despite the fact that these painted black and white corrugated metal crash barriers occurred throughout Britain, Molly had thought the one near her road end was a unique landmark. When they finally got her home quite some considerable time later that night, they had "turned left at every damned Tartan Dyke in Leeds and district."

While the London audiences were turning out in large numbers to see this play that had some considerable substance as well as high entertainment value, Scotland was about to have greatness thrust upon her as a new centre for an international clamjamfry of the Arts; the first Edinburgh Festival was to take place in the summer of 1947.

During the London run of *Dr Angelus*, the Old Vic had been considering another Bridie play to be presented at the first Edinburgh Festival. This was *John Knox*, and it must be admitted a play about the great leader of the Reformation in Scotland would have been a paradoxically apt dramatic offering, since it was from his lips that came that condemnation of plays and players so resounding as to cause the theatre in Scotland to stand still for two centuries. In addition, the Union of the Crowns of Scotland and England in 1603 meant the withdrawal of the court to London, and thereby the withdrawal of a major source of patronage of the arts. As William Power said in an article in the *Evening News* on 18 March 1947:

Sir David Lindsay's Satire of 'The Three Estates' acted in the open air before the Court and large crowds at Linlithgow, Cupar and Edinburgh in 1539-40, was the most effective socio-political "Morality" produced in Europe down to that time. A reference in one of Dunbar's poems shows that there had been plays in Scotland before 1500.

The withdrawal of the Court gave social sway to the Kirk, which, regarding the stage as a rival pulpit, banned the theatre and inoculated the mass of the people with an unreasoning animus against drama . . .

The governors of the Old Vic, after due deliberation, rejected *John Knox*. As *The Bulletin* said: 'A new Scottish play which had been written by James Bridie specially for the International Festival of Music and Drama in Edinburgh in August, is not after all to be produced there by the Old Vic Company.' (8 May 1947)

Bridie courteously accepted what must be seen as a rejection slip on a colossal scale, saying that the Old Vic had to stage a play that could be continued in their autumn repertoire in London. The governors had pointed out that the main difficulty was in finding enough players in their company to play the large number of Scottish characters in the play. This discovery is one that might have been made earlier than the May preceding the festival. Anyway, denied the piquancy of a drama about Knox as the first Festival dramatic offering, the audiences enjoyed an excellent production of Shakespeare's *Richard II*, a worthy choice, but somewhat lacking in relevance.

Another change of personnel had taken place at the Citizens'. John Casson, son of Sir Lewis Casson and Dame Sybil Thorndike, had taken over from Matthew Forsyth as director of production. He had joined the company as an actor in 1946, after demobilisation; during the war he had kept up his fellow prisoners' spirits in Stalag Luft 3 by many gallant productions in makeshift conditions, some of them acting as cover for escape bids by his comrades. A member of one of our most distinguished theatrical families, he was doubly welcome, in Bridie's eyes, since it was the fine series of productions staged by Lewis Casson for the Glasgow Repertory Players so many years ago that helped to fire love of the drama in O.H. Mavor, then a university student. This looked like the solution to all the problems of an emerging company. Bridie wanted to be able to choose plays without any restriction and it seemed as if a Casson at the helm might help to eradicate some of the criticisms that he had taken to heart over the theatre's policy. A.S. Wallace, *The Observer's* Scottish correspondent, had something to say about the company's strengths and inadequacies in an article 'The Citizens' in Perspective' which he contributed to a booklet *The Story of Glasgow's Citizens' Theatre, 1943-48* (Stage and Screen Press Ltd.):

> The Citizens' has no such bracing wind blowing about it to quicken its blood and stir its audiences. It is quite unsuited for presenting the sophisticated "West End success" — the English "society" play of the Lonsdale-Coward type. I recall its attempt at Barrie's tense little drama of the "spivs" of his day — "Shall We Join the Ladies?" That gruesome dinner party might conceivably have occurred in Hillhead, certainly not in the Home Counties. But in really great drama this lack of a particular sort of polish matters not at all. Macbeth may acceptably have a Scottish accent that would ruin the Marquis of Mayfair.
>
> For tackling the play that is universal in its theme the Theatre is, I think, adequately equipped in its directions and in its cast.

For Molly, leaving the *Dr Angelus* company at the end of the run and the tour, there was no work at the Citizens', the company being well into its autumn and winter season. However, never one to waste time, she settled down to a real flurry of domesticity, getting back to her rug-making, upholstering chairs, knitting sweaters for Willie and Jim, and enjoying with her husband and son some all too rare holidays and visits to family and friends. Her confidence in her career prospects perhaps did falter a bit, since at this period she took up writing as a hobby — and indeed did try her hand at a play, which she never had time to finish, since in the late spring of 1948, Tyrone Guthrie, who had gained fame with his work in the Old Vic and at Covent Garden Opera House, returned to Scotland to discuss what was to be a really innovatory idea for drama at the second Edinburgh Festival, a production of *The Satire of the Three Estates*, the sixteenth century Scottish play by Sir David Lyndsay, in a skilfully edited version by playwright Robert Kemp.

This venture was viewed with scepticism in many quarters. Any Scottish play had been considered too esoteric for an international festival programme, even one written by a contemporary writer. David Lyndsay, born in 1486 in Monimail, Fife, was the tutor of the young James V of Scotland. He was knighted upon his appointment as Lord Lyon King of Arms in 1542. An ambassador to the courts of Europe and London, his duties also included supervision of the formal pageants and masques that were a regular feature of court entertainment on great occasions; indeed he himself wrote the masque which was staged to welcome the Queen, Marie of Lorraine, mother of Mary, Queen of Scots, to St Andrews in 1538.

His great work, a spectacular morality play that is peopled with characters representing every vice and virtue in the turbulent tapestry that was sixteenth century Scotland, has been claimed as the 'satire that re-made Scotland'. So said *The Scotsman's* critic Charles Graves, in an article in the *Scots Review* of September 1948:

> Those who have already seen the play have, almost to a man, marvelled at the audacity with which Lyndsay attacked the follies and vices of his age in high places. His audacity was, however, perhaps more apparent than real. He had always felt himself as much at liberty to warn the King whom he had dandled on his knee of the folly of wantonness as to sue him for a new coat.

It was a heaven-sent opportunity Lyndsay's work gave the players who had become identified, by the public anyway, as key figures in the Scottish theatre. The cast included Bryden Murdoch as the young king, Douglas Campbell and Peter MacDonell as Wantoness and Placebo, Jean Taylor Smith as Chastitie and perhaps the most inspired casting of all, Macrae, doubling as the Pardoner and Flatterie, Archie Duncan as John the Commonweal and Molly as Dame Sensualitie.

Tyrone Guthrie, who had known the Scottish theatre movement from its grass-roots beginnings, having been the producer of the Scottish National Players on a legendary tour in tents through a wet Scottish summer in 1927, summoned his company, unerringly choosing for these larger than life characters players of high individuality in the Scottish style. His keenly intelligent direction illustrated when necessary by what actor Moultrie Kelsall, described as 'the extraordinary anglo-saxon attitudes into which he contorts himself when he's showing someone how he wants it done' led the group to a complete understanding of the dramatic statement. Their portrayals were polished into a three dimensional brilliance, since the stage to be used was three level thrust, Elizabethan type platform, constructed, with a nice appropriacy, within the Assembly Hall of the Church of Scotland, so that each and every patron had to enter past the forecourt statue of John Knox, his hand held up in benediction.

The costumes were lavishly designed by Molly McEwen, Dame Sensualitie's costume was in ermine-trimmed, white slipper satin, low neck, long slashed sleeves lined with gold lame, and a skirt flowing from a high waist in twenty shining yards of a train. Long red gloves and a stylised head-dress with a wimple completed the creation. Its wearer looked superb. Her full figure suited the costume to perfection, and the vitality that surrounded her like an aura brought a kind of lusty cheerfulness to the part that called from one critic the apt description 'an amusing blend of Doll Tearsheet and Venus'.

There was great excitement during rehearsals, but the situation at the box office was gloomy. Less than twenty per cent of the seats had been booked, and it seemed as if a huge financial loss would be sustained. Guthrie had built the entrance of Sensualitie elaborately, she was to come down the aisle through the audience in a cloud of Chanel No 5, which he actually wanted to permeate the air from scent sprays held by her and her attendants. When he heard of the poor response, he cancelled that extravagance. Molly suggested a cheaper fragrance — "Don't be silly, woman. We can't spray a Festival audience with cheap scent!" Her opening speech had worried Molly a little. It began:

Lovers awake! Behauld the fiery sphere
Behauld, the natural dochter of Venus!
Behauld, lovers, this lusty lady clear,
The fresh fountain of knightes amorous!'

and going on to bid the audience: 'Behauld my paps of pulchritude perfyte!'

"Tony, how can I *say* that? In the Assembly Hall too!"

"Just fix your eye on the nearest clerical collar, and throw them at him, darling!"

(A French photographer later called to take pictures of the production for *Paris Match*. He spoke to Guthrie about the possibility of photographing Sensualitie 'topless'. "Why not go and ask her?"

said Tony wickedly. If the poor man didn't know what a 'flea in his ear' was before he came to Scotland, he soon learned, for he came catapulting out of Molly's dressing room as if on a reflex spring! "Imagine," she said to me later, "half of Scotland on a package holiday in Paris and he thought I'd consent to be photographed 'bare scuddy'. Well he'd another think coming to him!"

The doubting Thomases who had murmured that Guthrie would never succeed had to eat their words. After the first night, the booking increased ten fold and the play was the surprise hit of the Festival. The public adored it, and the critics, in scarce concealed astonishment, brought out their superlatives to endorse that opinion. And the French perfume was added as planned!

The Bulletin remarked, 'To many, it will be a pleasant revelation to realise what fine native actors Scotland possesses. It is difficult to single out particular performers where so high a standard is maintained. Molly Urquhart as Sensualitie acted most beautifully and the suppleness of her voice was a joy — never a word lost, despite the exigencies of the apron stage.'

Stephen Watts, in the *Sunday Express*, 'learned to my delighted surprise that foreigners (and I don't mean merely English, but Americans and even French) had found the old Scots speech of "The Three Estates" no hindrance to their enjoyment. The whole action and import of Tyrone Guthrie's brilliant production was vivid enough to make every meaning substantially clear. Incidentally, while John Gielgud's *Medea* (played by Eileen Herlie) is awaited in London with much interest, "The Three Estates" is the talk of the "Theatrical Town".'

Kenneth Tynan visiting the Festival was delighted. He said:

> The Scottish Theatre in 'The Three Estates'. This tough, beaky old sixteenth-century morality by Sir David Lyndsay has been given a virile cast and hectically good production by Tyrone Guthrie, whose handling of crowds has never looked more masterful. The play is in two parts, the first an allegory of the salvation of the individual, the second a piece of symbolism dealing with the cure of the realm. The scene is set first in the mind of King Humanitie, and then expands to cover his whole empire: it is very seldom that both techniques are to be found in the same play, and the result is to make the stage wholly elastic both in space and time. The production erupted with good things, for example, the splendidly

voluptuous entrance of Sensualitie, to beguiling and insidious
music. This buxom, tomato-cheeked trull was beautifully cast:
setting aside modern notions of sensual luxury, Mr Guthrie chose
the ample, rubicund sort of woman for whom Henry VIII or any
of the Canterbury Pilgrims would have run mad. Two inventive
displays of pantomime-dame flamboyance were frisked through
by Mr Duncan Macrae, as Flatterie and a Pardoner; and above the
whole play sat a leprous, bloated huddle of Catholic prelates,
whose manifold hypocrisies were superbly shamed in the scene
where John the Common Weal, challenged as a heretic, responds
by giving his own credo:

> 'I believe in God, that all has wrocht,
> And create every thing of nocht . . .'

The actor delivered this speech with most moving resolution.
(Kenneth Tynan: The Play's the Thing.)

Everything seemed to be falling into place. A Scots classic had
started an awareness of a dramatic tradition going back over
centuries, and a French writer, M. Najeau de Bevere, was planning a
French translation, many people acclaimed the unique Scottish
company, and Tyrone Guthrie had gone far to establish his own
claim that the production 'should do much to dispel the inferiority
complex that had characterised Scottish dramatic endeavour in
recent years'.

It seemed as if the past had brought new life to the present.

A new A.S.M. at Citizens' for the season 1947-48 was a young
Scot, James Gilbert, now Director of Television Light Entertainment for B.B.C. London. Having done two years at R.A.D.A. after
serving in the R.A.F., he came to the resident company, who were
opening the season with Barrie's *Dear Brutus*. He recalls his
impression of *The Three Estates*:

> I was A.S.M. for the resident company which was doing "Dear
> Brutus" but the bulk of the company was in the Festival in "The
> Three Estates". Duncan Macrae was playing the Pardoner, Molly
> was Dame Sensualitie, Douglas Campbell, John Stewart, Jean
> Taylor Smith and Archie Duncan as "John the Commonweel" and
> I remember going over to the first night, the great excitement of it
> all — this *was* the Company! And when they came back, the
> atmosphere was transformed! Instead of it being a rather small,

quiet, rather conventional rep., when this great flood of actors came back, all enormously friendly and full of energy, the atmosphere just lifted — it was like the home team coming home victorious. And there was the feeling that this was going to be the basis of a new national theatre in Scotland. You felt a tremendous feeling of excitement at just being part of it.

John Casson took up his challenge whole-heartedly. He had the staunch backing of his parents, who not only gave him advice, but on several occasions came to play in the Citizens' season, an act of integration much appreciated by Glasgow playgoers. His sister Ann and her Scottish husband, Douglas Campbell, were with the company, and he had, naturally plenty of contacts with other English actors of standing to help out as the plays demanded. He had voiced firm views about Scottish speech. John Casson, addressing a meeting of the Glasgow branch of the Scottish Association for the Speaking of Verse, said 'A Scotsman should talk in his own language, otherwise he is out of his depth.' He added that he could not bear to find someone with a beautiful way of speaking which belonged to his own environment who — for snobbish or social reasons — took lessons to remove that quality from his speech.

Yet for a career in the theatre, it was, of course, necessary to acquire and sustain an English R.P. accent, if one's sights were upon roles in the English and World dramatic classics, as well as on modern West End plays.

Molly, that season, had accepted an engagement at Dundee where Michael Whatmore was producing *Jane*, the Somerset Maugham play, in which she played the title part, created by Yvonne Arnaud in London. She was never particularly happy with John Casson as a director. The feeling was mutual, since he had said to her, in polite but real perplexity, "I find you very difficult to cast." So it was at Dundee she received a telephone call from Alistair Sim who wanted her to play Mary Paterson in a revival of *The Anatomist*, in the Westminster Theatre in London. Sim was to direct and play Dr Knox, the lecturer in Anatomy at the University of Edinburgh, who, in his search for subjects to dissect, had received bodies obtained, not from the resurrectionists, but by the infamous murderers, Burke and Hare.

Mary Paterson is a fascinating character. Strikingly handsome,

with long auburn hair, she is a spirited woman, of proud bearing, who, though lacking in education and refinement, has in her the shreds of a simple dignity. The scene in which she sets her cap at young Dr Walter Anderson, Knox's assistant, who has gone into the Three Tuns Tavern to drown his sorrows after a quarrel with his young lady, gives her a wonderful line. Drawing her shawl around her, with some pretensions of gentility to try to impress the young doctor, Mary says in tones of fearful refinement:
"The evenings is beginning to draw in."
Ian Wallace, who played the landlord, recalls how night after night, the impact this had on the West End audience.

> If you try to analyse it, you could give Bridie a lot of credit for writing a splendid line. But it wasn't just that. It was because Molly never forgot the woman who existed within the girl. In its way it was a very moving line. A lot of actresses would not have seen it as a little bit of gentility that perhaps had survived from an existence before she had gone on the street or an attempt to make her present existence seem a little more refined.
>
> This was one of her great strengths. This is the sign of the great actress, the capacity to go from comedy to tragedy in one effortless move. And she could do that without any doubt at all.
>
> Molly was a person of tremendous warmth. Although many people can convey in a public performance, Molly conveyed it all the time. A lot of her success depended upon her giving a performance of complete sincerity and genuineness, and I'm certain she was incapable of any other approach to life at all.
>
> But I don't mean that she wouldn't express herself forcibly against something she disagreed with; she could give the same warmth to disapproval as she would to approval!

As the young doctor drinks himself into a stupor, Mary gathers him in her arms in a gesture of almost maternal tenderness and sings to him the old Scots lullaby:

> Can ye sew cushions and can ye sew sheets,
> And can ye sing Balaloo
> When the bairn greets?
> Then ho and baw birdie
> Then ho and baw lamb,
> Then ho and baw birdie, my bonnie wee lamb.

The rhythm changes from the soothing three beats to the four beats of the gently jogging strathspey rhythm to which Scots mothers have lulled their babies for countless years:

> Hey, oh hyooch oh, what'll I dae wi ye?
> Black's the life I lead wi the hale o' ye.
> Mony o' ye and little to gie ye.
> Hey, oh hyooch oh, what'll I dae wi ye?

As she sang the refrain again, with its wistful pentatonic lift, Molly brought into her voice a sighing weariness with the life she had come to know in the wynds and taverns of Edinburgh's Canongate. As she cradled the young drunken doctor in her arms, her long auburn hair falling forward to veil both their faces, she brought the audience to an awareness of the lonely despair to which poverty could reduce such an unfortunate as the doomed Mary Paterson.

The critics acknowledged this, but a more memorable tribute came from another actress, who in her own career has given us so many memorable performances of illumination and warmth.

The part of Janet, the timid little creature who is Molly's unwilling companion on her visit to the Three Tuns, a disreputable enough place, which no respectable girl of the period would contemplate visiting, was played by Carmel McSharry, then a youthful newcomer to the stage, who recalls with affection how Molly's cheerful presence at rehearsals soon put her at her ease:

> My first meeting with Molly was in the second professional company I was to work with. I was working at the Duchess Theatre in a play with Dame Sybil Thorndike and Sir Lewis Casson. Then I got the chance to go into "The Anatomist" at the Westminster Theatre.
>
> Molly was playing Mary Paterson. I was Janet, who doesn't have much to say although obviously she had to have a Scottish accent. Molly really took me under her wing, as the character does. She seemed such a homely body in the daytime when we were rehearsing, but then in the spectacular auburn wig, that wonderful red hair which is part of the story . . . I remember on that first night as she came down the passageway, she said to me, "Are you wi' me, hen?" and I really was the little child walking behind her. And she tossed her head with that red hair . . . I always thought that it grew on her when she played the part. I always thought of

A CITIZENS' PERSON

Molly Urquhart as that character. That is as she will always be to me.

In Act 2 in the Three Tuns Tavern, when Molly is enticed and made drunk by the two terrible men, Burke and Hare — that was one of my first moments of theatre that took over — it was so frightening. Liam Redmond and Michael Ripper played the parts. When they entice her over, she's been drinking and she has to traverse from stage L. to stage R. — the stage is dim and I suppose grows dimmer — this was the body they wanted. As she left me and I'm saying in my Scottish accent — that Molly had taught me! — 'Come on away hame' — I used to mean it. I was really terrified, leaving that stage, going up the long ladder-type stair, looking back down at Molly sprawled there with that lovely red hair and that low-cut dress that secretly I thought rather awesome, rather risqué. It was a wonderful piece of theatre. I thought she was smashing. I can never think of that play without that cast — almost a definitive cast.

I always remember the little song. As we came upstairs (— we used to have to mount a ladder in order to go *down* onto the set — it was a very risky business. How actresses ever survive these rickety off-stage contraptions I'll never know—). We had to be two girls going out together, with the poor little Janet hanging back saying, "Oh, don't go in there!" It's the equivalent of two girls visiting Soho, one who'd been there many times and the little one saying, "Ooh, we can't go in there!" The other replies, "Geraway! Come on. Come *on!*" And she suddenly started to sing, "Oh my love is like a red, red rose". We used to sing it together as we mounted the ladder. Later when the body is delivered to the Anatomy Lab. they push on the basket — and there is a lock of that red hair hanging from it in a pool of light.

I know Molly played lots and lots and lots of parts and I saw her many times on TV — her wonderful housekeeper types — yet even then I knew she would have a career that would get richer and richer and richer. She seemed to me like an actress waiting to come into her prime. The part was right for her, she was right to look at, the setting was right.

. . . She would always make time to talk to me. I thought it was awfully kind. Like most young actresses in this business, I was very open to influence, and being with a leading actress as she was — it's like a laying on of hands — something is passed on.

She was not a vain woman. Or if she was vain, God knows where the vanity was, because you could never see it! It was like a transformation, rehearsing with this rather jolly-faced lady, and

171

then entering with this really beautiful Scottish woman — and it took over. It took us both over, and I just toddled along. I mean — poor Janet! I think all she ever says is "Come on away hame" — but I spent my time gawping at her — at all of them.

The critical reaction to the play was somewhat varied. Molly's performance was acclaimed:

> Miss Molly Urquhart invests a doomed trollop with endearing warmth. (Peter Fleming: *The Spectator*)

> . . . gives a rich and glowing performance as one of the "subjects" that help to make Dr Knox great. (Stephen Williams: *Evening News*)

George Cole, likewise, gave a sterling performance, then, as always, bringing 'life and humour' in Stephen Williams' words to the 'colourless' Dr Walter Paterson.

The reaction to Alistair Sim's performance was mixed. *The Evening Standard* said 'it is Alistair Sim's evening', while Peter Fleming said his performance 'leaves us with a slight feeling of inconclusiveness. His production, on the other hand, is above criticism'.

An unusual incident occurred on the first night of *The Anatomist*. Alistair Sim had been nominated by a group of students to stand for election as the Lord Rector of the University of Edinburgh. He was elected by the students with a large majority. Mrs Sim, knowing full well the pressures of a first night, had made it quite clear that her husband should not be told the result, whatever it was, before the performance. Ian Wallace, who was playing the landlord, was among the group who listened with incredulity to the announcement made just before curtain up by the publicity representative, a man usually calmly competent, but who seemed to have been overcome by this gesture from the Groves of Academe, that "Mr Alistair Sim has just been elected Lord Rector of the University of Edinburgh."

The comparative irrelevance of this information was one thing; the fact that the central character Dr Knox was a lecturer in that same university meant that the announcement had an all too distracting relevance during the action of the play. And the fear that the information might have been taken amiss by some of the critics was borne out; at least three of them mentioned the Rectorship in their notices. It was seen, in some quarters, as a kind of publicity stunt, and Alistair Sim, that most modest of men, had to bear the brunt of a piece of news imparted without his consent in untimely fashion.

At his installation as Rector, Alistair Sim later addressed the assembled Senate and students of his old university in a manner that illustrated the unassuming brilliance of the man: 'In having been gracious to a mere mummer, you have at one stroke dispersed the snobbishness of two worlds. By that I do not mean that Athens has embraced Bohemia. Between ourselves, I am not a very typical Bohemian. You have done more daringly than that—the scholar has honoured the truant; the cap-and-gown has exalted the cap-and-bells.'

Despite the vagaries of the opening night, *The Anatomist* ran successfully over the Christmas and New Year period. During the run Liam Redmond had to leave the cast to go to America, and Ian Wallace tentatively approached Alistair to see if he might try for Liam's part as Burke, one of the body snatchers. Alistair expressed grave doubts as to whether he could manage the Irish accent, but after some rehearsing he found Ian's performance acceptable and he got the part. During his first few performances, Sim, always the anxious perfectionist, was surreptitiously creeping along behind the set of the 'Three Tuns' tavern, where Dr Knox certainly never appeared, to make sure Ian was coping. Molly was annoyed by this, and finally tackled the situation. "Alistair, can you not leave the laddie alone. He's doing fine." Dr Knox retreated hastily to his lecture room.

When the run at the Westminster Theatre ended, Molly returned to the Citizens' while the theatre's first *Macbeth* was running. John Casson had been rehearsing the company in this, their first Shakespearean tragedy, while the Christmas show, a revival of *The Forrigan Reel* was playing. Duncan Macrae was to appear as Macbeth. Perhaps to those who recall his performances in the kind of parts in which he excelled, those he later defined in his entry in *Who's Who in the Theatre* (Fourteenth Edition) as his favourite roles of 'dignified fools', he may not seem ideal casting for the Thane of Cawdor. Yet he had been playing leading roles in the theatre for four seasons and his tall dark presence and his resonant Scottish voice equipped him as well as any other for a part which he longed to play.

The production was a considerable undertaking for John Casson. In his biography of his parents, *Lewis and Sybil* he explained how grateful he was for the invaluable coaching in the interpretation of the work given so patiently by his father, Sir Lewis Casson, who was in Glasgow along with Dame Sybil, to play again their original roles in J.B. Priestley's *The Linden Tree*. They acted with the company not only in Glasgow but also on a touring date in the Gaiety Theatre, Ayr, much to the delight of the Scottish audiences who were quick to appreciate this gesture.

One does wonder, however, what made John Casson look beyond his own company for a Lady Macbeth. He invited Margaretta Scott to make a guest appearance. She agreed, and was, of course, a suitable choice. But it seems strange, in retrospect, to think that from a company that had in its midst such competent actresses as Madeleine Christie, Ann Casson, and Lennox Milne, as well as Molly Urquhart, he could not have fielded a leading lady from the home team to play alongside a Scottish Macbeth.

In any event, that particular tragedy and its long association with theatrical disaster took its usual toll. Macrae broke his ankle during rehearsals, and played the first three nights with his leg in a plaster cast before he sadly relinquished the throne of Scotland to John Casson, who took on the part at, amazingly, five days' notice.

Erik Linklater, the witty intellectual Orcadian had written the next play, *Love in Albania*, a comedy in which a Military Policeman in the American army, Sergeant Dohda, invades the Mayfair flat of a somewhat staid civil servant and his wife, intent on avenging the death of his daughter who was murdered by a comrade in arms whose advances she rejected while they were serving with the guerilla movement in Albania. The suspect he is pursuing is an eccentric poet who also drifts in and out of this household, hopelessly and lyrically in love with the wife, and in his turn the object of the secret yearnings of their treasure of a housekeeper, one Flora McIvor, ex-A.T.S. artillery gunner. The unlikely ingredients allowed Linklater to toss around light-hearted debates on love, war, democracy and poetry, and the play was full of what one critic called 'shafts of wit'.

Eric Capon had been invited back as guest producer on this occasion. Since his earlier work in Glasgow, he had gone on variously to direct at Liverpool Old Vic, to tour America on a Rockefeller scholarship, and to direct some documentary films for the Crown Film Unit. He immediately sought out Molly to play Flora McIvor. An article in the *Evening Times* called it 'old home week', reminding the public that it had been Capon who had first invited Molly to come from the MSU Theatre to play in *Is Life Worth Living?* at the Citizens' in 1943.

The play went down well in Glasgow, its highly individual quality being best described by Robins Millar in the *Daily Express*: '. . . Can a play have barely two minutes of credibility and yet entertain by wit? The comedy joggles all over its roadway, like a flitting on a barrow, holding together by a miracle. It is sustained by Linklater's sagacity, his bravura and something of that hay-wire zest which makes Scots win Rugby Internationals.' The *Glasgow Herald* had this to say: 'Molly Urquhart's Flora is among the best things she's done'.

The play caught the attention of a London management. The 'Company of Four' decided to tour it and take it into town to the Lyric, Hammersmith. Peter Ustinov, then as now one of the most consistently interesting and exciting actor-directors, was to direct and star as Sergeant Dohda.

Molly, who now had a London agent, learned that she could have an audition for her original part as Flora. Despite the fact that she had so far met with considerable success in the West End, she took a dim view of her chances in direct competition with the other well-established actresses who were also being considered for the role. Her three previous West End appearances had been in productions by Alistair Sim who knew her work well, but this was to be a London-based English company.

However, a family interest played some part in motivating her to make the trip south. Her sister Lexy had, when she left the women's services in 1944, married a handsome Polish officer, Ted Rostek, and had gone to live in Wroclaw. It was an extremely happy marriage, despite the desperate conditions of life in war-ravaged Poland, and the family were sustained by the constant stream of parcels of clothes and other supplies which Molly and Willie sent, often enlisting many other Scottish friends to despatch similar gifts to help the Rosteks and their friends through a very difficult time. Lexy, with their first-born son, Tadeusz, had managed to come home for a short trip to

Scotland in the spring of 1949 to visit her parents and family; her mother's health was beginning at this time to fail rapidly. She was due to go home by sea, sailing from Tilbury. Molly decided therefore, to try the audition, and travelled to London with her overnight. They parted at the station, Lexy to go ahead to the ship, and Molly declaring that since it wasn't at all likely she'd be kept long at the theatre, she'd catch up before her departure.

She arrived promptly at the theatre where the auditions were to be held, but though she should have been heard straight away, one of the selection committee was late and there was a half hour delay. With growing irritation, increased by the belief that her chances were negligible, she waited. When she was finally called on stage to face the young man who was to read in the part of Dohda, she had a gleam in her eye that her friends and family would have recognised as a sign to 'gang warily'.

They started the scene, but the youth read ineffectively with little pace and much stumbling over words. She did what she could for a few moments, then decided to relinquish the whole business.

"I'm sorry, but I can't possibly give a performance if you can't pick it up a bit and give me my cues."

She put her script aside, bowed into the shadowy red plush auditorium where a small, cold silence reigned. One voice spoke up "Will I do to read with you?"

Stating a fact, rather than being in any way malicious, Molly, peering into the darkness, replied simply, "I don't know. I've never heard you read."

Whereupon a chuckling Peter Ustinov bounded on to the stage. They read the scene at a cracking pace. She thanked him sincerely and took her leave, without any comment from the invisible auditors. "That's that", she thought, as she hailed a taxi to catch up with her departing sister.

Two days later she found she had the part. The company included Brenda Bruce, Robin Bailey and Peter Jones as well as Peter Ustinov. In his autobiography, *Dear Me*, Ustinov remembers the play as an 'affectionate kind of literary comedy'. Crisply directed and played with bravura by all the small company, it enjoyed a considerable success. Perhaps more than any other, this was the performance that established Molly Urquhart as a West End actress. Flora is described by the author as 'a strongly built, robust, and hearty woman of about thirty-five. She speaks in a well marked Highland accent. There is no subservience in her attitude to the Lawns — her employers — but her independence is not offensive because she had naturally good manners.' Her berating of Sergeant Dohda who has been lounging, complete with boots, on the silk counterpane of the bed causes him to ask, "What's eating you, sister?"

Flora replies with Highland rhetoric: "It's not me that's your sister and don't you insult my father by suggesting it. If you were a brother of mine you might or you might not be better looking, but you *would* have better manners. Now get off that bed and go and sit decently on a chair."

There follows a neatly written scene, when she reveals to Dohda that during her time as a gunner in the 536 Ack Ack Regiment of the Royal Artillery she received a leg wound, which she displays decorously, and another she's not prepared to show. Dohda is mightily impressed "to meet up with a moll that's been wounded in the 'bosoom' for democracy". The line became a catch-phrase of Molly's and the scene was particularly memorable because of one occasion when a bunch of soldiers from the Royal Artillery crowded the dress circle and punctuated the action with a series of appreciative cheers, sending her later a huge bouquet of flowers in the regimental colours. It was Remembrance Sunday the following weekend, and she took the flowers to the church she attended; choosing a name at random from the list of those who gave their lives in the war, she inscribed a card 'To Private Green, in remembrance and respect from Molly Urquhart'.

The young soldier's father was touched by the gesture and traced her to the theatre where he called to thank her, and to give her, from the little antique shop he had, two quaint theatrical prints which she took home to Glasgow where they remained in the lounge of her flat for the rest of her life.

Because, of course, home she went, as soon as possible, to Willie and young Jim who was being looked after by his Aunt Kit and Elizabeth. Molly always had the most amazing knack of coming back and taking up a conversation almost where she left off. She had early on worked out her *modus vivendi*: as soon as she stepped off the train or plane on her return home, she immediately left all thoughts of theatre behind, and was wondering about something really

177

important, such as whether she could get to her favourite fishmonger's before it closed that evening. She was sorry for the kind of actor who confined himself to the limited world of the profession. She had resolved always to have her private life to herself and the actress became the housewife and mother as soon as she set foot on her own home ground.

She had enjoyed great personal success in London for three years running, in three parts that gave tremendous scope to an actress who had decided all those years ago to try to make her name as a Scottish actress or not at all. These roles were cornerstones in her career. Her agent realised that more offers would inevitably come, especially if she were London based. She rejected this idea absolutely; even if she had been on her own, this would never have been part of the scheme of things. "If they want me, they'll phone for me" was her simple response.

Each of the West End plays had given her the opportunity to select from the great range of Scottish accents. Bridie and Linklater were playwrights who provided interesting work for Scots, far from the stock cooks and housekeepers for women, and hirsute gardeners and chief engineers (the multitudinous 'Jocks') for the men, who might occasionally find a part of a doctor, qualified in Edinburgh.

That Scots-English language could be used for a wide range of dramatic expression was an idea that did not find acceptance easily either north or south of the border. Scots dialect was always claimed to be perplexing to English audiences, despite the fact that they seemed to understand without apparent difficulty the regional voices of Yorkshire, Northumbria, Liverpool or indeed the highly inventive thickly accented London Cockney. Since these could all be understood with ease north of the border, critical reaction to the Glasgow Citizens' Theatre Company production in the Embassy of *L'Ecole des Femmes*, ingeniously adapted by Robert Kemp into the Scots of eighteenth century Edinburgh and named *Let Wives Tak Tent*, seems a little surprising. The play had been successful in Glasgow and Edinburgh, and the performances, particularly those of Duncan Macrae, James Gibson, Lennox Milne and Gudrun Ure, were likewise acclaimed in the London press.

The language, which the critic of the *Scotsman* had used these lines of Wordsworth to describe:

A CITIZENS' PERSON

Choice words, and measured phrase, above the reach
Of ordinary men; a stately speech;
Such as grave Livers do in Scotland use

was met by diverse reactions. W.A. Darlington in the *Daily Telegraph* found it 'a Caledonian dialect rather more difficult than French to understand', while Leonard Mosley in the *Daily Express* found it 'a dialect that soon comes easy' which made 'The London audience laugh long and hard'. The compositors of the *Evening Standard* must have been perplexed over the enthusiastic attempt by Beverley Baxter to emulate, helped, no doubt, by the glossary provided in the programme: 'Moliere wha hae! A muckle aumry and a rare whummle of guid things awaits ye Sassenachs on the banks of Sweess Cottage.'

An anecdote of this visit is worth recording. Duncan Macrae, whose droll sense of humour enlivened many, many theatrical occasions, went to lunch with a group of fellow Scots at the Savoy, where he was approached by an excessively dignified waiter who enquired in tones so lordly as to be almost patronising what he wished to eat. Without a flicker, Macrae replied in the resonantly affected tones of the best Kelvinside West End of Glasgow accent, "A cup of tea and a pheasant."

When the various members of the company came back home in the autumn, Bridie was already turning over in his mind ideas for what was to be one of the most uninhibited flourishes of Scots comic creativity theatre in the west of Scotland has ever known, the first pantomime specially devised for the coming festive season.

In the season 1949-50, the company was about ninety per cent Scots. The list includes names such as Rona Anderson, Stanley Baxter, Douglas Campbell, Madeleine Christie, Fiona Clyne, James Gibson, James Gilbert, Andrew Keir, Lennox Milne, Fulton MacKay, Roddy Macmillan, Gudrun Ure (later known as Ann Gudrun), Robert Urquhart and John Young. These actors were sizzling with talent and energy and they had seized every opportunity the season had offered, making it a memorable one for the patrons. A judicious mixture of plays had been presented. Terence Rattigan's *Adventure Story* opened the season, its stylish account of the life of Alexander the Great much enhanced by the playing of the handsome Douglas Campbell in the lead. A premiere of

Vineyard Street by George Munro, a neglected Scottish dramatist, came next, to be followed by one of the finest of Bridie's plays *Gog and Magog* in which Duncan Macrae was sublime as Harry Magog, a McGonagall-type poet whose adventures allowed fascinating dramatic debate on the nature of poetic inspiration and the intellectual snobbery of some literary critics. Tenessee Williams' *The Glass Menagerie* followed with Ann Casson in the lead ('Ann is the new Dame Sybil' enthused one critic) Sheridan's *The Rivals* and Priestley's *Laburnum Grove* took the season up to Christmas, during which time Bridie, George Munro and others had been putting together ingredients for a new and heady brew of light entertainment.

Bridie was highly skilled in writing Scots. As must now be evident, the use of that Scottish dialect as a medium for drama in the Scotland of that time was in certain quarters considered somehow vulgar in the pejorative sense, a lesser kind of language that 'wasn't quite the thing'. This is something altogether apart from the problems some non-Scots claim to have with its comprehension: what existed and does exist, was a belief that native linguistic expression was second class, a belief that was, unfortunately, nurtured by the policy of our educationists in rejecting not only the use of dialect words in the speech of young children coming from homes where they were in daily usage, but also in drawing up a literature syllabus that allowed only a few novels by Scott and a handful of Burns' poems to represent the whole of Scottish literature.

Bridie was certainly not unaware of these prejudices and indeed had brought a hornets' nest about his own ears when in 1948 he had rewritten in Scots the scenes for the Mechanicals in *A Midsummer Night's Dream*. As well as this innovation, the mortals strode through their scenes in Athens and the magic wood nearby, in modern dress.

The school children who crowded to the special matinees were absolutely enchanted, and being new theatre-goers, took no offence at the comedy, which they found delightful, especially the performance of Duncan Macrae as Quince, a Glasgow working man enthused with the excitement of amateur theatricals.

The adults, those paid-up members of the educated audience whom Bridie had so often implored to support the theatre, did not all approve, especially those who had preconceived expectations of what a Shakespearean production ought to be.

An extract from a letter sent to the *Glasgow Herald* signed 'Stratford' gives us an insight into Bridie's emendations and the shattering effect they had on some playgoers:

> May I suggest more strongly still that all lovers of the play cannot but condemn the attitude that made it possible for some member, or members, of the Citizens' Theatre to "improve" Shakespeare by tampering with the text? I think most of us would prefer the original: "Have you the lion's part written? Pray you, if it be, give it me, for I am slow of study" to "For Goad's sake, see's a look at it" etc. Quince's words: "We shall be dogged with company and our devices known" are hardly improved in this guise: "We'll hae a hale wheen o' lang-nebbit buddies keekin' in on us." Changes of this type which I have rendered as accurately as I can remember after one hearing, and dozens of others with which the "mechanical" scenes are crammed, are not only offensive but unnecessary even to the modern dress convention, and serve only to establish a thoroughly mischievous precedent.

The writer goes on to lament that at the school matinees 'the greatest appreciation was shown not at the exquisite poetic passages, which produced a slight but very definite restiveness, but at the cheap clowning that all producers seem to regard as essential to the performance of Pyramus and Thisbe before the duke. A large and mixed audience of school children will invariably find slapstick amusing.'

Another letter in the same columns, this time signed 'Hippolyta' gives us a further tantalising glimpse of what liberties were taken with the Bard:

> Must the uninitiated — young as well as old — go away with the idea that Shakespeare was the composer of the tune "The Red Flag"; that a "blue do" is Shakespearean in origin; that a number of Scots artisans were "translated" (the asses!) to act in these essentially "English" plays? Whaur's yer Wullie Shakespeare noo?

Reading those letters, as well as some accounts of other less highbrow witnesses who recall the Mechanicals' scenes to this day with undiluted mirth, I regret that I did not see this version. The idea of the 'Pyramus and Thisbe' drama being played in 'put-on' polite

English by Macrae and company, has great appeal.

Perhaps this fracas about Scots language, along with the many others of similar nature that had provided a constant secondary theme since the theatre's inception, was one that had echoed in Bridie's mind when he thought of a pantomime story. Also a Christmas pantomime, it was hoped, would be a money-spinner, since the theatre had lost £4000 in the summer of 1949, and Bridie was ready to do everything in his power to make good this loss. Since he never ever took royalties from the Citizens' for his own plays, *Gog and Magog*, which had done very well at the box office as well as being an artistic success of high order, was a gift. (It is sad to reflect that this great play too has not yet been published.)

Among the notices this verse appeared in the feature page of the *Evening Times*, in the style of the great, eccentric poet. It indicates the general appeal a Scottish play and player had for the average Glaswegian, who, though not necessarily a patron, held 'his' theatre south of the river in affectionate esteem:

McGONAGALL'S ODE TO THE CITIZENS'
O wonderful city of Glasgow, where the pubs are always
    packed on Friday,
And they also have a famous playwright called mister James
    Bridie,
Who has the wit that many things he puts upon the stage,
Which are often very funny, but sometimes put you in a rage,
Now at his Citizens' Theatre, which is a great thing to have
    when you want to get out of the fog,
Glasgow can go for to see his latest play which is called "Gog
    and Magog",
Which is about a poet of very great fame
Who everybody in Scotland and the U.S.A. should know
    McGonagall is the name;
And to the Gorbals you ought to go to see this play
Because there is an actor called Duncan Macrae
Who is very funny and most wonderful to be seen
Nearby the River Clyde and the Glasgow Green;
O wonderful city of Glasgow, where the people were kinder to
    me even than Dundee,
I hope you will go this wonderful play for to see,
And when you get there I hope it will fill your hearts with
    delight

A CITIZENS' PERSON

When seated in the theatre on a cold winter's night.
And some of you, no doubt, will let a silent tear fall,
In dear remembrance of WILLIAM McGONAGALL.
(*Evening Times* — Thursday 27 October, 1949)

The theatre now had a new manager who took up his appointment in September 1949. The press announced, 'Inspector William MacIntosh, of the Glasgow police has resigned from the force to become manager of the Citizens' Theatre, in place of Mr Colin White who went to take up an appointment in the film world in London.' As the report went on 'the combined business acumen of Mr MacIntosh and the artistic sense of his wife Miss Molly Urquhart had been responsible for the success of the MSU Theatre.' He, in a way, had missed the Rutherglen venture more than his wife did, since her work at Citizens' immediately filled the gap. He saw her act whenever he could, if possible, several times in each new production, and they constantly discussed and analysed her work. He was always her most trusted friend and critic, as well as her husband. His career in the force of twenty five years, was one of real distinction, and he had gained the respect of all sections of the community.

He was scrupulously fair and conducted all matters with the impeccable good manners of the Highlander. One incident may serve to illustrate this. On one occasion, he was making an arrest at a Glasgow apartment which can best be described in the old-fashioned term, as 'a house of ill-fame'. When the formal charges had been made, and the police were waiting to escort the occupants to the waiting van, the owner of the establishment suddenly went to a cupboard and brought out a fine copy of *The Rubaiyat of Omar Khayyam* which he thrust into Willie's hands saying, "You've been so polite about the whole business."

With Willie's encouragement the board of directors planned what they hoped might be a show that could be staged inexpensively and prove sufficiently attractive to the public to increase the box office takings. The pantomime had the traditional thirteen letter title, *The Tintock Cup*.

Chapter Thirteen

'The Tintock Cup'

'The ancient and now forgotten pastime of high jinks'
(Scott: *Guy Mannering*)

> On Tintock Tap there is a mist,
> And in that mist there is a kist,
> And in the kist there is a cup,
> And in the cup there is a drap,
> Take up the cup and drink the drap
> That stands abune on Tintock Tap.

That old rhyme, a piece of folk-lore about Tinto Hill in Lanarkshire had all the necessary ingredients of a tale on which to base a pantomime; a quest to find a mysterious cup, a command, fraught with danger, to sup thereof — a promise of magic and who knows what else!

Bridie himself didn't know, because on his own confession, after having airily offered to write the pantomime, he did not settle to the task easily;

> Months rolled by. At last, impelled not by inspiration but by my sense of honour I began to churn out some turgid stuff on my typewriter. I called in George Munro to help and at last faced the company with a script neither John Casson nor I dared to read to them. I told my clowns that they must by no means consider what was set down for them. They must go out on their own for laughs. They took me at my word ('Random Ideas About How To Compose a Pantomime' from *The Prompter*)

John Casson was faced with a mass of material that was local in the extreme. He quickly enlisted the help of Stanley Baxter, then in his second season with the company, who not only had a good deal of experience of producing and writing amateur revues but was an able, Glasgow-born interpreter of those parts of the dialogue that were somewhat esoteric to anyone who did not actually hail from that city. With confidence and assurance Stanley proceeded to streamline the very funny, highly literate book into a workable shape. The task must have been daunting, or might have daunted anyone other than a twenty-two year old who even then was showing signs of becoming one of the greatest comedy character actors Scotland has ever produced.

The elements of traditional pantomime were to be the framework, but from there, the show, like Stephen Leacock's horseman, went 'galloping off in all directions'. The cast list is memorable in itself:

"THE TINTOCK CUP"
A XMAS EXTRAVAGANZA

Some of the Characters—

The Dame	DUNCAN MACRAE
The Principal Boy	MOLLY URQUHART
The Warlock King	LAURENCE HARDY
The Fairy Queen	ANN CASSON
Wullie	FULTON MACKAY
Maggie	GUDRUN URE
The Broker's Men	DOUGLAS CAMPBELL STANLEY BAXTER
The Shop Steward	JAMES GIBSON
The Cat	JAMES STUART

And All the Rest
JOHN YOUNG, JOHN HUMPHRY, JAMES GILBERT,
ABE BARKER, LEA ASHTON, JOAN KENNY, FIONA
CLYNE, PENELOPE CASSON, JANE CASSON.

With the Chorus
MOIRA ROBERTSON, WENDY NOEL, MOYRA CHAL-
MERS, PAT GREEN, JEAN MACKIE, MARGARET RUS-
SELL.

PRODUCED BY JOHN CASSON

SETTINGS DESIGNED AND PAINTED BY MOLLY
MACEWEN

As well as a good sized sept of the Clan Casson, there is a quite
amazing conglomeration of talent there. Four of the original songs
were composed by another comparative newcomer, James Gilbert, a
composer with a fine sense of musical parody, who had been singing
send-up versions of the songs from *The Forrigan Reel* at an after show
party during the autumn season, when Bridie bore down upon him,
not to admonish, but to suggest he write some music for a lyric he
had written that contained all the turbulent history of Scotland's
Stuart Kings in six neat verses, with James First and Sixth informing
the audience:

> I'm Jamie the Saxt,
> Ye'll hae mind o' my Maw and my bairn —
>   they wis axed.
> For a' that they ca' me a bit of a fule,
> I won a' the medals they had at the schule
> I had Latin and Greek and I lippened what art meant
> In England, they made me a Heid o' Department . . .

And what was such subject matter to do with pantomime? You
might as well ask why the quest of the principal boy and girl, Wullie
and Maggie, in search of the magical cup, should have involved them
with Hamlet, Robert the Bruce, Catherine the Great, as well as the
ubiquitous Mary Queen of Scots.

The show was a whirling melange of widely diverse incidents made

coincident in an explosion of satire and near surrealistic comedy.
When in the opening scene Fulton Mackay, playing the boy Wullie,
finds the principal girl Maggie (Gudrun Ure) in the mist near Tinto
Hill, before they go on the quest for the magical 'drap' in the cup, he
has to save her, not merely from the clutches of the leering baritone
Warlock King of Laurence Hardy, but from a sacrificial pyre built by
a berobed band who chant in procession, mingling with the small
corps de ballet performing, in all earnestness, something claiming to
be a Mosquito Dance:

> O hot, O cold, O solids, O fluids,
> Make way for the Druids,
> Make way for the Druids.

The young pair are rescued by a regally authoritarian Fairy Queen,
played with Mrs Siddons-like panache by Ann Casson, who gives
them an amulet to keep them safe, sings 'My Ain Folk', and exits,
returning periodically to guide the hapless pair through the
complicated book. At one point, they arrive in the Hebrides, where
they encounter Dougal and Donald (James Gibson and John Young)
two ancients who have made a small fortune as extras in the new
wave of films set in Scotland, (recalling *Whisky Galore.* which
seemed to involve the whole population of the Isle of Barra):

> Donald: They are saying that the Islands is the true challenge to
> Hollywood.
> Dougal: They are, they are, Compton MacKenzie bethanket.
> Donald: I was hearing that Hollywood is no' a very moral spot,
> Dougal.
> Dougal: So they were saying. But we could give them a good
> game here, whatever.

Then there enters, on the run from the Redcoats, Bonnie Prince
Charlie, in the comely Principal Boy form of Molly, who having
uttered the following couplets:

> In this impasse, I fail to see the fun,
> The rightful King of Scotland on the run,
> I can't but feel that the occasion merits
> A little ditty to keep up our spirits. —

187

bursts Ethel Merman-like into a 'razzamatazz' Broadway style number which almost stopped the show:

> I'm gonna take a trip to Cali-for-ni-a
> California in the U.S.A.

A somewhat cheerier Charlie than he is usually portrayed.

Macrae's Dame was a unique creation. A protean role this, he moved from the traditional dress of bunchy skirts, striped stockings and elastic-sided boots, to the full court regalia of Catherine the Great of Russia in a hitherto unrecorded meeting with Mary, Queen of Scots, in Red Square, Moscow.

Perhaps the most memorable of Macrae's many impersonations was a single scene written for him by Stanley Baxter, 'Polly at the Palais'. In a slinky black evening dress that accentuated his tall angular build, this brassy blonde dancehall wall-flower waiting for her boy friend who never appears, remains in the memory not only as a comic figure, but one with all the tragic magic and pathos of Chaplin. Some of the lines, uttered as 'she' peoples the empty stage with dancers were the essence of Glasgow in expression and intonation. When she rejects an unwanted partner with a shrug, suggesting, "Take ma pal. Ah'm sweatin'", the line employed was one actually overheard at the near-by Barrowland dance hall. And her searing condemnation of a rather smooth, wolf-like individual from whose clutches she extricated herself — "Champ dancer? Dampt chancer!" — has become a classic.

Another scene had Stanley Baxter as Joe McClout, a Glasgow boxer who, after winning a championship at Madison Square Gardens, New York, gave the retort laconic to the interviewers' standard question, "What do you think of the U.S.A.?"

"S'aw right. Nae fish'n'chip shops, but."

This engulfed the audience in mirth in a way that the gallant, bewildered John Casson could never have foreseen.

So many vignettes have remained in the memory of fellow Glaswegians. Duncan Macrae and James Gibson as two wifies used the opposite stage boxes, as windows from which to observe and comment on the passers by, in the traditional custom known as a 'hing'. On seeing a very smart young lady emerge from the 'close mouth', they comment as follows:

1st wife: There's Sandra McGuffie.
2nd wife: I don't think Sandra McGuffie's a very glamourous name, do you?
1st wife: Naw. I've heard glamourouser.
2nd wife: Whit's that she's got on her hands?
1st wife: Gloves!
(This last was uttered in tones of surprised condemnation of such airs and graces that are impossible to convey.)

Each of the players approached the script presented with a lively assurance that seemed almost divinely inspired.

Jack House found Molly's principal boy memorable. He reminds us that even in 1950 certain luxury goods were hard to come by, and related how John Casson who had determined his principal boy would be traditionally dressed, had to appeal to Jack Barton of Ayr Gaiety who produced from their wardrobe:

> a really beautiful pair of fish-net tights, which are now really beautifully displayed by Molly Urquhart.
> Personally, I think Molly Urquhart is the best principal boy in Glasgow this season. She has the panache that so many of our rather 'naice' principal boys lack today. I've been feeling that the great days of the principal boy were passing, but Molly Urquhart has renewed my faith in the boys of the old brigade. When I see her, I think fondly of the days when I was enraptured by Clarice Mayne, Florrie Ford, Victoria Carmen and Nellie Wigley.
> In fact, if I'd only known how well Miss Urquhart was equipped for the part of principal boy, I'd never have made the mistake I did when I wrote a pantomime for her Rutherglen theatre away back in 1940. I cast her as the dame.

Stanley Baxter recalled her approach during rehearsals:

> Aware that Bridie's burlesque of a principal boy might be 'toned down' by the "Tintock Cup's" English producer, she rehearsed it for two weeks in a slightly Kelvinside accent with only two or three lapses into broad vernacular. On the first night, though, she was pure Doris Droy. Or do I misinterpret what happened? From the word "go" on that incredible opening night no one could do any wrong. Success has never seemed to be so palpable. And the Glaswegian dialect was eliciting the biggest roars of laughter. Perhaps her decision to broaden came after the curtain went up.

We'll never know. For "The Tintock Cup" I'd written a number
for Molly. In a dressing room at Ayr during the preceeding
autumn season I'd said to Lennox Milne, "Wouldn't it be funny at
some point in this panto we're going to do at Christmas to have
Molly as a bedraggled follower of Bacchus complete with grapes
and animal skins?" Lennox said, "A sort of tatty Bacchante?" That
did it. I wrote it that night.

As for 'Sour Grapes' as Stanley's number was called, it was a
resounding hit. The melody, by Ian Gourlay, had a keening,
bibulous lilt which gave her every possible opportunity to
reproduce, in perfect vocal verisimilitude, the resonant, plangent
sound known in Glasgow as 'back court singing' from the style of
those impoverished choristers who used regularly to give voice in
the washing greens in the well of tenement buildings, to collect the
odd pennies thrown from the windows by kindly housewives.

Dressed in a leopard skin, vine leaves twining through her flowing
dark hair, a bunch of grapes held desultorily in her hand, the shapely
legs that had sported those fishnet tights throughout the rest of the
evening, drably encased in thick lisle stockings, her feet comfortable
in 'granny' slippers complete with pom-pom (— this last inspired
detail was her own idea —) she stands forever in the memory of all
who saw her, a cross between a wee Glasgow wife who enjoys 'a
refreshment' and a classical wine bibber:

I'm Tatty Bacchante — I'm everyone's auntie,
The darling of all who love beer,
I eat grapes by the dozen, and look like that cousin
That turns up blind-drunk at New Year.
Oh I used to get toasted in Athens and Rome
And Senators fought to see who'd take me home,
In those days the men blew the beer off the foam —
Tatty Bacchante's yer auntie.
Spare a wee hauf at New Year.

I'm Tatty Bacchante — I'm everyone's auntie,
The Greek word for "out on the skite".
Every new tax on liquor has made me feel sicker
They're ruining ma Setterday night.
In the black-out I had a great time with a Pole,
But now that exporting our whisky's the goal

THE TINTOCK CUP

It's New York for me — or I'm back on the dole —
Tatty Bacchante's yer auntie
Spare a wee hauf at New Year.

I'm Tatty Bacchante — I'm everyone's auntie,
The Priestess of Pim's No. One,
Though I look a tough heathen — no kiddin' — I'm freezin'!
A leopard's skin isnae aw fun!
A Hollywood Goddess can turn up in mink
And tipple till all hours — it does make ye think,
The nine-thirty closing will drive me to drink —
Tatty Bacchante's yer auntie
Spare a wee hauf at New Year.

I'm Tatty Bacchante I'm everyone's auntie
The Bosom companion of Zeus
I suppose it was fate that the plasterer's mate
Got too plastered to finish oor hoose
Bacchanalian orgies and nights on the spree
Are exempted from tax for Miss Vivien Leigh,
I wish the Arts Council would just sponsor ME.
Tatty Bacchante's yer auntie
Spare a wee hauf at New Year.

I'm Tatty Bacchante — I'm everyone's auntie
Except for the man that's T.T.
With some tax off the wine, we can have a rare time,
Come up any time and see me;
If you'll just name the place where you'd like us to meet
As long as it's licensed my day is complete
Though you may have to cart me home to Vineyard Street
Tatty Bacchante's yer Auntie
Spare a wee hauf at New Year!

(Reproduced by permission of Stanley Baxter)

The reviews were panegyric in the extreme:

'Shades of Princess' pantomimes of other days must have been
in the wings last night, inciting, encouraging and applauding.
(*Evening Times*)

'— a script which for all its outlandish nonsense cannot conceal a
sound theatre and cultured background.' (*The Glasgow Herald*)

'— moved swiftly and faultlessly from slapstick to sincerity.'
(*Scottish Daily Express*)

' "Tintock Cup" a riot of fun.'

After the opening night on 20 December 1950, the box office was besieged by the biggest crowds that the theatre had ever attracted. The show was the talk of the town; everyone wanted to see it, and having seen it wanted to go again, its subtleties, and there were many, proving the more delightful on a second or even a third hearing. Bridie's comment on the first night was disarmingly modest, saying that his clowns, taking him at his word, had jettisoned Mr Munro's script and his own:

> On the first night my pleasure in the entertainment was heightened by the touching consciousness that here and there a few lines had been allowed to remain.
>
> They allowed me to put on a bold face when knowing people shook me by the hand and congratulated me on my handiwork and themselves on their perspicuity. But of course I had nothing at all to do with it.

Macrae, in particular, was hailed as a new pantomime discovery, and by the beginning of January had been approached by a commercial management who had put forward a 'lucrative offer' to engage him for a Tom Arnold pantomime the following Christmas season. This for him seemed an ideal solution; it would mean some financial reward, yet allow him to act in the rest of the Citizens' season. Meanwhile, he and Molly and the rest of the company were drawing the people of Glasgow in ever increasing numbers to their own repertory theatre.

The new manager, Willie McIntosh, was solidly in favour of letting the show run on. Scheduled to run for four weeks, it was extended till the end of February, then finally played to capacity audiences for fifteen weeks finishing, appropriately enough, on April the first. Each extension was granted only after a long discussion with the Arts Council. The grant which the theatre received was, the Council reminded them, so that they should produce a season of plays. Their money-spinner which netted in all of £22,000, was somewhat of an embarrassment to the Board of Directors.

Yet Bridie, who had been in hospital with pleurisy over New Year, must have been relieved to know that the £4,000 deficit with which the season had opened was well and truly wiped out, and the profits would be a nest egg such as the theatre had never before enjoyed.

But more than that, the Glasgow people were finding themselves at home in their neat little Victorian playhouse. Willie McIntosh was always in the foyer; a theatre manager in the good old-fashioned style, he considered it a much as part of the job to be there to welcome the patrons as they went in to the auditorium and to see his 'house' out, as attending to the business side. His experience at Rutherglen had given him a practical down-to-earth approach to his task; as he saw it, to try to ensure the season was a success financially as well as artistically. The newcomers to the theatre found their visit enhanced by his presence, a handsome ambassador-like figure, receiving them with quiet courtesy, recognising regular patrons, listening to opinions, and giving advice about everything from transport to tea intervals. The manager of a theatre is a key figure, and it cannot be too strongly stressed that a theatre will gain incalculable benefit if he sees his post as a public relations exercise, as well as a business and financial one. Members of the Citizens' Theatre Society, the supporters' club, doubled during those months.

The theatre issued some statistical evidence of the show's appeal. There were 116 performances, and 585 curtain calls. The takings amounted to £22,000 over 15 weeks. 140,000 people attended, 20,000 seeing the show from the Unreserved Gallery (known as 'The Woods', since it offered the simplest of benches for the public to sit on, from which, however, could be obtained a good view of the stage, and, in those days, perfect audibility) while 1,740 people had taken standing room! At a conservative estimate of five laughs a minute, this indicated there were 104,400 'audience' laughs during the run, giving in all, 14,500,000 individual laughs.

Harry McKelvie would have loved that.

For the individual members of the company, it meant that reputations were made. Macrae had already been booked for the Glasgow Alhambra next season. Stanley Baxter declined offers made, saying he had joined the Citizens' to learn as much as he could about acting.

James Gilbert went on composing music for two further pantomimes. He acknowledged that working on the scores, and being involved with writing songs for Molly and Duncan Macrae and Stanley Baxter gave him the encouragement as well as the practical experience he needed to develop the flair that enabled him to take on the job of writing musicals with his next company, Windsor Repertory. After a successful musical show there for Beryl Reid, he wrote the score for *Grab me a Gondola* which transferred to the West End. Thereafter he got his first job in the B.B.C. as a Light Entertainment producer. He acknowledges in affectionate and generous manner the impetus his time at Citizens' gave him in his career:

> My first success down here was again as a result of Citizens' days, because Eric Maschwitz who was director of Light Entertainment then suggested I do a revue. At that time, it was thought that the revue format wouldn't work on television, whereas now, since TW3, Monty Python, The Two Ronnies, there are numerous "revue" programmes. I had a complete "carte blanche" because I had a similar show running in the West End, so I said I wanted Stanley Baxter because he was quite unknown here. And I got Betty Marsden and David Kiernan and a whole batch of writers including Richard Waring. "On the Bright Side" was a huge success. Then we did two "Stanley Baxter" shows and he and I both won awards for them — and that again was entirely due to the acting and writing experience that started off our careers in the Citizens' "Tintock Cup".
>
> It was a tremendous mainspring — Fulton Mackay, Roddy Macmillan, John Fraser, Gudrun Ure, Douglas Campbell — such a huge background of experience at a time just after the war when so many people were determined to make a success of their careers in the theatre. It was a growth point.
>
> I was also invited to direct the musical episodes from "Cavalcade" which was being presented at the Academy (the Royal Scottish Academy of Dramatic Art) where John Grieve, John Cairney, Ellen McIntosh, Bob Baird and Andy Stewart were all students.
>
> Molly had such a vigorous, physical approach to a number. I remember once we were invited to do a charity cabaret in a night club. Molly with her supreme confidence in being able to belt a number from the stage right to the back of the hall rejected the microphone that was a permanent feature of the tiny performance area. But as it was a night club, everything was sound insulated and there was no feed-back at all. "Bump it up a bit", she hissed to me, thinking a higher key might help. But it was no use. That was the

only failure I ever saw Molly have — it was as if she were singing in a velvet box.

She was very good in straight stuff too, a super actresss, but it was that drive and timing and energy that made her impossible to by-pass in comedy.

Molly had made a triumphant return to the company and was happy to be back in the theatre where she felt so at home.

The pantomime programmes had published a warmly expressed invitation to the audiences:

> Do you know that most of the players you will be seeing in "The Tintock Cup" are members of our company which plays in this theatre for nine months of the year?
>
> There is nothing highfalutin' about the plays they work in. They are plays of all kinds and but for us they might not be seen by Glasgow audiences. But please remember, whatever the show, we like to feel that we are offering you something that will entertain you.

The public were ready to respond. Unfortunately, the play that followed was a world premiere, a play by Tyrone Guthrie, identified in the *Evening Citizen* report as 'The Three Estates' man. Edgar Wallace's thriller *On the Spot*, Paul Vincent Carroll's *The Old Foolishness* and Shakespeare's *The Merchant of Venice* all had been considered as possible follow-ups when, as the report said 'their money-spinner . . . is reluctantly hauled off'. But it was finally decided to give Guthrie's *Top of the Ladder*. Guthrie's foreword announces his intention:

> The play is much concerned with symbols: key, box, ladder, window, railway, river, garden and so on. All are intended to convey a shadow meaning larger but vaguer than their literal meaning. These symbols are not intended to be precisely interpreted. They carry many possible meanings and many people will interpret them in different ways.

The Stage hailed the production and with enthusiasm going on to say: 'As Mr Guthrie fully acknowledges, this is not a commercial play, and yet we owe a debt of thanks to Mr Guthrie for introducing us to something novel in the way of an experimental play.'

But despite the 'gallant acting' of fine players like Laurence Hardy, Douglas Campbell and Madeleine Christie, the play was thought-provoking to the seasoned play-goer, and downright perplexing to the new patrons who, urged on by the cheerful invitation on the pantomime programme, had returned to see a play, that whatever other qualities it had was positively 'high-falutin'.

It is sad in retrospect that the breathing space afforded by a fifteen weeks' successful run could not have allowed the board to scrap their plans for the rest of the season and evolve a programme that might have enabled the many new visitors to the theatre to continue to feel at home there. In fact, the Guthrie play was undoubtedly one of the most abstrusely intellectual ever to be presented.

Many of the 'new' audience retreated in confusion.

The Tintock Cup has become a legend among shows. 'A tremendous mainspring', James Gilbert called it. There is no doubt about it, to the company, it provided a new outlook, just as in the legend 'Tinto Hill' was a vantage point from which to see what lay beyond.

In the version told by Marion Lochhead in her book of Scottish tales called *On Tintock Tap* (The Moray Press) the drink that the boy got from the cup had a strange effect:

> The mist had lifted, and all around him it was more bright than noon-tide or the full light of the moon. He looked down at his own home, and, although it was so far beneath him and so tiny, it was clear in every detail. He could see all that was going on, inside the house as well as out-bye; as if the walls were made of glass.

In the pantomime version, the Cup contained happiness, and certainly Molly, as well as Stanley Baxter and Duncan Macrae had thoroughly enjoyed the reaction of the happy audiences that thronged into the theatre during that phenomenal run. "I like to hear people laugh" was her simple answer to an interviewer who queried the trend her career took in this and subsequent seasons towards comedy, both in plays and in pantomime and revue.

Molly quickly became established in the public eye as a comedienne who very definitely belonged to Glasgow. She was much in demand, making appearances in charity shows and student revues, opening sales of work and choosing beauty queens; deluged by these invitations that are the inevitable accompaniment to public popularity.

Her next appearance in the theatre was in *The Scientific Singers*, a new play by Robert Kemp. Set in the University of Aberdeen in the year 1753, this comedy told of the reverberations that shook 'town and gown' when a musical Professor of Natural Philosophy (James Gibson) introduced a choir and part singing (known as 'scientific singing') to King's College Chapel in place of the usual precentor who had hitherto led the praise in solemn sonorous vein. Based on an actual incident, the play gave Robert Kemp ample scope for humour expressed in the Doric, and young Fulton Mackay got his best opportunity to date as the shy student who suddenly realises his fine tenor voice is a powerful pawn in the game to bargain with the 'solemn singing' champion, the Professor of Greek, and the scientific singing enthusiast, in order to win passes in both subjects.

Molly played the Professor's wife.

Molly Urquhart looking extremely sonsie as his very Scots wife played up magnificently, *Scottish Daily Mail.*

Molly Urquhart revels in repartée as the couthy wife with a lashing tongue, *Evening Times.*

The Glasgow Herald disagreed:

Molly Urquhart is in her own period and region an excellent actress, but it is her misfortune to throw the play out of its century by making her dialogue hoarse and modern, and reminding me too strongly of her Tatty Bacchante, who was so admirable in the recent pantomime.

On the other hand, the *Evening Citizens'* critic who applauds the play for its success in obtaining 'a continuous ripple of laughter from the audience' rejoices in its being 'full of pithy Scots phrases — "as helpless as a coupit tup" — and they get their full value from such players as James Gibson, Molly Urquhart and Fulton Mackay.'

There is little doubt that the demands made on the Scots actor were manifold. He had to aim for the current West End style for a play like Rodney Ackland's *Before the Party*, to acquire the requisite pure English for a play such as *The Merchant of Venice*, and be able to assume the appropriate tones for historical plays, written in archaic Scots and set in various parts of the country.

This dilemma had been acknowledged when, on 15 September 1950, the Royal Scottish Academy of Music in Buchanan Street had 'and Drama' added to its name and function.

The first principal of the Drama School, Colin Chandler, gave a spirited address assuring press and public that 'students of Scotland's first College of Drama will be taught to be "bi-lingual" to acquire an acceptable English accent without losing any individuality or pride in their native Scots' tongue'.

Dame Sybil Thorndike, who with her husband was a patron of the new establishment, said, in a subsequent speech, 'You want your own vernacular. That is something you can give which no other nation has got in the same way — strong speech with strong vowels and consonants.'

Classes in Scots dialect were set up as a compulsory part of every student's course. The dialect that was hardly ever required of an actor, except in pantomime, was the present day urban working-class speech of Glasgow and Edinburgh.

There were, of course, in existence working class plays. The Unity Theatre had been formed in 1941 by a coming together of members of many Glasgow clubs, notably the Jewish Institute Players, the Clarion Players, the Workers' Theatre Group and the Transport Players. In turn, the group became professional in 1946, by the simple means whereby those members who decided to risk giving up their jobs, got together and announced they were now professional actors. Andrew Keir, Roddy Macmillan, Russell Hunter and Marjory Thomson were all Unity Players who had acted in such socially committed plays as Robert McLeish's *The Gorbals Story* and James Barke's *Major Operation*, adapted from his novel about the relationship between employers and employees in a Clydeside repair dockyard. Not surprisingly, the group revered O'Casey's work and were quick to point out that the Glasgow Citizens' Theatre was in no way fulfilling its early promise when it had been occasionally compared to Dublin's Abbey Theatre.

In an article in Unity's magazine, *The Scottish Stage*, Joseph MacLeod, one of their producers, said:

In the new Scottish theatre there are two divisions: primarily middle class repertories and writers, whose art is seen in Perth, the Glasgow Citizens' Theatre and elsewhere: and the tougher working class drama and performances to be seen in Glasgow Unity Theatre.

Certainly the only new play dealing with a working class Glasgow family in several years was *All in Good Faith* by Roddy Macmillan. Incidentally, although presented in Citizens' in 1954, this work has only just been published in 1980, subsequent to his highly acclaimed comedy drama *The Bevellers* which dealt with the initiation of a young boy into an apprenticeship in the glass bevelling trade. It was presented first in 1975, and received such approbation nation wide, that the Scottish Society of Playwrights took the opportunity of bringing out the earlier work, a gesture which, sadly, turned out to be a posthumous tribute to Roddy, whose sudden death in 1979 at the age of 58 left the Scottish Theatre with a gap that cannot easily be filled.

Molly loved *All in Good Faith* — it was very much 'her kind of play', but by the time the board decided to present it, she was no longer a full member of the company.

At a time when there were murmurs that playing in pantomime had broadened her style irretrievably it is interesting to note that the medium in which she, and many other Scottish actors had become involved was film. She had always loved the cinema, and in fact in the early nineteen thirties she had been involved in an unfinished project, a film called *The Bullet and the Alibi* with script by Joe Corrie that was a thriller to be shot around Loch Lomondside with a Scottish cast. Apart from the occasional appearance in short documentaries made for information purposes, her film debut had been as Thirza, the Yorkshire housekeeper to Margaret Johnston's Clare in the somewhat sentimental family saga *Portrait of Clare* directed by Lance Comfort and released in 1949.

In 1954, during the time that Roddy's *All in Good Faith* received its premiere and ran successfully for its statutory fortnight in the season, she was playing the mother in *Geordie* that simple folk tale type story of how a wee Scots boy, despairing of his insignificant size and strength, takes a correspondence course in body building and ends up competing in the Olympic games. Shot, under Frank Lander's direction, the cast, led by Bill Travers, included Alistair Sim, Stanley

Baxter and an outstanding character comedian from the Scottish variety stage, Jack Radcliffe.

All of them enjoyed the experience, and although the movie has been consistently slated by the critics, it has been issued and reissued, as well as being a perennial on television. Critics, who often give opinions that are perfectly sound and valid in their own circles, where experience of film-going is at a very sophisticated level, forget that this story is a stereotype that has been successful since *Jack and the Beanstalk* became one of the hits in the oral folk tradition many centuries ago. It is certainly wish-fulfilment fantasy that the weak little hero eventually becomes the champion, but it is a kind of escapism that delights the type of audience who also enjoy the stories of Perseus, Beowulf and even James Bond.

Molly came, shortly after the film's release, to talk to a group of teenagers in a school theatre club. She had given them a vigorous and amusing speech about the work of an actress. When there was an opportunity given for questions, one of those bedazzled silences reigned, until a shy little girl, who had seen *Geordie*, asked, "What did you think the first time you seen yourself on the screen?" Molly beamed at her, then admitted with that disarming, reasoning candour that made everyone feel at home in her company, "I wanted to go and drown myself!"

It was true, she confided to me later. She had, in her forties, with the hearty appetite she freely acknowledged as one of her worst failings, grown very stout. "I made up my mind no one would ever see that fat gudge again!" (Gudge, n: anything short and thick; a short, thick set person. *Chambers Scots Dictionary*.)

True it was she had put on weight in a comely enough way. 'Sonsie' was the adjective frequently used to describe her; another Scots word, Chambers Scots Dictionary again gives a meaning that shows in detail how apt the epithet was. 'Sonsie, adj: lucky, fortunate, happy; thriving; plump; buxom, stout; jolly; placid; tractable; good-tempered; comfortable; plentiful; cordial.'

In 1951, that was more or less true of her. It is a strange thing in the theatre, that actors often become moulded by the roles to which they are summoned, not the other way about. And when Thalia, Muse of Comedy was calling the tune, Molly did, as it were, forget to make the effort to stay as slim as she would have needed to be for the serious, sombre heroines that followed Melpomene's banner.

But film, with its all-revealing lens was different, and she did, after *Geordie* go on a slimming diet that trimmed her figure down again to 'sonsie' instead of 'gudge'.

But the subtlety that would be needed later for film was put aside as the second Bridie pantomime was planned for Christmas 1951. He had outlined a book for *Red Riding Hood* that allowed Glaswegian vitality to break loose again on the boards of the old Princess Theatre. Enhanced by a delightful set of songs by James Gilbert, this was again a kind of parody on pantomime form, giving a few nods to tradition in that it had a Fairy, a Demon King (Laurence Hardy again, as Lord Miracle of the Gorbals) and Molly resplendent in tights once more as Robin Hood, who had a band of brothers, notably Roddy Macmillan, Fulton Mackay and Lea Ashton as Lively, Likely and Monks Hood respectively. There was of course, the obligatory rhyming couplet or two; Moira Robertson as the heroine announcing firmly and frequently: '. . . I canny/Find ma Granny.'

It was a jolly show, good seasonal fare and much enjoyed by happy audiences who filled the theatre. It did not measure up to *The Tintock Cup*, but it served to establish Stanley Baxter as a Pantomime Dame who made a more than worthy successor to Macrae (who was playing an Ugly Sister in Tom Arnold's *Cinderella* at the Alhambra). He played Granny McNiven, sought by the heroine, Teeny from Tahiti, Gloria, the first of his many posh 'Kelvinside' Glasgow ladies, and a Miss Yvonne McLafferty, a would-be Glasgow beauty contestant. The *Evening News* endorsed the audience's reaction — 'Baxter's Miss or Mrs comes from Glasgow . . . pawky, gawky, sometimes glamorous . . . He is fresh, brisk, genuinely new as a new penny and his work is plainly his pleasure.'

Molly wandered through a variety of guises, ranging from a Cleopatra from West Nile Street, Glasgow, to a principal boy à la Napoleon, hat and all. She didn't have quite the same opportunities in the script as previously, but she made the most of what was there. It still was the brightest show in town.

On 29 January, 1951, during the run of this last *jeu d'esprit* that brought laughter to so many, James Bridie died at the age of 63. He had been admitted to the Edinburgh Royal Infirmary a week earlier, suffering from a vascular condition. Over forty plays had been his provision for the actors of his country. He had seen his theatre born and established, he had seen a company of Scottish actors working successfully along the lines described in the theatre's charter, and the College of Drama he had envisaged was now a reality.

The company each felt the loss personally.

Never a remote figure he was frequently in and around the theatre, and knew all of them. Their reaction was voiced by Duncan Macrae:

> I have lost an honest friend. The theatre in Scotland grew by his tireless efforts. He was a Scot known and respected throughout the world and his loss is irreparable.
>
> His ain folk were perhaps shy to praise him as he deserved. Let us devote ourselves now to the cause he always held dear.

The newspaper tributes were thoughtful and fair, fairer perhaps than the critical assessment of *The Queen's Comedy*, which had been his first to be included in the official Edinburgh Festival programme in the summer of 1950. Directed by Guthrie, the Citizens' company had performed with verve this stylish and amusing play which shows the Gods of Olympus using the Greeks and Trojans like so many puppets; it deplores the futility of war and the exploitation of the finest human courage that it calls upon. Bridie wrote in a letter to fellow dramatist St John Ervine:

> As to "The Queen's Comedy", the London newspaper notices made it quite certain that London won't see it and I have a pleasant feeling that I have the laugh of them there.

The funeral service which was held in the Chapel of Glasgow University was attended by over four hundred mourners including the Principal and Senate of the University in formal academic dress.

Alistair Sim who was one of the pall-bearers at the interment at the Western Necropolis said, "Proud as I was to work with him and for him, I was proudest of all of his friendship — the most valued and inspiring I have ever known."

Alistair, standing near Willie and Molly McIntosh as they watched the solemn procedure of the service unfolding, said, with a half sob, half smile, "Jimmy would have loved this."

Fulton Mackay avers that subsequently whenever there was a play by Bridie produced in the Glasgow Citizens' Theatre, those of the company who had known him felt very strongly that the playwright was there. Whatever O.H. Mavor might have thought of that contingency, there is no doubt at all, that James Bridie, if it is at all possible, would indeed be there.

"Molly's grotesques" observed Stanley Baxter, "anticipated Monty Python's adenoidal characters by many years. Like theirs, hers were cartoons incarnate."
Coincidentally, a young Scotsman who was later to direct the Monty Python series for B.B.C. TV, Ian Macnaughton, from 1950-52 a member of the Citizens' Theatre Company, was playing supporting roles in two of the pantomimes while Stanley and Molly worked their way in partnership through a series of memorable characterisations.

They seemed at first an unlikely pair, the volatile, dark-haired, young intellectual who already was one of the best character actors the company had ever known, and the well-established, unassuming matronly actress, who had quietly made theatre live in the west of Scotland for well over a decade. Stanley who believed in maintaining as much sartorial elegance as he could on his £6 a week, was somewhat bemused by Molly's life-style. He remembers her worka-day wardrobe as a haphazard affair, looking as if it came from the Salvation Army.

Certainly Molly did not ever worry about having an image; yet when she dressed up for a special occasion she could dazzle her friends who were used to seeing her in comfortable clothes, suitably warm to defeat the multiple draughts of Citizens' backstage. She always had to have her feet comfortable, whatever else, and would rehearse in her slippers until she got the appropriate footwear for the play 'broken in'. Once in later life, when making a personal appear-ance for some charity, she was resplendent in her mink coat and a rose pink silk dress. Arriving at the function, her escort pointed out in alarm that her feet were still encased in her furry moccasins. Unperturbed, she announced, "Never mind. We'll go in with an air and nobody'll notice." With her famous grin wreathing her features as she made her way on to the platform, she just might have been right.

Stanley found her an intriguing mixture of motherliness, enthu-siasm and sensuality "with a frugality in life style reminiscent of Lilian Baylis' penny pinching". While Molly could be generous in the extreme to her family, she seldom spent anything on herself without considerable conscience-searching. Her unpbringing had taught her the necessity for an organised personal and domestic economy, she considered it extravagance to spend any more than was absolutely necessary. In later times of hardship this skill was something that helped her through.

> Though she was never unco-guid in the lace curtains and aspidistra sense, all religion had a great appeal for her. But I always felt it was a gipsy's feeling for the supernatural rather than faith in the Christian sense. Her own heart was big and emotional and certainly was in step with Jesus and in its empathy with life's underprivileged.

That note from Stanley Baxter perhaps explains the quality of warmth she could bring to the comedy singles and sketches which she played so successfully. She did not leave her sensitivity behind when it came to pantomime and revue but as Stanley was quick to recognise, her talent was something really special: "she worked totally by instinct but that instinct was accurate and secure".

So it was as actors as well as fully paid up members of the 'Celtic lunatic fringe' (a definition that could include all the Scots actors who kicked free of the traces during the annual pantomime) that the two of them continued for the next few years in a remarkable partnership.

John Casson, having left to take up a post in the Australian theatre, the new director was Peter Potter who had previously been at Salisbury Rep. He started the season with a brisk production of *Tartuffe* with Duncan Macrae in the lead and Molly as Dorine. Molière suits Scots actors, and the company scored a success with this version in the Miles Malleson translation, with no Doric overlay.

The Christmas show, *The Happy Hapny*, contained a sketch called 'They also Serve' about two waitresses in a café to which a wedding party of four Glaswegians had come straight from the Registry Office in Martha Street to celebrate with a pie and chips bridal supper. Waitress service in Glasgow has always had its share of characters. A certain unwillingness to conform to the requisite ideal of unobtrusive efficiency, coupled with warmth, and excessive tendency towards motherliness and a highly original sense of humour has resulted in a proliferation of anecdotes about them. The owner of the careless hands that inadvertently scattered the remains of the vegetable dish about the gown and hood of a distinguished academic at a university luncheon, gave vent to the cry of concern, 'Aw, sir, I've spilt some peas in yer pixie hood'. And another, bringing an order of side dishes, three broccoli, one cauliflower, one spinach to accompany the main course of a dinner to which a group of high-powered business men sat down, greeted them with the cheerful cry of "Which one of youse is Popeye?"

The pair that were depicted in the sketch were certainly carica- tures, but they had the ring of authenticity about them. Stanley recalled:

> My own characterisation was no understated cameo. I was leggy, Bridgeton Cross spoken and in drag. How do you keep upsides with that? Molly was in no doubt. Her waitress acquired hair like dead eels, a speech defect, a hump back and cross eyes that didn't once correct themselves during the fourteen minutes the sketch sometimes ran. At the first rehearsal the dismayed director fresh from Salisbury, declared that no-one could find our disgusting exhibition funny. "Nose wiping, soup serving and this . . ." he pointed at Molly, "pitiful creature. Oh they won't laugh, will they?" "Like drains," I said, with firm twenty-three year old confidence. And they did, through till the spring the following year.

But the caricatures were not completely cruel. There was a warmth of concern for that excessively plain lassie, who could look astigmatically on the cheap fashionableness of the bride in her C & A Modes costume, and say, in generous sincerity, "She's lovely, sure she is."

"Aye. You canny beat the powder blue. Looks nice at the time and dyes nice after," was the rejoinder from her more down-to-earth companion.

The characters Molly played in this and subsequent shows all were marked with this basic true-to-real-life quality. She could not have played them otherwise. A highly original spot was one written by R. Crichton for the next pantomime *Carrie the Queen of the Caurs*. The lady tram drivers and conductresses had 'manned' Glasgow's trams both in the First and Second World Wars. (It was in 1916 when it was still a novel occurrence to have women doing such work that the

Transport Department, in order to warn off anyone who might refuse to yield up the fare to the lady officials, put up posters with the admonitory legend: 'No boy with pride — would steal a ride.')

The 'Carrie' number had every mark of a winner, but Molly was not happy with her interpretation. She was rehearsing it as a rather dowdy, harassed body, who looked as if she would be more at home in an apron than in the bottle green uniform with red piping of the Glasgow Transport Service.

"I'm not right," she confided to Willie as they went home on the subway after a very late rehearsal. "I'm not getting the character."

As she spoke, the train stopped at West Street, and on walked a goddess. Blonde, beautifully and colourfully made up, with slim, nylon-clad legs that high heeled, platform ankle-strap shoes showed to advantage, she too wore the green uniform, the little peaked cap almost invisible amid her fashionable bouffant hair-do. She was followed by a small man, also green uniformed, to whom she complained with towering indignation about a bus inspector who had been 'putting it on to her'.

"He's not getting away with it. Treating me like that! I'll show him. Talking to me as if I was dirt. I'm going to report him first thing the morrow, so I am."

Such strength she had that one trembled for the over officious man, as she continued her monologue of threats and revenge, punctuated by the short, acquiescent remarks of her companion, "That's right, Betty" — "You tell him, hen" — "Don't you take it".

Entranced, Molly and Willie unobtrusively observed this living inspiration until, entourage in tow, she strode majestically from the train. By this time, the observers had not only gone past their own stop, but found that, as it was the last train, it had reached the terminus The taxi fare home was a cheap price to pay. "That's it," they both agreed and ordered a blonde wig first thing next morning.

Carrie was a triumph. From her entry, on a magnificent full-size tram which came crashing through the depot doors on to the stage, her opening remark was received with roars of delighted recognition. As she staggered towards the footlights, she said, "It isny as if I wisny experienced. I've been driving for mair nor a fortnight."

Other numbers included a plump little nearly forty 'White Bride', all aglow with pride at the prospect of matrimonial status, carolling, 'Everything comes to her that waits'; a devastating send up of 'Lord

206

Ullin's Daughter'; a Ruth Draper-like monologue 'Jenny a' things' about a corner shop keeper — and 'Fairy Cake' a comic pantomime fairy that was the first of many items written for her by Jim Macnair and Jim Waters, two young seafaring men who had become her fans, and spent their off duty time on the light ship in the middle of the North Sea planning a series of comic singles that were to be her principal source of material over the next few years. Those portraits, executed boldly and with real human warmth were a gallery of Glaswegian personalities, reminiscent of those County and Cockney ladies that the late Joyce Grenfell used to create so well.

Comedy, then, became the predominant element in her work. Although she was happy to have the opportunity to play Mary Paterson in the production of *The Anatomist* that began the James Bridie Memorial season at the beginning of the 1952 season. Alistair Sim and George Cole came to Citizens' to appear in the roles they had played in the West End in 1948, and the production was extremely popular with the public. Alistair Sim was by this time better known than ever because of his appearance in a number of successful film comedies, as well by his performance as a delightfully macabre and sinister Captain Hook in the yearly tour of *Peter Pan* by J.M. Barrie.

Her only other appearance that season was in *Green Cars Go East* played for the first time by a professional company in Glasgow. Its fortnight's run enjoyed good houses, although one critic found it difficult to accept 'a school teacher daughter and student son living under the same squalid roof as a drunken father and slatternly mother'; while another found it 'native drama of good characterisation garnished with humour'.

The audiences liked it.

Molly's mother, whose increasing infirmity had made it impossible for her to travel any distance from their Earnock home in her later years had not been able to see her daughter on the stage, though all of Molly's last night bouquets were promptly taken to her mother the following Sunday.

Alasdair, who rose to the rank of Captain in the Lovat Scouts, had met and become engaged to a very beautiful Austrian girl. On his demob she travelled to Scotland, and their wedding in 1947 was held in the home of the Urquhart parents, so that the family could be together on that occasion.

Mrs Urquhart died in 1950. Mr Urquhart came to live with the McIntoshes, in the more spacious six-room flat, 12 Clifford Street, which they had bought.

Alasdair got work in the B.B.C. and he and Erika set up house in Glasgow in a flat in Hayburn Crescent, Partick. Alasdair was fascinated by his sister's success as a comedienne, and he it was who urged her take up the inevitable offer made by Howard and Wyndham's to join the cast of the *Five Past Eight Show*, playing in the Theatre Royal in the summer of 1953. This was a summer revue, that had retained the same format since its inception in 1933 — 'song, dance and laughter', but the essential keynote was comedy. The show pivoted around the expertise of Jack Radcliffe, one of the most versatile of Scottish comedians, whose range stretched from the well-groomed compere opening the show with brilliant *ad lib* wise-cracks, to splendidly rich comic characterisations of a variety of Scottish worthies. Ably partnered by Helen Norman, a talented actress as well as a song and dance lady of real distinction, he was the anchor man for the show. Stanley Baxter had scored a personal hit in the 1952 version, with George Lacey. Now Molly was to partner him.

Helen Norman remembers Molly as "a great actress, a great comedienne, a great person, who was completely dedicated to the business. She was sane and sensible; a wonderful booster if you were down. An original, good comedienne, she had the power and energy not there today. And she fitted in beautifully."

So well did she and Stanley fit in, that their contracts were renewed for the following summer, when a spectacular version of the show was to be presented in the Alhambra, the largest theatre in Glasgow. Having received the accolade of top billing in the Citizens' Christmas show in 1953 as Dame-cum-comedienne, Mrs Duff in *Tapsalteerie-o*, she went on with some trepidation to rehearse with a new director from England, Heath Joyce, for an all-Scottish revue that was to be staged in truly fabulous manner. There was something for everyone. Elaborate scenery and costume; ballet, operetta-type song 'scenas', sketches by new talented writers, as well as the comedy spots that individual performers had to supply for themselves.

The finale costumes were to be in chocolate brown and cream; top hats and tails for the men; bouffant creations, each individually designed in velvet and tulle for the ladies who had coquettish little hats to wear also. Molly never felt at home in 'stagey' costumes, and I remember being with her as she pinned on the frivolous hat for the finale. "How do I look?" she asked. "Lovely," I replied firmly. Raising that quizzical eyebrow of hers, she said, as she wafted out, "I think I'm like a cow looking over a dyke."

She was more at home in the outfit she wore for her solo spot, a multi-coloured knitted sweater, a dirndl skirt, high wedge heel shoes and a tammy hat. She was a wee plain Glasgow lassie, who had finally got a man. Dreamed up by the two Jimmies, this was a real character, simple, comical but lifted into a kind of homespun romantic radiance that almost brought a tear to the eyes, as she sang to the tune of 'Galway Bay':

> Oh Bella, tella fella that you love him
> Oh Bella, tella fella that you care.

The number was a hit. Alan Dent came up to review the opening for the *News Chronicle* observed immediately that the show was 'pure music hall in the guise of an elaborate revue'. He enjoyed Jack Radcliffe's drunk, whom his wife Helen is berating on the way home after an evening at the opera.

> She is furious: he is bibulous. "You had father standing around in the bar all evening as well" she rages. And he, with a bland grin, hiccups the reply "Your father never stood a round in his life!"
> Funnier still is Stanley Baxter telling intensely Glaswegian stories, and Molly Urquhart as a Glasgow trollop in a patchwork pullover who decides, after a trial at changing her name and style of dress, that she would on the whole much rather be Bella amorous than Stella glamorous. Miss Urquhart is that vanishing thing, a true comedienne.

The new formula show was a hit, not only for the established stars but for the newcomers. The first night had ended in a champagne supper and congratulations all round. As she came home, escorted by Willie and young Jim, both equally proud of her, her father came to the door to meet his daughter who beamed at him, her arms full of bouquets, "Molly," he said, "Molly — do you know there is not a bit of bread in the house?"

Throughout her life in the theatre, Molly averred that the way to remain happy was to keep one's home life separate, as a kind of stabiliser. With parental commonsense remarks like her father, it's obvious that she always managed to keep her feet on the ground! The season was a happy one, and her two 'boys', Jim Macnair and Jim Waters, kept on writing singles for her to perform. New material was necessary. The previous year, she had been persuaded to repeat the 'Tatty Bacchante' number. Though this delighted the fans who had seen it originally, it did not transfer to the more conventional format of *Five Past Eight*. But 'Bella' and other numbers from the same team were well received. It was Alasdair who first recognised the two writers had the kind of comic vision that would be right for Molly. She relied on her brother, Ali, more and more while she was working in revue, which can be a lonelier kind of existence than straight theatre. Alasdair was delighted to help her. He and Erika were an ideal couple: he was working on radio and at Citizens', and he had got a foothold in the film world, having acted as Scots dialect adviser for the Walt Disney productions film, *Rob Roy*.

The Citizens' first play after the summer recess was Bridie's *Marriage is no Joke* in which Alasdair was cast. He left the theatre in the afternoon, having had a chat to his brother-in-law in the office. Half an hour later, he collapsed with a heart attack within five hundred yards of his home, and died before an ambulance could get him to hospital. He was forty-one years of age.

At Arrochar, the graveside ceremony was witnessed by his stricken young wife, standing between old Mr Urquhart who suddenly seemed shrunken with age, and Molly trying to contain her own grief in order to comfort Erika.

Erika went back to Austria that autumn. Molly, knowing how much store Ali set by the cruel dictum that 'the show must go on', did not miss a performance. But she only played one more year in summer revue. The time for laughter seemed to be over.

Once at an Actors' Equity meeting where the subject under discussion was the over-crowding in the profession, the late Dame Sybil Thorndike remarked with a kind of naive sagacity, "There's plenty of room at the top". She was right, of course, but since Scotland has never managed to create a national theatre of her own, the Scots actor can obtain nationwide recognition only by success south of the border. And there, as any regional actor will find, it is difficult to avoid being typed.

In the mid nineteen-fifties the situation was the same; there was no superstructure in the Scottish Theatre, no 'Old Vic' where the best actors of the country could be concentrated to perform classics and indigenous drama.

Duncan Macrae and T.M. Watson did form a summer touring company, financed in part from the sizeable salary Macrae could command during the pantomime season. They presented Scottish plays in the larger cities, ending the run in the Palladium in Edinburgh during the Festival. Never an acknowledged part of the official programme, the plays presented over three years were popular with audiences and did give Scottish actors and writers a foothold among companies from other nations.

Impresario Henry Sherek mounted a season of Scottish plays in the summer of 1956 in the Lyceum Theatre in Edinburgh during June, July and August. Audiences built up satisfactorily as the season proceeded, and there was one new play of some distinction, *Voyage Ashore* by Alexander Reid which was a retelling of the story of Odysseus' return, in the lively poetic Scots that is a feature of this playwright's work.

Tall, handsome Andrew Keir played Odysseus with convincing strength, and Stanley Baxter scored as Telemachus, the young son trying in his father's absence to run the household which was besieged with suitors seeking his mother's hand. He was, in the words of the dramatist, 'mair a worrier than a warrior'.

The critic of the *Scottish Field* acclaimed the work as a worthwhile Scots treatment of a universal theme. He went on to say:

> Penelope was played by Molly Urquhart, who gave us a new conception of the hero's spouse endlessly torn between longing for her husband's return and the urge to forget him and marry one of the suitors who cluttered the halls of her palace. Something of the satirical, the tragic, the comic and the coy was skilfully introduced into Miss Urquhart's interpretation, upon which much of the appeal of the play depended.
> Jean Taylor Smith made an excellent Eurycleia, Odysseus' old nurse, a hobbling crone full of significant reminiscences and grim forebodings. The other men of the cast offered vigorous support as

sailors and noblemen, the latter speaking a suave Mayfair English that effectively underlined their foreignness and sinister intentions. They made a brave spectacle and obviously enjoyed their Homeric orgy in the palace hall and the culminating fight in which all are killed by the avenging Odysseus and Telemachus. (With the stage littered with bodies and discarded weapons and Odysseus departed in pursuit of a survivor, Penelope's horrified enquiry brings from Telemachus the laconic explanation, "Faither's hame!")

Stanley Baxter acknowledges the last line as the one in all his career that, night after night, was met with the most prolonged laughter.

Stanley was then invited to take part in a new television revue, which was collated and directed by his former colleague James Gilbert. It was called *On the Bright Side* and its resounding success established not only Jimmy Gilbert as a director but Stanley as a star whose career from there has become legend.

Molly returned to Citizens' to play in the first two plays of the season, a J.B. Priestley première, *These Our Actors* and *Mr Gillie*, James Bridie's last West End success. A gentle domestic drama, it tells about a school teacher, an intelligent, Quixotic visionary, who urges any of his pupils showing artistic tendencies to leave the dead-end little mining village in pursuit of their ambition. Most of his geese fail to swan along, but two of them, played by Phyllida Law and Fulton Mackay, come back, artistic failures but having gained considerable material success in less elevated spheres, which delights everyone except their idealistic former school master.

Andrew Keir played Gillie and Molly his wife. Michael Langham was a sympathetic director. Anyone who might have thought that pantomime and revue had diminished the subtlety of Molly's playing was proved wrong in this, possibly, her finest performance. As the fluttering, dowdy, lady-like, kindly wife, she was superb, and the scene in which she turns on her intelligent, witty, personable failure of a husband was specially memorable. She blames him for encouraging his two latest protegees to run off to London. His protest, 'I haven't got a guilty conscience' calls forth the following piece of homespun rhetoric:

> Mrs Gillie; Conscience? You never had a conscience, guilty or otherwise. Self, self, self, all through. That's you. You were the fine fellow at the university. I remember. I've cause to remember.

All the snotty wee geniuses with baggy trousers and their fingernails in mourning thought you were Jesus. You only got third class honours; but that was because the professors were so blooming ignorant. *They* couldn't understand you, let alone a poor household drudge like me. But it did no damage to your opinion of yourself. Not it. You got married on tuppence three farthings and dragged me away from all my friends and everything, up to a place the like of this with a coal bing in front of the parlour window. From that time on, it was always the fine things you were going to do. It never struck you to do the thing next your hand and make a job of school-mastering. Not it. Ten thousand a year and the Order of merit and T.S. Eliot and Winston Churchill calling you "Sir". You were the great Willie Gillie . . . my God, what a name.

That wonderful line where her voice lifts up on 'Willie Gillie', holding the name in the air during a long pause and, suddenly finding it ludicrous, exclaiming in genuine surprise, . . . "my God, what a name," was a classic moment; equalled only perhaps by the underlying poignancy of the first scene when crossing to draw the curtains, she says to her husband: ". . . Maybe if we had children, schoolmastering wouldn't be such a drudge for you." Mr Gillie answers cheerfully, "I've got plenty of children."

In an almost imperceptible movement, her hand on the curtain tightens, holding it an instant until she is enough recovered to turn towards him; she says, "I haven't!"

But he breezes on. "I know. It's hard on you. Why are you drawing the curtains?"

Memory is an inestimable critic. Somehow, over the years, the most telling moments of a performance remain crystal clear. Phyllida Law, remembers the tremendous camaraderie there was in that small cast, each of them very much what Lea Ashton calls 'a Citizens' person'. From their dressing rooms after the show, Molly or Fulton would start to sing some old Scots song, and Andy Keir, John Grieve and James Cairncross would join in, harmonising as they went along. In the echoing corridors of the musty old theatre, it seemed a ghostly version of the many parties that had taken place over the years.

Apart from appearing in the Christmas show later that season, this was the last occasion Molly was to act in the Citizens' Theatre. The company, under Michael Langham was extremely strong, and the revue *Merry-ma-tanzie* had a great cast; as well as Molly's special brand of comedy in two spots and two sketches, it had John Grieve, Roy Kinnear, Fulton Mackay and Clare Isbister, all making outstanding contributions to the fun, with an ingeniously amusing book, Ronald Emerson (the playwright, James Scotland) and music by Arthur Blake. And what theatre enthusiast would not be entranced to see Annette Crosbie, in anything but her Queen Victoria vein, singing 'Torch Song' and 'Biscuit Packing' Momma'.

On the back of the glossy souvenir programme for 'Mr Gillie' there was a message in Molly' hand. At a literary gathering, an acquaintance who had written a biography asked me, when he heard that I was working on this project, if Molly's literary estate contained many letters. "Not many," I said, truthfully. I didn't mention this one written in one of Jim's red crayons:

Dear William,
 FISH COOKED IN PAN
 Jim and I have gone to the flicks. Old Mr Paterson died and is being buried tomorrow. (— Just in case you were going to have a practice on your violin)
     Love,
     Molly

Chapter Fourteen

'All the World's a Stage'

"She was like the sun coming into a room." So said Dame Peggy Ashcroft, remembering Molly Urquhart. They had first met when, along with Audrey Hepburn and Dorothy Allison, they went on location to the Belgian Congo as it was then called, for the classic film *The Nun's Story* to be directed by Fred Zinnemann.

Molly had been playing in a cheerful little comedy, *Six Months' Grace* starring Yvonne Arnaud. Robert Morley, who was co-author and director of the piece, remembers her as ". . . dear Molly . . . a lovely, untidy actress with rather the same approach to the business as myself." She played Miss Ethel Sims, a dowdy company secretary who, when the directors decide in a fit of pique to leave their wives in charge, comes to the aid of the effervescent Miss Arnaud. Together they clear up some fraudulent doings that were draining off the profits, and Ethel who turns out to be a financial wizard, is made a director. Molly, like many other actors, always said that Robert Morley's presence ensured a very happy and contented company during a run. She got on well with Yvonne Arnaud, who was enduring rheumatic-type pains, and before every performance called on Molly, who had the knack of easing tension headaches. Dear Yvonne Arnaud, for whom a lifetime in the English Theatre had blessedly left undiminished her Gallic vivacity, scolded her once, when she was late, in the memorable reprimand, "Vere have zu been, zu naughty Haggis?" And Haggis remained her nickname during the run.

While she was in London at that time, her agent phoned to say there was a possibility of a part in the film to be made of Kathryn Hulme's autobiographical account of her experiences as a novice, *The Nun's Story*.

Fred Zinnemann explained to me how this kind of situation comes about: 'The normal procedure is that one looks at film or photographs of various actors. Robert Leonard, the casting director who had years of experience, showed me a piece of film when she played a police-woman.' (This was *Yield to the Night*, the film in which the young Diana Dors made an impressive debut in a dramatic role as a woman awaiting the death penalty for murder. Yvonne Mitchell and Molly played the more sympathetic and the sterner wardress respectively.) 'I liked the quality of her acting. I liked her personality. So from then on it was quite simple. I said, "Get her". We got her and took her to the Congo'.

The film has become something of a classic. The experiences of Sister Luke who enters convent life in Belgium then goes to work as a medical missionary in Africa, make a compelling story. The demands of the religious life, the nature of dedication, the variety of ways in which faithful service both of God and man may be expressed — all these are debated as subthemes to the main story line, related in a visually compelling way, recalling the great medieval frescoes in the churches where the scriptures are unfolded in a lucid manner, popular in the best sense of the word.

Molly, who admired Zinnemann's work tremendously, was thrilled at the prospect of this venture whose locations were to take her to Paris and Rome as well as Africa. With the thorough prepara-tion that characterises his work, Fred Zinnemann arranged that his actresses should have as immediate an experience as possible of convent life; so Molly found herself living in a convent in the suburbs of Paris, following the daily routine that would have been familiar to Sister Augustine the part she was going to play.

Mark Twain once said of himself, I was born excited. The buoyant enthusiasm with which she greeted every new experience convinces one that the same certainly could be said of Mary Sinclair Urquhart. She became completely involved in the everyday life of the convent, absorbing the details not only of dress and demeanour but of the pattern of worship and meditation, of prayer and sacrament. The sister who was appointed to be her guide found her a most willing novice, who even went so far as to admit and do penance for what was by then her habitual indulgence, smoking.

ALL THE WORLD'S A STAGE

The Mother Superior of a convent in Rome where some of the scenes were shot, complimented the nuns of the 'Demi-frère', as they nicknamed Fred Zinnemann, on their composure and dress. Peggy Ashcroft, Audrey Hepburn and Molly travelled together to the Congo. Peggy was an actress whose work, then as now, was one of the glories of the English stage and Audrey Hepburn, already an internationally famous film actress, was to find the part of Sister Luke, one of the most challenging and interesting roles she had had to date. Dorothy Allison made up the quartet, Audrey's skill as a linguist enabled them to laugh over the remarks of some of the Italian camera crew, who had looked them over, and said, *"Che razza di donne ci trovuamo fra i piedi in Congo?"*

The extraordinary capacity for being herself was something that never left the lady from Glasgow. She adored Africa — postcards to friends contained heartfelt assertions about the 'magic of Africa'. She had to be careful about the intensity of the sunlight, but soon got herself dresses made from the brilliantly hued lengths of cotton that were sold in the native market near Stanleyville. Mrs Renee Zinnemann remembers her wearing one in a particularly brilliant red as, pith helmet perched on her head, she explored the area making friends with everyone.

Filming in the jungle brought problems. During one scene in which Peggy Ashcroft as the Mother Superior talked with Sister Augustine under a rush covered hut, such an intense stillness emanated from the crew and show workers during the take that the ladies surmised that either they were playing superbly well or things were going sadly wrong. When the cameras stopped, it was gently broken to them that a particularly deadly snake was coiled on the roof just above their heads. Before there was time for them to hear the assurance that a crack shot standing by had everything under control, they leapt in a flurry of habits, with commendable agility well clear of their venomous scene-stealer.

They spent over four weeks on location, and filming in the white habits and veils of the order, often under the tin roof of the schoolhouse that was the set, was a trying experience.

There were days off, one memorable trip being taken up river where the ladies presented the certificates at the graduation ceremony marking the departure of the cleansed lepers from a Presbyterian mission. There they heard 'The Lord's my Shepherd' sung in the local dialect to the old Scottish tune of Crimond, in the green depths of the jungle.

In the evenings, some of the company joined the local people in Stanleyville where there was, of all things, a Scottish Country Dancing Society, who danced under the velvet night sky. An enterprising ciné enthusiast might have filmed a set of Petronella or a Dashing White Sergeant to records of Jimmy Shand and his Band in which the dancers included Peter Finch, Audrey Hepburn, Errol John and some of the Italian camera crew, with Molly calling instructions as required.

Peter Finch shared her enthusiasm for the ballads of R.W. Service, and often they recited reams of their favourite poems to each other. She treasured a beautiful little water-colour, an impression of the jungle, which he painted for her.

And often, the unit would come together in the lounge of the guesthouse, where most of them were accommodated, to have a sing-song, and her fund of songs and stories entertained the company during many a social evening.

"If people get bored and depressed on an isolated location like that, the fornication can be something terrible." This pronouncement made to me years later is one I have treasured as a unique 'Molly-ism'. One of the young Italian film crew said to her, "Molly *mia*, you send me back to my Mamma's as pure as I come!"

There is little doubt that both professionally and personally, she had been a hit. She coped very well with the medium of film. 'Just *think* the emotion. That'll be more than enough for the big screen' was her maxim.

Fred Zinnemann found her 'a marvellous actress which I like, because I'm very lazy by nature and I hate to have to work very hard with actors, but rather like them to know exactly what they are doing and I can just let them get on with it. And Molly was very much like that; she had great authority and she did her stuff very well. Extremely professional, extremely so.'

Having more than held her own in a major film with an international cast, home she came, laden with a multitude of curios of Africa for Jim, Willie and the family but that year she certainly felt the chill of a Scottish April.

In the late autumn, another break came her way, as a direct result of her work in *The Nun's Story*. Peggy Ashcroft was to play the lead in a modern play called *The Coast of Coromandel*, and Molly was invited to join a very strong cast including Alan Webb and Eric Porter. The plot had a sketchy parallel to Edward Lear's 'The Courtship of the Yonghy-Bonghy-Bo';

> On the coast of Coromandel,
> When the early pumpkins blow,
> In the middle of the woods
> Lived the Yonghy-Bonghy-Bo.

Dame Peggy, who had found Molly 'wonderful to play with, wonderful to be with', welcomed her to the company, rehearsals started just after New Year in London and the tour was due to play in Edinburgh in February.

On 9 January, 1959, Willie was driving home from a Citizens' Theatre function, when he suffered an aneurism and died instantly as his car swerved into a lamp post. There had been little or no warning of this. A few years earlier he had suffered a bad nose bleed, but on his recovery, had tended to dismiss the incident.

The police came to her London digs with the shattering news, Molly flew home in a distracted state. Jim, who was fourteen years old, seemed to grow up overnight. The funeral left from Clifford Street, winding through not only rows of actors from the theatre but a great number of ordinary folk come to pay their last respects to a man who had been held in high regard in every sphere in which he had ever worked. The Glasgow Police Pipe Band led off the cortege, playing a lament, which echoed in the ears of the mourners as the cars made their way slowly along the side of Loch Lomond to the Arrochar graveyard. Molly and Jim stood side by side, her son now taller than she was herself. Elizabeth was there of course, but Lexy was in Poland, and Kit, now married, was in Australia.

Jim and his mother talked long the next day. The only way was to go back. With Jim safely esconced with relatives Molly went on somehow with the tour. The support she received from the company, particularly from Dame Peggy and Eric Porter, helped immeasurably. When they came to Edinburgh, that most gracious leading lady ended her curtain speech by saying: "And we are so delighted to have in the company your dear — and now our dear Molly Urquhart."

The play, although an interesting drama, never quite took off, and did not go into a West End theatre, and it was a relief, in many ways to get home to make plans for the future. There is not much else an actor can do, other than act. At that time, Molly tried to find alternative work, but there really was little else available. She had to keep going for Jim's sake, though there is no doubt that her sense of loss did not ever leave her. When she had gone to London, it was always in the secure knowledge that not only was Willie looking after things at home, but his strong serenity and support was a harbour that was always there to welcome her back. Her ties to her country became even stronger after his death. She turned to the Church, often finding more comfort in the simple positive attitude of the little Mission Hall she attended sometimes, though she remained a communicant member of the local Church of Scotland and was always willing to help them in any dramatic enterprises.

She worked with a youth club in Glasgow, presenting them in a one act play by Joe Corrie, *Up in the Morning Early*. She loved the quick spontaneity of these youngsters, and when a post in community club work was advertised by Glasgow Corporation, she applied for it, only to be met with a politely expressed rejection on the grounds that she lacked formal qualifications for the work. This kind of system, which is even more prevalent today, makes one sigh for such opportunities lost.

At fifty-two, there were few opportunities for earning a living at home. Suddenly there came a second opportunity to work in a film. Fred Zinnemann was gathering a cast to make a film in Australia, *The Sundowners* by Jon Cleary. She was offered the part of Mrs Bateman, a farmer's wife with whom the travelling Sundowner and his wife, Robert Mitchum and Deborah Kerr stay for a while.

Since the location scenes were to be filmed in the summer, Jim would be able to spend the school holiday period with relations in the Black Isle and Inverness. Then Elizabeth, now a widow, with her own son married, would move in as a full-time housekeeper for the remaining few weeks.

It was exactly the right experience to help her through a difficult time. Not only were the few weeks' work much more financially rewarding than anything equivalent she could earn at home, but it presented a kind of solution, in that short spells of concentrated work would keep her financial situation secure, and would let her spend more time at home looking after her son. Also the trip would enable her to see her sister Kit and her Australian husband Len: something she could not have afforded in other circumstances. What was probably more important, it got her into professional work again, and in a film where the cast was of international standing. This acknowledgement of her standing as an actress was something she needed more than ever now that she was alone.

For the Zinnemanns, she had become almost a kind of mascot. Renee and she were great friends. Since *The Nun's Story* the habits and veil had become a kind of Zinnemann trademark, so the two 'token' nuns who were seen on the train in which Deborah Kerr, as Mrs Carmondy, was travelling, were, in fact, Renee and Molly.

The hot Australian sun was not the best climate for this kind of dress and they became terribly thirsty. The train stopped near a little township, just a cluster of wooden houses in the middle of the bush. "Perhaps there might be a cafe," suggested Molly. "Let's go and see."

As they looked down the one main street, they saw a saloon, where they decided they would surely get a soft drink of some sort. So they proceeded in that direction. As the benevolent, white presence glided down the dust track, the little groups of swagmen and sheepmen fell back in amazement. Old hats were doffed, horny hands tugged at forelocks, grizzled heads were bowed in reverence as the 'Sisters' passed by. The garb took over, and on reaching the swing doors of the little saloon, the sense of reality was such that they simply turned and walked back, still thirsty, to the train. They could not disillusion their public!

Robert Mitchum had been avoiding publicity during the filming, and tended to keep himself to himself on the set. Once while the cast not directly involved were sitting on canvas chairs, someone asked Molly if she would move along to make more room. "Certainly," she agreed, and moved to an uneven piece of ground and upon sitting down, tumbled chair and all 'over her wilkies' into the long grass. There was a shout of laughter, most of it coming from the gentleman who had come to help her up.

"Like Queen Victoria", she announced, "we are not amused."

"Well ma'am if you'd seen your backside and bloomers in the air, I reckon you'd be amused too," replied Bob Mitchum. He always came to chat to her after that and in fact, rode out one evening to join the musical parties she had got going, in the little hotel a bit away from the rest of the company, where she played the piano for the viola which the proprietor Miss Hackendorf played.

Molly always tended to find some smaller, less ostentatious accommodation, partly due to her sense of economy, but also because she wanted to get acquainted with the people in the area. In an edition of the *Cooma-Monaro Express* in which the film people are interviewed in the usual show business way, a feature on Molly is headlined, 'She's Busy Making Friends'. The article goes on:

> Perhaps none of 'The Sundowners' have made more Australian friends in such a short time as Scottish actress, Molly Urquhart.
> Middle aged, her smile, her laughing eyes, her very vim for life have made her a familiar figure among Cooma's townfolk.
> In the shops along the street, she stops and chats and her keen sense of humour has made her a popular identity.

She had gone to the rodeo, and attended the local Little Theatre's production of *Blithe Spirit* congratulating the cast and production team. In fact, wherever she went, be it Cooma, Australia, Shaftesbury Avenue, London, or Paisley Road West, Glasgow, Molly in a profession where there are a great number of people who take shelter behind a façade, often for reasons of shyness as much as for affectation, always remained herself. And though she always thought of herself as a very ordinary woman, this was one of the aspects of her character that made her a quite extraordinary one.

When she returned home, a fire, due to a wiring fault, had caused extensive damage to furnishings and carpets in the two public rooms of her flat. Fortunately Jim had awakened and summoned the fire brigade, and neither he nor Elizabeth were any the worse.

Then an unfortunate fall from some rocks near Dunoon, when her agent Joyce Edwards had come for a short holiday to Scotland, left her with a broken leg. The plaster cast had to be renewed for several months before it was properly mended and she graduated slowly from crutches to a walking stick. That and the physiotherapy sessions at the hospital put paid to any work for almost a year.

That made for a very lean time. She had, of course, her widow's pension as well as that, fortunately, afforded to her from the Police Force because of Willie's years of service there. But she realised the precarious existence she led, and immediately took out a sizeable insurance policy, which although the payments were for some time very taxing on her income, at least gave her peace of mind in that it would provide for Jim, if anything should happen to her. Although money was short, the house was still filled with laughter. Molly was always very resourceful, and she put her considerable inventiveness to the art of survival on a very tight budget. Jim, who was growing fast, remembered his mother's amazing renovations particularly his worn shirt collars, impeccably restored, with material trimmed from the shirt tail!

The first part she was able to accept was in a T.V. production of Patrick Hamilton's *Gaslight* in which Margaret Leighton played the lead. The Edwardian costume concealed the plaster cast that still supported her ankle, and she could leave aside the stick while she was on set. She met with tremendous kindness and consideration from the cast and production team, Margaret Leighton, especially, going out of her way to make things as easy as possible.

Although London offered the work and her head told her it would be sensible to move south, her heart was in Scotland and she never seriously considered such an uprooting of herself and Jim. She loved Glasgow, and the Ibrox district, like so many others in the city, had the atmosphere of a village, despite the tenements and traffic. She was extremely fond of the people in the neighbourhood, their ease of manner and quick sense of humour and she was popular with everyone. I never heard anyone in street or shop call her anything other than 'Molly', and they were extremely proud of her achievements, particularly in films. Once when she was washing down the paintwork in her kitchen, dressed in her oldest trousers and overalls, there was a ring at the door. Autograph books in hand, four youngsters looked at her doubtfully. "Does . . . does 'Geordie's' mother live here?" Immediately realising that she in no way measured up to how someone in a film should look, she replied "She's busy just now, but if you like to come back in the afternoon, she'll sign your book then." A spot of glamourisation and a plate of chocolate biscuits made all the difference to those children. "Mind you," Molly reflected, "I didn't think I looked all that special in Geordie. But it just shows what a sight I can look!"

Once while on a touring date with *Five Past Eight* in Aberdeen, she went one afternoon with her cousin Lily to see the film just after its Aberdeen première. There was a long queue, and since she had to get back in good time, she decided for once, to pull rank. She found the commissionaire. "I'm Geordie's mother in this film. Could we possibly get two seats?"

The man looked at her in disbelief. "I don't care if you're Geordie's granny. You'll wait in the queue." An agitated manager bore down on the contretemps and swept her in. But Lily and she were helpless with laughter, just as they had been in the matinees of long ago.

Elizabeth, her staunch friend, was the great standby whose readiness to step in at Clifford Street enabled her to get through the next few years while Jim was still at school. So she stood by her resolve, reiterating her maxim, "If they want me, they'll phone for me."

In 1961 she was cast as Maud Meakin, companion to Gladys Cooper's elegant Mrs Gantry in a play by Peter Mayne. Set in Kashmir, it had the lovely Diana Wynyard playing an anglo-Indian and in the part of Mrs Sharma, Attia Hosain, a beautiful, extremely gifted Indian journalist and radio actress made her stage début — somewhat unwillingly. She recalls how it came about:

> They needed an Indian actress; I had broadcast many radio plays in my language, so when they asked the B.B.C. they suggested me. When the man rang up, I began to laugh and said, "Look, I'm a broadcaster, I'm a writer — I'm not an actress!" So he seemed taken aback and he told me what the play was — "The Bird of Time" with Diana Wynyard. It was going to be at the Savoy Theatre, and I could think it over.

Her daughter and especially her son, who also worked in the theatre urged her to try the audition at least. She went along and to her amazement got the part. Sheer terror set in and it was only because of her son's enthusiasm that she went on with it. The first rehearsal was a nightmare full of incomprehensible stage jargon. Molly, realising the lady was ill at ease, soon found out what the trouble was.

> She said, "Don't be scared," and she came back with me to my flat. "Now, we'll work at this together". Most of my dialogue was with her. I knew nothing about timing — about anything — but with her help on one or two occasions, one obtained the reading that one wanted; the laughs, the desired effect, because Molly made it possible.

Even in my small part, she made me feel better by saying,
"Why, don't you understand that if it were not for you the scene
could be Bournemouth. You add reality, convince us the house-
boat setting really is in Kashmir."

We became such good friends. I don't think I would have been
able to go through with the rôle as I did, with such happiness, if it
had not been for Molly. She had this absolutely beautiful personality. It was the spirit. I don't think I ever saw Molly looking
anything but radiant — and I never heard her saying anything
unkind about anyone.

She was so unlike the general concept of an actress. You would
think — Ah, here's somebody's mother — somebody's best
friend. You wouldn't think for a minute that Molly had been in
key parts in the West End. Unassuming, not bothered to have an
image, just being herself.

She was so devoted to Jim. And then of course, my son Waris
loved and respected her so much. 'Her other wee boy' she used to
call him. She so hoped we could all act in a play together in
Scotland. And I feel, with her, I would have done it, and enjoyed it.

When Attia's son was beginning his career as a trainee drama
director with the B.B.C., he came up to Scotland to direct a TV play,
One Step from the Pavement and stayed with Molly and Jim at the
Clifford Street flat. Molly told me he was coming, "My friend
Attia's boy — he's going to be a great director." She always seemed
to have such amazing faith in people, but her judgement was shrewd
and this time, as on many other occasions. Her assessment of Waris
Hosain has been well borne out over the years. He remembers his first
visit to Glasgow with affection:

> One of my first chances to direct a television drama was a story
> called 'One Step From the Pavement' adapted from an H.G. Wells
> short story and I was able to ask Molly to play a gossipy neighbour
> to a small child who was supernaturally possessed. The neighbour
> provided a good role for Molly who played it with a mixture of
> humour and wariness.
>
> I stayed with Molly in Glasgow while we recorded the play over
> three days and I remember the warmth and pleasantness of her
> hospitality. She lived in a large old flat full of the memorabilia of
> her theatrical career and in spite of the hard work she was putting
> into her role she managed to be a marvellous hostess.
>
> After that we kept in touch mainly by phone. My next chance to

225

work with her was when I directed an episode in the series about the suffragettes called 'Shoulder to Shoulder' and Molly played a curious travelling beggar woman who met Annie Kenny (Georgia Brown) and told her about her travels and dreams. Molly was very good in the role. She was always concerned about giving her best.

The constant elements in all the various interviews and letters Molly's colleagues contributed to the researching of this biography were ones of affectionate admiration and remembered laughter. The elegant waspish stories that seem to go the rounds about many theatre personalities are noticeable by their absence.

Molly worked with three leading ladies in the glamour stakes. I wrote to each of them. Diana Dors remembers her from *Yield to the Night* as "the best of all my wardresses."

Margaret Lockwood, surely one of the enduring stars of British films, whose acknowledged beauty and sometimes underrated acting ability have lifted many an otherwise unmemorable script into some appearance of distinction, played a hotel proprietor in *The Flying Swan*, a B.B.C. television series, with Molly regularly featured as Jessie, the housekeeper. The ladies got on famously and Miss Lockwood not only remembered her as "a very good actress" but as "the dearest, nicest, sweetest person I've ever worked with — and I've worked with some." Julia Lockwood was fascinated by Molly 'reading the cards', whatever skill she had as a 'spey-wife' being certainly amplified by her ability to disclose the future in full dramatic vein!

Moira Lister, with whom she played in *The Very Merry Widow* T.V. series, scripted by Alan Melville, wrote:

> She was always smiling and witty and made rehearsals a joy. She was a consummate artist and extremely "giving" in her performances.
>
> I have only the most warm recollections of our time together.

Alan Melville explained how the casting for this last mentioned series came about:

> I wrote one comedy for B.B.C. TV called 'The Minister's Mallard' starring Moira Lister. It was agreed that Moira would be a right and fit person for a series, and there was a great long debate

about whom Moira's husband should be. Then one day, at one of those awful lunches when you just throw out ideas at each other, I said, "But why has she got to have a husband? Why isn't she a widow left with nothing but debts? But she's got somebody cosy — a housekeeper or something like that, who's been in the family for years". And that's how there arrived the series 'The Very Merry Widow' — and we did three series of those. I had a sort of say in the casting. I wrote in a cosy, lively, sensible amusing Scots housekeeper, who would be a lovely foil to Moira's rather glamorous flibbertigibbety-getting-into-terrible scrapes character. And when she got home, sensibility would rage; the housekeeper perhaps giving her a little ticking off — "Now, come along dear, pull yourself together". And they said "Who do you think?" And I said "Oh, there's only one person in the world, and that's Molly Urquhart." And Molly came down. And this is the terrible thing about a character like Molly — it's much easier to give stories about nasty people, or people who misbehave or say outrageous nasty things — we all absolutely adored her. It was a fairly permanent little company of about six or seven regular characters week after week. Very hard work as weekly television usually is, starting on the Monday morning, putting it in the can the following Sunday and then off again on the Monday morning. And big parts and a lot of location work and pre-filming and all those costume fittings and make-up — and publicity, and all the rest of it; so it really is a very arduous job. We did three lots of seven, twenty-one shows altogether.

Molly established herself or was just unanimously cast as "Mum" of the whole company. It was — "Anything wrong?" — straight to Molly!

There was never *any* sign of flagging energy. I was always amazed at her stamina. When we did the TV series, seven weeks at a stretch, it was really heavy, even for a much younger woman. We were very lucky to have Moira and Molly. Moira is athletic, plays tennis and swims; behind all that glamour she keeps herself really fit. They didn't show any signs of strain, but I noticed some of the people who weren't having to do *nearly* so much, nearly as regularly week after week as Moira and Molly — by the end of the third week, they were beginning to wilt mentally and physically.

The television series as well as her films made her nationally known, and in her late fifties and sixties, she counted herself fortunate with the way her career had worked out. Her income had increased, and she was able to relax a little. Jim had finished his training and was working in the Civil Service. Like his parents, he loved the country and spent most weekends camping or sailing. Molly sometimes joined him on the boat, which he moored down at Luss, since on Aunt Effie's death, Molly had gone on renting the little cottage on Rossdhu Estate. She was still extremely fit, and ready to tackle anything. Not too many ladies her age get family birthday presents of oil skins and walking boots. Jim also spent two summers working in a kibbutz in Israel. Molly and he had visited Poland in 1961, and Ted and Lexy toured them all around. A visit to Auschwitz left an indelible impression, and any of the charity concerts Molly initiated after that were in aid of the building of the Children's Health Centre in Poland, that stands as a memorial to the children who died so terribly in the ghetto and in the concentration camps.

Her Polish friends still were living a life of considerable hardship during that visit, and when in 1962 she was working in the Mermaid Theatre, Phyllida Law recalls that Molly spoke so movingly of the shortages in Poland that the company gathered boxes of 'nearly new' clothes to send over. "She'd get the very shirt off your back", exclaimed one actor who found himself donating a favourite, rather stylish, navy overcoat with an astrakhan collar that gave a Polish doctor a much needed lift in spirits the following winter.

The Mermaid Theatre was putting on a season of Sean O'Casey's plays in his honour, beginning in August 1962. Molly was delighted to be asked to play Eeada in *Red Roses for Me* — and more especially Bessie Burgess, the robustly drawn Protestant woman who is killed by a bullet fired by a British soldier while she is trying to bring the young woman, Nora Clitheroe, to safety. She felt deeply gratified to be invited to take part in productions in O'Casey's honour. She had long revered his plays though her performance as Juno in her own MSU Theatre was the last time she had a part in one. Moreover, she was delighted, as a Scot to be invited to play alongside such wonderful Irish actors as Marie Kean, Harry Hutchinson and Donal Donnelly. Yet apart from George Colouris who was to play Peter Flynn in *The Plough and the Stars*, she alone in the company had received the accolade of being listed in Pitman's *Who's Who in the Theatre*, that classic reference book in which her achievements had been recorded since the edition of 1951.

Sean was not in good health at the time, though he did manage to look in on some rehearsals with his wife Eileen, who came to the opening nights and met the company.

The whole event was a source of great delight to Molly. She was especially well cast as Bessie Burgess, the ebullient northern Irish-woman who dies by a British soldier's bullet while trying to persuade the young, distracted Nora Clitheroe to come away from the window. With the vigour and vitality of her playing, her ability to move effortlessly from comedy to tragedy, her impeccable timing, she made this one of the great performances of her career. It says much for her stamina and fortitude that having sustained a severe kick in the ribs in a misjudged stage fight during rehearsal, she went on to play the first night and two subsequent performances before the excessive pain forced her to seek medical advice. A visit to hospital revealed that she had two cracked ribs. Needless to say, she did not miss a performance.

The Stage critic said she gave 'an earthy moving performance . . . despite an accent which veered in the direction of Glasgow'. Her effective performance' as Eeada in 'Red Roses for Me' was praised by R.B. Marriott, without similar reservation so perhaps the over-tones on the first night were due to the pain she was enduring, for the accent was one she could well sustain, and did, in the subsequent performance in both.'

Eileen O'Casey herself wrote in 1981: 'I do remember quite well Molly Urquhart playing Eeada in Red Roses for Me, and Bessie Burgess in The Plough and The Stars, and her giving a good performance in both.

The final speech when Bessie dies was one she often used to include in the occasional recitals she gave in colleges and art centres in her last years. Standing in the midst of the audience, in her everyday clothes, with neither props nor lighting, she slipped into the charac-terisation and in a few moments had her audience so completely under her spell that her final words left that long, sustained silence that comes before applause, when people have known a deeply moving dramatic experience.

During my researches, a few people said to me that it would be difficult getting around the fact that this career ended in a kind of anti-climax. When I looked at the synopsis I had made, there did appear to be many many moments when it seemed as if Molly was on the brink of a more generally acknowledged fame. I remembered Carmel McSharry looking at the photos of her as Mary Paterson in *The Anatomist*; photos that conveyed in some way the vitality of that portrayal; she went right to the heart of the matter when she said, "She seemed to me like an actress about to come into her prime."

That was a perceptive comment. For in the dozen or so years around that time she gave a series of performances that stand head and shoulders above anything that any other Scots actress can lay claim to; Mrs Grant in *The Forrigan Reel*; Mrs McCrimmon in *Mr Bolfry*; Jeanie in *Dr Angelus*; Dame Sensualitie in *The Three Estates*; Mary Paterson,; the marvellous series of characterisations in *The Tintock Cup*; the trauchled Mrs Lewis in *Green Cars Go East* at the Citizens' and in the Theatre Royal in Glasgow; Penelope in *Voyage Ashore*; the beautifully modulated, sepia portrait of Mrs Gillie; and her latter day work in the West End, culminating in the O'Casey plays. When one thinks of any notable actor, a batting average of ten highlights in as many years is very impressive. What if some of these performances were in repertory theatres to run for a short season of two or three weeks? It does not make them any less commendable than those which were given in a West End theatre where a longer run was made possible.

In addition to those aforementioned parts, there were a great number of other plays, dramas and situation comedy series on T.V. and the summer revue work in Scotland.

Her part in *The Nun's Story* was the first of five appearances in the films of Fred Zinnemann. Appearing in such major productions for the cinema is recognition of an international kind. Each role is cast with meticulous care, and one finds players like Vanessa Redgrave, Maurice Denham and Cathleen Nesbitt playing cameo parts, so that the total artistic statement be the more powerful.

It was Joan Bridge, the lady who was responsible for the superb costume in such films as *A Man for All Seasons, Day of the Jackal, Behold a Pale Horse* and *Julia*, who pointed out to me that Molly Urquhart had appeared in five Zinnemann films, and had been contacted about three others, which had, for one reason or another been shelved. "She was the only artist so acknowledged."

After playing Sister Augustine and Mrs Bateman, in 1963 she played the matron in *Behold a Pale Horse*, a drama about the Spanish Civil War with Gregory Peck and Anthony Quinn as the guerilla and the Spanish officer, with the young Omar Sharif— "Nice boy. He'll go far", — and was delighted by a clipping sent to her from *The Hollywood Reporter* column of a film magazine. The news item pointed out that 'Scots actress Molly Urquhart was to appear in her third Zinnemann movie, but since she used often to say, 'I've been in everything except a circus', it was the headline that amused her: 'URQUHART IN HORSE' Front end or back end, she wondered.

She also took on the small role of Sir Thomas More's housekeeper in *A Man for All Seasons*, that wonderful cinematic interpretation of Robert Bolt's play with Paul Schofield playing More. Sir Thomas, having incurred the king's disfavour in much straitened circumstances has to tell his assembled household regretfully that he cannot sustain them in further employment.

Fred Zinnemann remembered her performance:

> My difficulty always was that I didn't make very many films, and the parts I could offer her were small, which had nothing to do with my respect and admiration for her. In "A Man for All Seasons" she had to say a couple of lines, and burst into tears. Unhappily, we had to do the scene six or seven times. And she did it each time, beautifully. And that's marvellous, because you probably know that sometimes it is very difficult for an actor to produce tears.

Stanley Baxter told a story once about how Molly had come late for a rehearsal at Citizens':

> Her excuses when late could border on the surrealist. A whole circus parade held up her tram to the Gorbals by twenty minutes. As that was one of the earlier excuses, they had to — in her thinking — get more creative on future occasions. Her fantasies were often more gripping than the play in rehearsal.

I know exactly what he meant. Molly had a story-telling style of relating anecdotes and daily happenings that gave them a strangely fantastic flavour; often, I must admit, I too wondered if they were half-illusory. I think I have been proved wrong in almost every instance. I recall being dubious once when she talked of her film work, saying two locations she had been specially looking forward to visiting were Hawaii and China, but the projects had had to be shelved. During these researches, I have frequently made a silent prayer of apology to her; in this instance it was when Joan Bridge, talking of how Mr Zinnemann had been approached about the filming of James Michenor's *Hawaii*, but had not agreed to do so, since he said the substance of the novel was such that it would require two films to contain it. Also elaborate preparation had been made for a film of André Malraux's *Man's Estate*, for which he had tested all the artists, including Molly, and for which wardrobe, to the tune of 14,000 Chinese costumes had been prepared. These are still stored away, since Metro-Goldwyn-Mayer had to cancel only four days before the date planned for commencement. (And incidentally, there really was a circus parade in the streets of Glasgow at the time she mentioned. A father of a friend of mine took pictures of it!)

Perhaps it was her serene, unassuming quality that made all of us fall into the trap of underestimating her in many ways. She was always in dread of appearing to put on airs; any kind of attitudinising had been much frowned upon by her parents, and 'getting above oneself' was a cardinal sin. Once, during rehearsals for a radio play in B.B.C.'s Scottish studios in Queen Margaret Drive, someone asked her what she had been doing recently. "I did a wee scene with Jane Fonda in Fred Zinnemann's new film," she answered truthfully. "Would you listen to the name dropping!" said a lady Thespian, motivated by heavens know what emotion. Molly was deeply hurt, and put herself through a fearful cross-examination. "Was I name-dropping?" she asked me. "You were answering her question." I reassured her. Yet in her own district of Glasgow, the neighbours and her many acquaintances there loved to hear what she had been doing in the show business world, and a walk down the street for two or three purchases could easily keep her out of the house for an hour and a half, while the girls in Telford's Fish Shop or in Galbraith's grocery store asked her about the film or television show she had been in and the people she had met. In such situations, she spoke easily and naturally about her encounters. "The people enjoy hearing about all the celebrities", she would say, never dreaming for a moment they considered her a celebrity, but rather seeing herself as a kind of link between show business and the public.

She had become a household name, not just in Scotland but throughout Britain. Her appearances on such popular television comedy series as *Marriage Lines* and *My Wife Next Door* by Richard

Waring, in Yorkshire Television's *The Flaxton Boys* and as the redoubtable Matron of the Tannochbrae Cottage Hospital in Dr Finlay's Casebook made her work known to a wider public than ever before.

In her later years, when she was tied to home by family commitments and her own failing health, she made a few commercials. One those was for a fire precaution documentary, where she played a garrulous neighbour who keeps a young housewife chatting so long at the door that her chip pan goes on fire. So amusingly did Molly play this role and so anxious were her neighbourhood fans for a glimpse of her on television, that I think this must have been the biggest failure of an information film ever made. Once, accompanying her down Paisley Road West, I heard no fewer than three houswives in turn regaling her with a story of how they each had been so engrossed in watching her in this little essay in fire prevention that some similar incident had occurred in their kitchens, a kettle boiling dry, a pan burning or even, in one instance, a chip pan bursting into flames!

This also recalls one of the funniest documentaries ever made; the little two-minute cartoon warning the public against pick-pockets and shop-lifters. In it, cartoon figures of a mother and two villainous sons perpetrate every kind of petty theft. "That's my clever wee boys" chuckles the unmistakable Urquhart voice in reply to the reports of illicit loot given in the likewise easily identified tones of Roddy MacMillan and Fulton Mackay. I hope the message got across; it was certainly most enjoyably portrayed!

She had a wonderful natural ability to communicate with people, neighbours, people in the local shops, or with the busy transient groups that come together in the brief but intense camaraderie of the theatre and film world. Joan Bridge says again: "It was largely due to her personality as well as her ability that she fitted in film after film. In making films, one hardly ever gets to know anybody — but due to the impact of her personality, everyone knew Molly."

Ewan Roberts said to me, "She was a great pro., Molly, yet she was never stale. She retained the enthusiasm of the amateur completely." This was evident in the way she approached every new piece of work with a completely fresh enthusiasm, with a clean slate as it were. She integrated completely into the internationally selected casts of the films. Joan Bridge never thought of her as being an exclusively Scottish actress. She was one of a group of several close acquaintances who had come to know Molly very well during the latter part of her life, yet had only the most minimal awareness of the fact she had run her own little theatre for nearly five years, and had been a founder member of Citizens' as well as appearing in premières of plays by James Bridie and Eric Linklater. As Miss Bridge looked at the smudgy, time worn photographs of the MSU company, she likened them to the pioneers who broke ground in the early days of Hollywood. Molly would have been amazed, and deeply flattered too.

She did not act in a theatre south of the border during the remainder of the nineteen sixties. She thoroughly enjoyed playing on a few occasions in Jimmy Logan's New Metropole Theatre in Glasgow. In *Strictly for the Birds*, a Sam Cree comedy directed by Jimmy, she gave a devastating study of a 'weel aff' lady from Bearsden, a direct descendant of Aunt Purdie in *Wee Macgregor*. (When someone from the wardrobe had suggested her costume should include brightly coloured directoire knickers and a hat with a ridiculous feather, she dismissed the suggestion fiercely, "If I can't get a laugh without that, it's time I chucked it.") But she loved that theatre, and much admired Jimmy's efforts to keep it going.

It is difficult to say exactly when that superhuman energy had begun to diminish. The enthusiasm and verve for life were still there. The more concentrated but less constant demands of film and television commitments allowed her time for more holidays and also to help a few amateur theatrical ventures in Glasgow. Unlike many actors, she never considered herself 'above' the amateur movement. She had the greatest respect for what it could achieve, but she had absolutely no time for slipshod work and bad attendance at rehearsal and although she would go to any length to help a keen group, she was scornful of any who did not take their hobby seriously.

She had got together herself with a little group of ladies, Jenny Sawers, Ros McCulloch, May Sinclair, Molly Blair, Irene Thomson, Isobel McIntyre, Nan Welsh and Barbara Blackwood, who formed a small revue company, called 'The Ladies in White' named after their opening number, a skit on a Scottish Country Dancing group which Molly had written. They played at Women's Guilds and raised a considerable amount of money for charity.

She also wrote *Sing a Song of Glasgow* a historical pageant about the city she loved so much. This was staged quite magnificently by Bruce Whitelaw, a leading producer in the amateur movement, who with his wife Nettie, had formed a little theatre group. Close friends of Molly, they had put a great effort into producing her show as a tribute to her, and that was one of the proudest moments of her life.

When the National Bible Society launched a 'Feed the Minds' campaign, the organiser, Jessie Adamson, who was Lexy's lifelong friend, had enlisted a representative from all walks of society to read a few verses from consecutive books of the Bible. Molly and Duncan Macrae agreed to help, and on this, the last occasion they were to meet and appear together, they read from the scriptures to a handful of people who huddled around an open air platform in George Square during one of the wettest afternoons of the summmer of 1965.

During a visit to Poland, she and Jim went with Lexy, Ted and their two boys to a kind of holiday camp in the mountains near Skarska Poremba. Sure enough, despite language barriers, she organised a sing song and it must have been quite something to witness her leading campers through the chorus of 'Mine Eyes have seen the Glory'. The Polish mountains cannot have resounded often to hundreds of voices, singing 'Glory, Glory, Hallelujah!'

Her last play in England was one that had been written by Alan Melville in 1971:

An ill-fated play called 'Darling, you were Wonderful' was presented at Richmond by Ray Cooney and was the story of a glamorous actress who had just ripped off 'This is Your Life' — a part meant for Moira Lister. All her relatives had come from all over the world at enormous expense, cousins, uncles and all the rest of it, and they'd done all that kissing lark that goes on — 'How wonderful to see you' etc. and they'd all stayed on and hated each other. And the leading lady said "But when are they going to go? We can't get rid of them!" Molly again was the sensible, lovely, cosy woman who had to cope with all this intrusion. Well in the end, Moira unfortunately couldn't play it; she had something else to do. So we got an actress who was both miscast and misbehaving. Now I was on fairly late — and I'd a long scene to play with her and not one word did I get. We opened at Richmond, struggled through it for two or three nights, and things were obviously getting worse and worse. I listened on the Wednesday and realised

235

that this was disaster, and I remember dear Molly had to bear the brunt in the first act with her — she opened the play with her. There came a little tap on my dressing-room door and Molly put her head round to say, "Alan dear, I don't think ...... is quite herself tonight". It was the biggest understatement ever and the leading lady disappeared that night. So it was tragedy. But this wonderful typical Molly way of putting it — I mean, she wasn't going to say "The woman's drunk, drugged or incapable!" — "I don't think she's quite herself tonight!" She was sorry for her. I'm afraid at the time I was very, very angry. One should have been sorry for her but I saw people being thrown out of work, including Molly, at the end of the fortnight.

A lovely lady. And that is the trouble. There's no hard, critical, nasty bitchy things you could ever say about that one.

Her timing was wonderful. Wonderful timer of lines. And she had — all her life, I presume, a beautiful face. Still at the time of the 'Widow' a very lovely face, which, I must say, could register the most incredible disapproval. Because there was one character in 'The Widow' she didn't approve of at all. And when he popped up, you thought "Poor soul — he hasn't a chance! Mrs Frayle's going to get him right out." It was a face that was very expressive — for what was fundamentally a very gentle face.

Her accent? — It was a very endearing and a lovely asset. I can write good dialogue to suit the lilt, the musical lilt that she had (having lived and worked in Scotland so long) so I don't remember one syllable ever being altered. It's an easy thing if you've the knack of doing it — and a lovely bonus to the part. A gentle accent and no trouble at all ever about understanding her.

A very strong personality — A lovely lady.

Chapter Fifteen

Epilogue

When Molly had her seventieth birthday on 21 January 1976, the newspapers pounced on the information and a series of small features and paragraphs appeared about her. I had not seen her for some months and went to call with a few flowers. I was staggered to see how thin she had become. "They've discovered I've got diabetes," she told me. "I've been on this strict diet. I haven't been so slim for years!"

She had lost about three stones, which pleased the hospital clinic she was attending though her family and friends found it a bit alarming. Still, her vitality, which had been on a somewhat low ebb, had improved. Jim had married Marion Stewart, a lecturer in modern studies, in 1975. Molly proudly showed me the photographs, taken in the grounds of the hotel at the Lake of Menteith, after the wedding conducted by cousin David Stewart, then minister of Gartmore Church. Even in these, she looked noticeably slimmer.

She had been down to London to see a television director who was casting for a proposed serial version of *Anna Karenina*, with Diana Rigg in the name part. "My agent put me forward for the part of the nanny, but I'd rather play the old midwife. She's only in two episodes, so I'd not need to spend such a long time in London. I'm tired of all that."

This did not sound typical either. She had been greeted by the director in tones of surprise, "But you're Scots."

"I make no apology for that" she retorted.

In any event Diana Rigg was not available to take the lead, so the project was postponed.

Scotland began to acknowledge her presence. Groups of students sought her advice on Scots dialect. Some young undergraduates called occasionally to talk about Bridie's plays. She used to laugh

237

when she told the story of how one young man had said to her, with disarming frankness "I'm afraid I've never heard of you, Miss Urquhart. Are you what's known as a bit player?" Dr Sarah Davies, the Chairman of the Citizens' Theatre Society invited her to give a talk. She prepared a programme consisting of speeches from the Bridie plays and Bessie Burgess' last speech, linking it with the anecdotes she could recount so well. It was a huge success and she was honestly amazed by the warmth of the reception and the speech their committee member Jean Adams gave, claiming her as 'our own special actress'.

That day was tinged with sadness too. As she looked into the manager's room that had been Willie's, her eyes filled with tears, and her face drained of its animation and became remote and still, just as it did on her regular visits to his grave at Arrochar. She had lived long with this sense of loss.

She had been involved in radio drama over the years, and was delighted to be invited by Stewart Conn to play in *Primrose Wing* a play by a new writer, Moira Heritage, which he was to direct. She was playing an elderly lady who had given up her own house. Moira Heritage recalls how movingly she played the scene where she realises that she would never leave the nursing home "Even the technicians stopped to listen".

A few more recitals followed, to students and at arts society meetings. She was genuinely delighted at these being of such interest. One given in conjunction with the Scottish soprano Dorothy Robertson, as an entertainment to delegates attending a conference on Scots Language at Hamilton College of Education, gave her the chance to do Dame Sensualitie's great speech from *The Three Estates*. She also made a noble attempt at the Widow's speech from Dunbar's, *The Twa Mairrit Weemen and a Widow*. She was vexed that she could not commit these lines to memory; this surprised me more than I admitted to her. But she was amused to see the academic gathering laughing loud and long at the final item she slipped in, the 'Bella' number, in broad Glasgow.

The pattern that was gradually completed during the last year of her life was not one we noticed being worked out at the time. She took a notion to visit Inverasdale once more. I drove her north, the journey being memorably enlivened for me by her running commentary on the passing scene, as she changed her accent according to the part through which we were passing. The weather was beautiful, the rich colours of a Scottish autumn enhanced the lovely coastline of Loch Ewe where her own croft land is. Her cousins Katie and Nora gave us the warmest of Highland welcomes, and Molly seemed more like her old self again, as she showed me her old haunts.

When she returned, there was a message from Fred Zinnemann asking if she would play a small part in his new film *Julia*, adapted from Lillian Hellmann's autobiographical book *Pentimento*.

Molly's reaction was one of absolute joy. "I'll see my dear friends Renee and Fred once more." That 'once more' struck an oddly disturbing note.

She went off to London looking radiant. She thoroughly enjoyed the few days' work under Fred's direction. She met Joan Bridge again and visited Renee for several hours of chat and reminiscence. She was most impressed with Jane Fonda who played Lillian Hellmann in the film. She admired her acting and her straight forward, down-to-earth personality. Both fighting ladies in their own way, they saw eye to eye.

In September she visited Pitlochry Festival Theatre to see a splendid production of *The Forrigan Reel*, with Walter Carr excellent as Donald McAlpin. Although she intended to be as unobtrusive as ever, she was most touched when Dr Kenneth Ireland spotted her. He had a genuine enthusiastic appreciation of the part she had played in Scottish theatrical history, took her to meet the cast and feted her at a party afterwards.

Early in 1977, she was delighted to play 'Aunt Florrie' in a new play by C.P. Taylor, *You're a Good Boy, Son*, skilfully directed by Robert Love for STV. The cast included Jack Short, who had managed the New Metropole, and, by an amazing coincidence, Betty Cardno, her understudy in her West End plays, also Andrew Crawford, with whom she had scrubbed out the little theatre in Rutherglen so long ago. Although she had found the rehearsals in the Territorial Drill Hall taxing because of the extremely cold weather, the occasion was one of happy reunion. One old soldier, fascinated both by her playing and by the lightning dexterity with which she rolled her own cigarettes, exclaimed in simple sincerity, "You're lovely, so you are". He gave her a little tin box which he had decorated himself to keep her tobacco in, a gift that she greatly treasured.

In the spring, she attended an amateur production in Rutherglen *Dr Angelus* directed by Haydn Davies for an enthusiastic group who were trying to revive the Rutherglen Rep. tradition. They made a very good job of it. Although far from well that evening, she went round to speak to every one of the cast.

Perhaps for me, the strangest coincidence took place at a meeting of Airdrie Arts Club. I had been invited, as I thought, to give a talk on the Music Hall in Scotland. By some misunderstanding, this was billed as an event to be held in their Little Theatre. I realised that some sort of entertainment was expected, and at only four days' notice, sought the help of the 'Melody Makers', a first rate local amateur group led by a fine musician, Dorothy Kjelgaard. She offered to come along with some of her singers. I was telling Molly about my dilemma; "I'll come with you, if you like," she said. I was deeply touched by this gesture, made so spontaneously out of friendship.

That evening, the last on which she was to appear on any stage, she somehow got the adrenalin going, and delighted the audience, who were quite astonished to find the first lady of the Scottish theatre suddenly appearing, all unannounced on the programme. She gave them 'Bella', then her Marie Lloyd impression in 'My Old Man', and as an encore, 'The Miner's Dream of Home', the same old ballad that she had sung the very first time I had ever seen her in *The Pyrate's Den* way back in 1946. She was entranced with the talent and professional approach of the Melody Makers, made friends immediately with Dorothy, agreeing to be a guest at her next show, the profits which were to go to any charity of her choice. This was to be, of course, the Children's Health Centre in Warsaw.

One final television engagement was in a new situation comedy by Richard Waring, *Miss Jones and Son*, featuring Paula Wilcox. It was to be recorded at Teddington, and somehow she managed the journey though she didn't have the energy to stop off in London to see Joyce Edwards, as she had hoped.

When she came back, she was exhausted. Yet she was anxious to hear about a demonstration march through Glasgow in which I along with hundreds of my teaching colleagues had protested about some particularly savage education cuts.

"No 'ifs', no 'buts' — no more education cuts", had been the slogan.

"What a pity I was away!" she said. "But if you go out again, I'll march with you."

I looked at her. She seemed so frail and tired. "Why on earth should you?"

The grey-blue eyes widened in surprise. "I could shout louder," she said.

She visited Poland with her cousin Jean to attend the wedding of William, her younger nephew, to Teresa, a beautiful Polish girl. That was the last family occasion she took part in. They had a fearful journey back, with strikes and hold-ups at the airports, and a series of flights, going by Zurich, Paris and London, instead of the straight Warsaw-Glasgow route.

After making a radio recording of *Autograms*, a personal choice of records, she had to give in and rest at home. She still managed to continue her work in the local community council; she had persuaded the authorities to give double glazing grants to all the Clifford Street householders whose peace had been shattered by a new motorway built nearby. She was nominated and elected their community councillor by a resounding majority.

In July, she went into the Southern General Hospital. After two months' intensive tests, a scanner revealed a cyst on the pancreas. She underwent an operation on the ninth of September. 'An obstruction was found, but it has been by-passed' was the far from reassuring report. She came through the operation with a fighting spirit and it was thought at first she would have perhaps another two years of life.

She kept heart right to the end, and when I visited her, used to show me the notes she had made for the autobiography she had never had time to write. "We'll do it together," she declared.

She was adamant that the profession should not be told she was ill. "Wait till I'm a bit more like myself." There were plenty of visitors; indeed they had to be prevented from coming since talking was obviously exhausting her.

She died four weeks after the operation with her son and her sister Lexy beside her. There had been much suffering and no complaint. A little nurse said to me, "She was a lovely lady. She always called me 'darling', but she said it as if it was my name."

The day of the funeral was bright with the most glorious autumn sunshine. When the cars went along the road beside her beloved Loch Lomond, its waters, which can so often be grey and surly, sparkled in a blue brilliance. As the coffin was taken into the little churchyard at Arrochar, the last wisp of cloud cleared from the top of the Cobbler Mountain, and the wreaths of flowers that banked the grave seemed to have sprung from the earth in response to the sun. When she was laid to rest beside her husband it was as if the pattern was complete. Yet what I remember most clearly was the expression on her face when her body was brought home to Clifford Street. She had looked strangely young again, and there was the beginning of that familiar smile, her chin lifting in the old familiar way, as if she had just seen someone she knew.

Fred Zinnemann wrote to me:

It is almost a year to the day that Molly and I worked together on 'Julia'. She did a splendid job, as usual.

He had said earlier of her role in that film:

It was a cameo part which again she did beautifully, because you could read so much more on her face. She was one of those people who could make you understand how they feel and what they think without having to say anything. And that was tremendously important in that scene.

His letter continued:

My wife and I are both deeply sad and grieving, especially since we had not known Molly had been ill for so long.
We will remember her with affection for the rest of our lives.

Jane Fonda wrote from California: 'I'm sad to learn of Molly's death. Though we only worked together one day, I remember her as a warm, serious, open, energetic woman. And I meant it when I said to her I'd like to be like her when I get to be 71'.

When I spoke with Roddy MacMillan some months later, he made the following remarks:

. . . People like Molly and myself always felt, in order to get the best expression out of ourselves, we had to work as near as possible to the kind of background that we came out of — it's as simple as that.

Oddly enough, you see, this is not denied to other people. I mean, it's not denied any more to the Irish, though it was for a long time. People used to mock those who wanted to have any kind of native theatre in Ireland, saying, "Don't be silly. What a ridiculous idea." But then, through time, they came to see it was a good thing.

A great deal of lip service is paid to the idea of allowing the artist to do what he wants. If it so happens that the artist in the theatre wants to make his work and his expression here in Scotland about his own background, is he to be denied that? I mean it seems to me ridiculous that people with so-called universal ideas will gladly accept the universal maxim, that people ought to be allowed to express themselves in the way they want, yet when it comes to facing up to it, in terms of their own people, they rather ridicule the idea — and that seems to me to be awful. They seem to be breaking cardinal laws there.

Anyway, lots of us feel we do our best work nearer to ourselves, and nearer to our homes, to our background, nearer to our feelings.

But perhaps Peggy Ashcroft expressed it best for all of us who knew her: "She was like the sun coming into a room."

List of Subscribers
at time of going to press August 28 1981

Aberdeen College of Education Library, Aberdeen.
Jean Adams, Glasgow.
Jessie G. Adamson, Glasgow.
Mrs Marianne Adler-Bell, Glasgow.
Mr Kenneth John Aitken, Edinburgh.
Mrs Kathryn Atkins, Dallas, Texas.
Graham Alison, Glasgow.
William Andrew, Glasgow.
Prof James Arnott, Glasgow.
A Bald, Conon Bridge, Ross-shire.
Bill Bamford, Stirling.
Y M Parry, Glasgow.
Mrs F Batchelor, Leeds.
Nina Bawden, London.
Ida Schuster Berkeley, Glasgow.
Lord Birsay, Edinburgh.
Mrs B E Blackwood, Glasgow.
Mrs Molly Blair, Slough, Berks.
Sheila Blane, Ayr.
Miss I T Boyd, Hamilton.
British Actors Equity Assoc., Secretary Alex Clark, Glasgow.
Mrs Elizabeth Brittin, Strathaven.
Isabel C Brown, Glasgow.
Mrs Rosemary H C Brown, Airdrie.
Dr C C Budge, Glasgow.
Mrs A Burgess, Campbeltown, Argyll.
Agnes Burns, Hamilton.
Mrs Joan Busby, Ormiston.
Mr James Cairncross, London.
Mr John Cairney, Glasgow.
Mrs Grace B Calder, Glasgow.
C G M Campbell, Stranraer.
Nora E Carmichael, Glasgow.
Citizens Theatre Society, Glasgow.

The Clan Urquhart Association, Jefferson, Louisiana, USA.
Mrs Margaret Clarke, Milton-under-Wychwood.
Margaret M Coghlan, Milngavie.
George Cole, Oxon.
Harry Cook, Glasgow.
Stewart Conn, Edinburgh.
Robert Cooper, Glasgow.
Andrew Crawford, London.
Andrew Cruickshank, London.
Mrs J Cumming, Glasgow.
Dr Sarah Davies, Glasgow.
Mr J Dennis, Glasgow.
Dundee College of Education, Dundee.
Dundee Writers' Circle, Dundee.
Mrs M Dunn, Hamilton.
Elizabeth W Dunnet, Paisley.
Lynne Dunnet, Glasgow.
Dr H S Dunsmore, Glasgow.
Mrs Dorothy Edwards, Surrey.
Ms Joyce Edwards, London.
Miss Lillian Fairgrieve, Glasgow.
Mr J F Forbes, Glasgow.
Elizabeth Anne Gallagher, Renfrew.
Moira Geddes, Monkton, Ayrshire.
James Gilbert, London.
Mr Iain Mark Gilchrist, Edinburgh.
Anne Gilmore, Lenzie.
Stan Gilmore, Lenzie.
Glasgow Theatre Club, Glasgow.
Librarian, Glasgow University, Glasgow.
Alistair R Gordon, Rutherglen, Glasgow.
Mrs Lilian Graham, Glasgow.

LIST OF SUBSCRIBERS

Attia Habibullah & Waris Hussein, London.
J Ross Harper, Glasgow.
Charles Hart, Glasgow.
Mrs Margaret Hawthorn, Glasgow.
Allan Henderson, Glasgow.
Mrs Lily M Hepburn, Inverness.
Mrs R C Houston, Greenock.
Mrs Mary M Hughes, Glasgow.
David Hutchison, Glasgow.
Dr Kenneth Ireland, Pitlochry.
Marion Jack, Glasgow.
Gordon Jackson, London.
William Jackson, East Kilbride.
D Jenkins, Glasgow.
Crena Joyce, Linlithgow.
Kenneth R Kelly, Doncaster.
L Kelly, Glenrothes.
Mrs M Kerr, Leeds.
Mrs Ivy Kerr, East Kilbride.
Mrs Edina M Kirkman, Kippen, Stirling.
Mrs Dorothy Kjelgaard, Lesmahagow, Lanarks.
Miss June Laidlaw, Edinburgh.
Miss Catherine Lindsay, East Kilbride.
Frederick Lindsay, Edinburgh.
Jimmy Logan, Glasgow.
Robert Love, Glasgow.
Mrs Elspeth A Mabbott, Glasgow.
E J P Mace, Glasgow.
Ronald Mavor, Edinburgh.
Elizabeth Mansill, New Zealand.
Elizabeth Marshall, Glasgow.
Mrs M B Melchior, Glasgow.
Elizabeth Meldrum, Glasgow.
William Michael, Glasgow.
Mrs Anne Miller, Inverness.
Stewart M Miller, Glasgow.
Anne M MacArthur, Glasgow.
Mrs Margaret McConnell, Glasgow.
Mrs Ethel McCracken, Glasgow.
Rosina McCulloch, Glasgow.
Miss A B MacDonald, Motherwell.
Ian MacDonald, Menstrie.
Lilian M de P MacDonald, Glasgow.

Miss M MacDonald, Edinburgh.
Peter MacDonell, Fortrose.
James McFarlane, Glasgow.
James U McIntosh, Glasgow.
Miss I B McIntyre, Glasgow.
E M McKay, London.
Fulton Mackay, London.
Linda Macenney, Edinburgh.
George Grant MacKenzie, Glasgow.
J Milne Mackenzie, Glasgow.
James Mackenzie, Rutherglen, Glasgow.
John Mackenzie, Glasgow.
Dr Roy Mackenzie, Edinburgh.
Mrs Beatrice MacLean, Glasgow.
Mrs Catherine McMillan, Hamilton.
Misses MacNair, Glasgow.
Duncan MacRae Memorial Trust, Glasgow.
Catherine M MacQueen, Glasgow.
Carmel McSharry, London.
Miss J G Moffett, Glasgow.
James Molloy, Glasgow.
E Moore, St John's, Newfoundland, Canada.
Miss J Morrison, Hamilton.
Miss J R Mowat, Glasgow.
Joan Munro, Glasgow.
B & M Murray, Fair Isle, Shetland.
Mrs Jean Murrie, Glasgow.
Mrs Norah Napiontek, Glasgow.
M M Nicoll, Glasgow.
The Librarian, Notre Dame College, Glasgow.
Nicholas Parsons, Reading.
T W Paterson, Burnside.
Tony Paterson, Glasgow.
Robert Pollock, Rutherglen, Glasgow.
Thelma Pollock, Glasgow.
Hugh C Rae, Balfron Station, Stirlingshire.
Mrs C B Reid, Bothwell.
Jean M Reid, Glasgow.
Ros Richardson, Edinburgh.
Ewan Roberts, London.
Dorothy Robertson, Edinburgh.

Rosina Robertson, Paisley.
Gillian Rodger, Glasgow.
Mrs Dorothy Roger, Glasgow.
A W Ross, Glasgow.
Royal Lyceum Theatre Co,
  Edinburgh.
Herbert W Russell, Lundin Links,
  Fife.
Jean Rutherford, Glasgow.
Alex Sawers, Largs.
Miss Norah Scott, Glasgow.
Scottish Society of Playwrights,
  Glasgow.
Scottish Theatre Trust, Glasgow.
E Doris Sey, Edinburgh.
J J Sharp, Portugal Cove,
  Newfoundland, Canada.
Mrs M Sinclair, Paisley.
George Singleton, Helensburgh.
Mrs M R Smith, Glasgow.
Bob Somerville, Edinburgh.
Mrs I M Stewart, Ardrishaig,
  Argyll.
Mrs Moira Stirling, Johnstone,
  Renfrewshire.
Miss E M Sutter, Glasgow.
Anna Taylor, Glasgow.

Mrs Catherine L Taylor,
  Grantown-on-Spey.
Mrs Silvie Taylor, Dundee.
Phyllida Thompson, London.
Mrs I Thomson, Glasgow.
Miss Margaret Tomlinson, Giffnock.
Robert Trotter, Glasgow.
Mrs E Tulloch, Dumfries.
Mr I G Urquhart, Edinburgh.
Kenneth Trist Urquhart of
  Urquhart, Louisiana, USA.
Mairi M Urquhart, Glasgow.
Brenda Vernon, Tobermory, Isle of
  Mull.
Ian Wallace, London.
Barbara Waring, Conon Bridge,
  Ross-shire.
Mrs Jenny Watson, Airdrie.
Mrs Brenda Williams, Glasgow.
Mrs Margaret Williams, Dumfries.
Mrs M B Winks, Glasgow.
Doreen Winning, Glasgow.
Mrs M P Wood, Glasgow.
Dr E I Young, Inverness.
Mrs Fred Zinnemann, London.
Zonta Club, Secretary Iris Grant,
  Glasgow.

Further Subscribers
at proof stage October 23 1981

Dr & Mrs Clifford Anderton, St Johns, Newfoundland, Canada.
Borderline Theatre Company, Irvine.
Edward Boyd, Glasgow.
The Citizen's Theatre, Glasgow.
Margaret M Coghlan, Milngavie.
Comunn Na Drama Chaidhlig, Stornoway.
Mrs A W Connell, Glasgow.
Evelyn Cowan, Glasgow.
Nancy & Bill Davidson, Glasgow.
Mrs B G D Dickson, Glasgow.
Lt Col Gayre of Gayre and Nigg, Minard Castle, Inveraray.
Allan Henderson, Rutherglen.
Mary Henderson, East Kilbride.
Michael Ireland, Glasgow.
Austen Kark, London.
Mrs D Lynch, Glasgow.
Nan & Iain McFarlane, Stirling.

Miss Anne McNeely, Glasgow.
Mrs E Miller, Ayr.
Mrs Margaret Morgan, Glasgow.
Miss Margaret B Napier, Rutherglen.
John Paterson, Newton Mearns.
Queen Margaret College, Edinburgh.
Edna I Robertson, Glasgow.
J L Russell, Glasgow.
St John's Dramatic Club, Paisley.
Scottish Theatre Company, Glasgow.
7 : 84 Theatre Company, Edinburgh.
Miss H R Stewart, Glasgow.
Mrs Beth Thomson, Glasgow.
The Clan Urquhart Association, Louisiana, USA.
John M Whitehead, Dundee.
R Bruce Whitelaw, Glasgow.
Dorothy Whittington, Co. Antrim.

INDEX

INDEX

INDEX